Penelope Leach

Child Care Today

Penelope Leach was educated at Cambridge University and at the London School of Economics, where she received her Ph.D. in psychology, after which she studied many aspects of child development and child rearing under the auspices of Britain's Medical Research Council. A Fellow of the British Psychological Society and a founding member of the U.K. branch of the World Association for Infant Mental Health, she works on both sides of the Atlantic in various capacities for organizations concerned with prenatal care and birth, family-friendly working practices, day care, and early years education. She has recently codirected a major program of research in the United Kingdom into the effects of various forms and combinations of care on children's development from birth to school age. Penelope Leach has two children and six grandchildren and lives in Lewes, England.

Children First
The First Six Months
Your Growing Child
Your Baby and Child
Babyhood

Child Care Today

Child Care Today

Getting It Right for Everyone

PENELOPE LEACH

Vintage Books
A Division of Random House, Inc.
New York

Contents

Part Three: QUALITY OF CARE

Part Four: MOVING ON

Introduction

This book is about child care. In the book and in most of the research it reports, child care means just that: the care of children. It includes what used to be referred to as "day care" but is by no means confined to it. The distinction is important. To many people, perhaps especially North Americans, "day care" refers only to child care provided by people other than parents for children below school age while their mothers are out at work and mainly to care that takes place in group settings such as nurseries or centers. The real world of child care is a lot more diverse and complicated than that. For a start, even when a child is in child care for many hours and her mother, as well as her father, works a fifty-hour week, she will still spend more time with her parents and be far more intensely and lastingly influenced by them than by her other caregivers. Then, for many families child care is not a clear-cut either-or between home or child care setting but a jigsaw puzzle of people and places, family and nonfamily, paid and unpaid, in the child's home, in someone else's home, or in a professional setting. To complicate matters further, not all nonmaternal care is nonparental; there are increasing numbers of fathers caring for their children. And not all nonmaternal care is chosen to enable mothers to work or study, either. Some women are based at home and available to their children but want some separate time for their own benefit or for the child's. Some fathers and mothers want to share children's care or to have one or the other of them solely responsible for it, and some grandparents want to spend time with children that's as much sociable as useful. We need to be aware of all that complexity, because if child care research is to inform public or personal policies usefully, it needs to be about identifying ways of caring for children that fulfill the needs and fit the changed and changing lifestyles of both children and adults.

Child care is a very large and wide-ranging topic, so this book covers a lot of ground and is crammed with facts and figures, not all of which will seem relevant to every reader. American parents thinking about nonparental care for their own child may not care what is provided in Europe or Australia or how researchers judge the quality of a children's center; they may want to start with Chapter 4, read about different types of child care in Chapters 5–12, and then go to Chapters 14–16 on judging and choosing child care, and Chapter 20 for some suggestions on making it work for whole families. However, those same parents, thinking about child care as taxpayers and voters, may welcome the discussion of political and policy issues in Part One, of the research that tells us what we know and what we still need to know about child care in Chapter 13, and of how American child care and its funding compares with that of other countries in Chapters 17–19.

Child care is not only a big topic but also one that is dangerously hot to handle. Tapping into parents' desperate desire to do the best for their children and the hair trigger of their guilt when that is in question, child care stories are widely reported in all the media, whether they are individual scare stories, dry reports from the Office for Standards in Education, Children's Services and Skills (OFSTED) in the United Kingdom, sober findings from the National Institute of Child Health and Human Development (NICHD) Early Child Care Research Network studies in the United States, or accounts of their own experiences from parents who took part in the Families, Children and Child Care (FCCC) study in the United Kingdom. And, judging by TV shows, Web sites, radio phone-ins, and letters to editors, such stories all get a huge response from their audiences. Unfortunately, that wide interest and coverage says more about increasingly intense concern about child care than about widespread or growing understanding of it. There is more written but less understood about child care than about almost any other single topic that is relevant to almost everyone. And the more sensitive the topic becomes, the more difficult it is to present objective facts or measured accounts, to identify gaps in our knowledge, and to open honest debate, as this book hopes to do.

The topic of child care is becoming more sensitive because, after two generations of startlingly rapid social change and almost a decade into the new millennium, we are still looking at it backward, treating the sole mother care that was typical of white middle-class families for a generation after the Second World War as a gold standard against which to measure (and decry) today's child care and sometimes look askance at today's parents. It is difficult to imagine a less useful mind-set. Rapid social change is the context for many parents' problems and the starting point for this book, but it is neither a diagnosis nor a cure. Understanding more about how things have changed will not, in itself, make it much easier to cope with the way things are. And looking at the differences between today and yesterday, between our children and our childhoods, will neither resolve regrets nor produce solutions. History never runs backward. We don't get a second shot but have to try to figure out how to live with and enjoy what we've got in the time and place that we're in, and perhaps exert some control over where we're going.

Whatever the brief period between the end of the Second World War and the 1970s when sole full-time mother care was the social expectation or aspiration meant to children, it meant isolation and discrimination to many of their mothers and hastened its own ending by helping to power them into the women's movement. Modern sociology recognizes that in each society some women want to give priority to children and home rather than to paid work, but wide acceptance of that particular form of nuclear-family living and gendered division of labor is over. We know that modern economies absolutely require women's work as well as men's, that of parents as well as those without children, yet we are still arguing about whether it is bad for children to have "working mothers." Looking regretfully over our shoulders at a rose-tinted past stops us from making realistic assessments of the present or looking forward to how we could make a better future, and both are urgent. The reality is that nonmaternal child care is a fundamental part of modern societies; until we acknowledge that, we shall not recognize, let alone address, the unpalatable reality that much child care, especially for children under three, is currently of dismally low quality. We know this; anyone who reads research studies or reports of them from North America, Australia, or the United Kingdom knows it— including millions of anxious parents who would rather not. Less known, though, and far more shameful is that we know how to improve the quality of child care, and we are not doing it.

If we stopped pretending that parents are solely responsible for child care; stopped implying that if nonparental care isn't good, the only alternative open to good parents (mostly mothers) is to care for children themselves full-time, whether or not that is what they want to do, we could stop looking back and use what we know to move forward. Some countries have already moved farther forward than others. Countries need to learn from one another. The United States is unique among Western countries in having no federally mandated paid maternity or parental leave, and its programs to assist poor parents with child care fees are underfunded. In contrast, parental leave in Finland is so generous and well paid that having a parent at home with a baby or toddler is a realistic alternative to child care, which is freely available to all parents who choose it and, like later schooling, financed out of general taxation. Between these extremes, child care in the United Kingdom must still be paid for by the parents who use it, but paid maternity leave can now last nine months for any employed mother, and every three- and four-year-old is entitled to free half-time preschool education. We need answers to positive questions: What are the real issues in combining the human essentials of earning and caregiving? What types of child care are there? What is high-quality child care like—for which children in which families and when? How can it be provided and paid for?

These are some of the questions this book addresses.

Part One

CHILD CARE TODAY

1. The Context for Child Care

This ought to be the best time to become a parent that there has ever been. The stream of scientific information about fetal, infant, and child development is at an all-time high and still rising. There's more government and media interest in families, parenting, and small-child-related issues than ever before, and parents and stepparents—grandparents, too—are increasingly thoughtful about what and how they are doing.

Not everyone is interested in becoming a parent, of course, but not everyone has to. This millennium-spanning generation of women has an unprecedented amount of control over its childbearing. An active sex life and no children is socially acceptable and physiologically possible in most of the developed world, and many people opt for it. Low fertility (or no male partner) and children is not quite so easy, but assisted conception is now available in most of the Western world (though whether as a right or a big business depends on where you live) and is astonishingly widely used, often by individuals who would not have seen themselves as prospective parents a generation ago, including women past menopause and gay couples.

Throughout the postindustrial world, however, women are having fewer babies than ever before, and while mondially falling birth rates may do something to slow the overpopulation of the planet, falling birth rates in developed areas mean "aging populations" and, thirty years into the future, a real threat to economies. The 2006 Canadian census shows that the number of people over age sixty-five has gone up by almost 12 percent since 2001, while the number under age fifteen has dropped more than 2 percent in the same period. An aging population, better described as a shortage of young people, not only means that a larger proportion of the population will be retired and dependent on pensions and care arrangements that a smaller proportion of people of working age are going to have to finance; it also means fewer young people acquiring and disseminating the new skills on which employment will increasingly depend. So, in the long term, we need our populations to produce the next generation of workers, and countries that do—such as the United States, which saw a fractional increase from 64 infants per 1,000 women of childbearing age in 1996 to 66.3 in 2004—will be at an enormous advantage if it is maintained. The assumption that countries with very low birth rates can turn to migrants instead ignores the real math. If a country such as Italy continued with its current fertility rate of about 1.3 (instead of the 2.0 that would replace each couple with two offspring) for more than a generation, its labor supply would drop by about 10 million workers. It is inconceivable that Italy, or indeed any nation, could attract such a large number of employable immigrants or absorb them.

It is difficult to see a future shortage of labor as an urgent problem in countries where unemployment rates are high, as they have been, for example, in Germany and Spain. However, it is now generally realized that current unemployment comes about less because there are too many workers than because too few of the available workers have the requisite skills. Indeed, if the birth rate stayed so low that there was a catastrophic shortage of labor in thirty years, there would probably still be a high rate of unemployment among inadequately skilled workers, many of them approaching retirement age, who were no longer employable in the jobs available.

What do birth rates now and labor supplies in the future have to do with child care? The link is women's participation in the labor market. A generation ago, the women who didn't work outside their homes were the ones who had the most children, and that is still the case in some parts of the world. In most countries, though, that sit-

> "In Germany the phenomenon of shrinking families has been going on for the past 30 years. This problem doesn't just affect Magdeburg, or Germany, it affects the whole of Western Europe. . . . Having children just doesn't seem to fit with modern lifestyles. . . . Some people have become less tolerant of children. They see them as loud and stressful and a bit of a pain."
> Lutz Trumper, mayor of Magdeburg, Germany, 2005

uation has now reversed so that it is countries with high rates of female employment that have higher fertility rates. In Iceland, for example, 90 percent of women are employed, and it has the highest birth rate in Europe—two children per woman. Countries that have lower rates of female employment have low fertility rates because the governments do not make it possible for mothers to work. Germany, which has a low birth rate and fewer women working than Iceland, is addressing the issue with new tax breaks and state-funded welfare programs. France has instigated even more direct incentives to childbearing: not only well-paid maternity leave and some paternity leave but monetary benefits up to a child's third birthday and a presidential medal for parents of several children!

More and more countries are announcing direct financial incentives for having an "extra" child. In Australia, there is a baby bonus of $4,133 per child, and there is soon to be a "bumper baby bonus" of $10,000 on the birth of a third or subsequent child. The governor of the Russian province of Ulyanovsky went even further, suggesting September 12 be designated a public holiday on which to conceive a baby. It was announced that on June 12, 2008, a refrigerator or television would be awarded to anyone giving birth on that day—exactly nine months later. It is not clear if this actually happened, but in Russia as a whole, Putin's government gave vouchers worth about $8,500 (£10,500) to any woman having a second or third child.

While about 20 percent of women do not want children and 20 percent want to have children and not work outside the home, 60 percent of women want to combine the two. For individual women making decisions about their personal fertility, the key issue is often the difficulty of reconciling roles and associated images of self as a mother or as a working woman rather than the monetary cost of having a child—wages lost during time away from work and costs of caring for another family member. In a national poll of U.K. adults in 2006, 63 percent said that career pressures that made it difficult to have children were the main reason for the low birth rate, while in 2008, Harriet Harman, then deputy leader of the Labour Party in power, stressed that it is not only middle-class "career women" who feel torn between work and home: "This is a particular problem for women who are in low-paid, low-status jobs. If you're the boss or in senior management you have choices. You don't if you're in a cleaning job or on a production line."

Individual decisions are often affected, therefore, by the extent to which national policies make it possible for women who are mothers to stay connected to their workplaces, through paid maternity leave, good-quality child care, and part-time and flexible working arrangements. The long-term effect on a country's fertility is very limited, however, because even the most mother-friendly employment package is not going to induce a woman to have children if she is one of the 20 percent who don't want any. Nevertheless, such measures do have marginal effects on fertility, and the margins are critical, as demographer Peter McDonald explains:

> It's really about people who, at the margin, make a decision not to have an extra child. The difference between a fertility rate of 1.65 and 1.4 (per couple) is 25 per cent of women having one child (rather than two) so we're talking affecting fertility rates at the margin. And it does seem that the policies that have been introduced in the northern European countries, and in France and the Netherlands, actually do that. They provide enough incentive for enough women to have that one extra child.

If there are more women than ever before who opt to remain childless and regard themselves as child free, there are also many people who want children and have them but find themselves unable to revel in being parents. Most parents devote to their children a huge proportion of whatever energy, efforts, and resources they may have, yet many of them still don't feel like good-enough parents with happy-enough (and perhaps "good-enough") children.

All Western countries are aware of a multiplicity of parents' problems—selected and colorful versions of which fill hours of prime TV viewing time with sitcoms and "reality TV"—and make at least token attempts to address them. "Help" programs sprout like seedlings in a hothouse. There are preparation-for-parenthood courses as well as physical preparation for birth; parent support groups for coping with everything from newborn crying through toddler tantrums to adolescent challenges. There are networks of interventions concerned with making sure parents bond with newborns, stimulate the brains of babies, read books with toddlers, and take (very) early years education seriously. Educational groups for parents are even sometimes made compulsory. But many seedling initiatives damp-off and die at an early stage, and even those that grow from project status into the real world don't always get the funding they need to keep them sustainable. Most of these efforts are welcomed by some parents, but, so far at least, few have made major impacts on overall outcomes.

It sometimes seems that we are having such trouble with children, child care, and family life because children have changed. Parents and grandparents say, with considerable truth, that they would never have behaved as disrespectfully, aggressively, greedily, or heedlessly as the children they love. However, children are part of the same puzzle as the rest of us, so of course their behavior and their expectations have changed in line with what they see other people do and have, and adults don't like that. Adults' images of childhood often reflect their own experiences a generation before more closely than they reflect their own children's lives, and the differences—often as trivial as they are dramatic—always evoke nostalgia for some lost innocence. We don't want children to do as we do; we want them to do as we say and as we feel we used to do. We long for them to espouse values that have become almost old-fashioned in adult lives—rigorous personal honesty, for instance. We wish they would eschew behaviors that have become almost universal, such as using "bad" language, casually and almost continually, and join us in whatever position we happen to take on current ethical confusions. So what if we drink alcohol, hunt animals, and insist on citizens' right to carry guns? We still want our children to believe that we are against drugs and violence, and to act as if we really are.

Changes in generations of children are almost always more apparent than real. What has changed most for this generation, and is still changing rapidly, is the jigsaw puzzle of family, community, and society in which they are included. Children seem different because they take up differently shaped pieces of the overall picture. And the most differently shaped piece of all is their daily, hourly, minute-by-minute care.

The immediate context for our acute concern with child care, then, is extraordinarily rapid social change affecting women and

Western economies directly and children only indirectly. A crucial and often-ignored part of that change is that the advent of oral contraception not only increased the reliability of birth control but put it into the hands of women for the first time. That is background to the fact that the economic survival of commercially active nations now depends as much on women's as on men's lifelong labor and resulting earnings, taxes, and spending, while children's survival still depends on somebody taking care of them every minute of every twenty-four hours for at least a decade. So who is going to do that? Mothers tend to answer "me"; a lot of fathers answer "us." But when most able adults are in paid work, much of the day-to-day hands-on care of children has to *be* paid work. Questions about how much time which children spend in whose care for how much money from what source are basic to modern life. It is a pity that not every nation or community recognizes that resolving those questions is not just a familial responsibility but a social one that crosses both gender and generation boundaries.

CHANGES IN FAMILIES AND WORK

Changes in family roles are obvious and well rehearsed: we're all aware of the socioeconomic and demographic developments since the Second World War that phased out many unskilled jobs in heavy industry and kicked off an expanding labor market for women. We all know that along with sociopolitical developments associated with the women's movement, these altered the roles and expectations of all family members, putting mothers, even those with very small children, on a par with other women. The once-traditional division of labor in which employed fathers brought in money from outside to support mothers caring for children inside the home is no longer common practice nor widespread aspiration.

Patterns of employment and earning have not only changed for mothers and for all women but for everybody, with men's and women's patterns actually reversing in some communities. With fewer jobs in the heavy industries that traditionally employed men and many more in a booming service sector traditionally employing women in less steady and lower-paid jobs, work can be easier for women to find, and to lose, than it is for men. Few communities are

> *Highlights of changes in U.K. families*
> *and their functioning for children*
>
> - The replacement average of 2.4 children per couple has dropped to 1.66. Barring a hiccup in 1977, this is the lowest figure since records started in 1924 (*Population Trends*, 2001).
>
> - Fewer children overall means that there are fewer siblings, cousins, and neighbors. Playmates are mostly from school or from playdates arranged by adults, while hours at home are mostly adult-centered or solitary.
>
> - An increase in single parents, stepparents, older parents, and parents starting second families means that there are more half siblings and stepsiblings, often widely separated in age, and that extended families are more complex.
>
> - There are more longer-surviving grandparents, and while many contribute to child care, there are also more parents carrying responsibility for aging parents at the same time as growing children.

sticking with those traditional gender roles, though, even outside the professions. While women's struggles for equal opportunities as long-distance truck drivers or members of the armed forces hit headlines, there's a quieter struggle going on for men's rights to work in child care or as secretaries and, for some, a more personal struggle to accept work that doesn't fit their male self-image.

In the United Kingdom and some other European countries, these changes in types of employment have been accompanied by large reductions in job security for almost everyone in almost every sector. It is not only that there are no longer jobs on the docks, in the steelworks, or in the mines for boys to start in their teens and stay with until retirement; it is also that there are almost no lifelong

> *"The last mines are closed. That life's over and I accept that. There's work in the new factory they say, women's work really but I can put cherries on top of muffins all day. I can even wear a cap to cover my hair. Can I do that for the next twenty years and be the daddy I meant to be, though? That's the question."*   Ex–coal miner, Wales

jobs left for anybody. Even in medicine or the military, in academia or the civil service, only a small percentage of people will ever achieve tenure, and the wait for it is long. Most jobs, even those at senior levels, are offered for short periods, on contracts, and this has changed people's roles and expectations. People have far less security, but with less to lose there can be more job mobility, more willingness to exercise rights, such as requesting flexible work hours, and to test the limits on unauthorized absenteeism (sometimes called "duvet days" in Britain).

The labor picture is different in the United States, where companies hire and fire to keep pace with economic conditions. Over the last decade, that has meant employment cuts in telecom technology, airlines, tourism, and media/advertising but a shortage of employees for skilled jobs in health care and some aspects of information technology. As in Europe, though, the net result has been uncertainty, sharpened in North America by anxiety about losing health benefits along with a job. After twenty years of corporate layoffs and downsizings, U.S. workers have learned that the days of employer-employee loyalty are gone and that they must at all costs keep their skills marketable and their résumés updated. Often the employee jumps before he or she can be pushed.

Changes at the national level have altered the working patterns of family members as well. On both sides of the Atlantic, two incomes are generally the norm for two-parent families—not only because people have high mortgages or aspire to a high standard of living but also because a future layoff or "early retirement" is a very real possibility, and divorce and single parenthood a statistical probability. For most single parents—whose numbers are still growing—two incomes are impossible, and one income is hard to achieve, so relative poverty is almost inevitable.

Grandparents are affected, too. Western populations are aging

---

A survey of American employers shows that annual voluntary employee turnover is 17 percent. Large employers (five thousand or more employees) report an average annual voluntary turnover of 25 percent.

Society for Human Resource Management, 2006

> *"The family is the bedrock of the welfare state. It is the family which cares for the new born, raises children, instils a sense of values, coaxes and encourages children to learn and thrive. It is the extended family—grandparents, aunts, uncles, godparents and family friends—who play a crucial caring role."* — John Hutton, secretary of state for work and pensions, United Kingdom, 2006

more rapidly than medical advances can produce healthy longevity; the real value of pensions is dwindling, the cost of elder care is soaring, and many older adults strive to stay longer in paid work. Some grandparents (and other older-generation relatives) who would like to provide support and help to young families have little spare time in which to do so. The many who do help, especially with informal child care, often do so at considerable financial cost.

Against a background of so much change, it is scarcely surprising that the composition of families and the ways they operate for children have also changed. Traditional ideas are not always easily shifted. Respectful lip service is still paid on both sides of the Atlantic to notions of "extended family," but once geographical mobility, informal partnerships, and marriage breakdown take their toll, few people are left with more relations than they can seat at a festive family dinner. The Canadian census for 2006 shows that for the first time more adults (52 percent) are single—unmarried (or in an informal partnership), divorced, separated, or widowed—than married.

Children in Western countries have traditionally been regarded as primarily family business, and it is still easily assumed—and sometimes loudly asserted—that families have a right to privacy and autonomy in exchange for children's care and upbringing. It sounds sensible and equitable, and for many generations it probably was, but are traditional views of responsibility for children viable now that there are so few traditional families left? That "children are family business" assertion used to mean that societies delegated child rearing to multigenerational networks of kin, microcosms of adult society and of their local communities. The same assertion today may mean leaving the care of a child to isolated couples or lone adolescents. No wonder the British government often finds

itself facing a justifiable charge of running a "nanny state," while the
U.S. government faces an equally justifiable charge of not doing so.

As societies become less hidebound by traditional families, much
is made of people's freedom to make new "families" in any way they
please. For children, though, that's easier said than lived. A woman
may exercise her freedom to decide that this man or woman, or
these several friends, constitute her family. But her little boy will not
feel that they are his family as long as their relationships with him
are based solely on their relationships with his mother and are
therefore vulnerable to changes in it. If a mother's lover or friends
choose to leave her, they can simply leave her child, who has become
an irrelevance to a failed relationship. In contrast, when a parent's

---

Stepfamilies and others

It is far more difficult than it might seem to know how many
stepfamilies there are in any particular society. In the United
States, a sixth of traditionally defined "mother-only" families are
said to be cohabiting two-parent families and the one-fourth of
current stepfamilies that are cohabiting are missed by marriage-
based definitions.

In the United Kingdom, the Office for National Statistics
counts 8 percent of all British families as stepfamilies, but that's
a major underestimate. Old data only counted as stepfamilies
those families in which married couples were bringing up children from previous marriages who were aged sixteen and under.
Even broadening the definition to include the never-married
does not go far enough because it still implies that a stepfamily is
only a stepfamily if it contains young children. The many, many
over-sixteens in stepfamilies vanish.

And half the parents are missing from those official statistics,
too. Many children live in two families after their parents have
separated or divorced. Instead of counting only families in
which there are children from a previous relationship, we should
surely count all the families to which those children belong.

Including half siblings and stepsiblings, aunts, uncles, ex-in-
laws, and grandparents, the estimated number of British people
involved in "the stepfamily experience" is around 18 million.

The Policy Studies Institute predicts that by the year 2010,
serial marriage will become the norm in Britain, with more families breaking down and restructuring than staying together.

spouse or sexual partner leaves, her child retains at least a vestigial identity as the formal or informal stepchild of that partnership.

"NEW MEN"

Fathers' roles have changed and are changing at least as radically as mothers'. Today's children often spend less time with their mothers than their own mothers spent with them when they were children, but many spend much more time with their fathers or men in fathering roles. Often willingly but sometimes reluctantly, men—fathers, stepfathers, partners—are playing an ever-larger role in their children's lives.

All fathers are toweringly important figures in their children's lives, real—in the present or the past—or fantasy. While there are still too many children who don't see or maybe even know their fathers, increasing, if small, numbers of fathers in two-parent fami-

---

Men, money, and home

Traditional gender inequities are under economic pressure. The current ratio of the time spent by women and men on housekeeping chores is around 3:1, and data from Britain suggests that for every extra hour women work outside the home, men work an extra 1.2 minutes inside it.

Recent commentators see couples operating competitively to avoid these chores rather than operating cooperatively to get them done. Some suggest that paychecks are used as bargaining chips: women who earn more do less household work; the difference is not picked up by men doing more but by paid labor bought with the extra income.

Twenty percent more women than men are now graduating from American universities. Professor Richard Freeman believes that "once you are graduating more women than men from universities you are really changing the whole nature of the job market."

Gary Becker, the Nobel Prize–winning American economist, says the outcome will be even smaller families, because as women earn more, they will be prepared to spend less time in the home. "If men can't cut it in the labor market, maybe one day it will be them staying home."

lies are their children's primary caregivers (see Chapter 7), and most are their backup caregivers. Some separated or divorced parents share their children between two homes. And in every kind of family, men are taking an active parenting role for granted, especially with young babies.

Led by the (expanding) European Union, along with expanding maternity rights, some countries are increasingly allowing paternity leave—still often only a token week or two. In many countries, including Britain, which has just granted all fathers two weeks' leave with (almost always) paternity pay, it will probably take a long war of attrition before that token becomes as substantial as the leave entitlements of Scandinavian fathers, but at least the idea of paternity leave is taken seriously, and there is serious discussion of allowing part of paid maternity leave to be taken by fathers as parental leave. In Australia, and in the United States, of course, with no federally mandated entitlement to paid maternity leave, paternity leave, other than a few days graciously allowed by an individual employer, is still blue-sky thinking. If fathers want to be at home while their new babies are settling in, they usually have to take precious vacation time or unpaid family leave.

DISCONTINUITY BETWEEN THE PARENT AND GRANDPARENT GENERATIONS

The expected social and cultural generation gap has been exacerbated by these changes so that today's young adults are even more likely than those of a generation earlier to feel that they live in a completely different world from their parents. Whether a particular aspect of today's lifestyle seems better or worse than yesterday's, just being different can make it uncomfortable. The difference between those worlds separates young people from their mothers and fathers; when they become parents, many cannot look to their own childhood experiences to understand those of their children, or look to their own parents' mothering and fathering as models for their own or for solutions to their own parenting conflicts. The differences are too great—and often even greater than they appear.

A mother may stay home with her child just as her own mother stayed home with her. But a woman who gave up paid employment

One hundred years of staying home with children

A generation or two ago, if your mother stayed home with you she was doing what was still ordinary and what many mothers did for a year or two at least. Nowadays, in many communities, if you stay home with your child for more than six months at most, you're doing something unexpected. You may be doing what your mother and grandmother did, but it's far more of a statement and more likely to be isolating, too.

Although many women of your mother's generation found full-time mothering limiting and frustrating and that played its part in the women's movement, their mothers and grandmothers had stayed home as a matter of course prior to the First World War and between the wars, and the experience was very different and far less isolating.

- Families used to be much bigger—and a family of four or five children did to some extent entertain and bring each other up, as well as keeping exhausted mothers' nests full for years.

- World War I left such a surplus of women that many households had unmarried aunts and cousins living in as part charity, part mother's helpers and companions.

- So scarce were jobs for women that even households that today would be regarded as poor employed servants. They were often no more than little girls themselves, but they were nevertheless people with whom babies could be left while mothers worked at other things.

when her first baby was born in the 1970s and stayed home until the last started school was doing what was socially acceptable, and there were probably other mothers living nearby who were doing the same thing. When her daughter stays home for several years today, she is doing what most women *don't* do, and that makes a big difference. Although there are communities in both the United States and the United Kingdom where women who go out to work are in the minority (and unable to get appointments to see teachers or doctors at hours they can keep), in most parts of both countries many stay-at-home mothers are both physically and emotionally lonely in their chosen lifestyle. In response, some adopt a militancy that all too easily sounds more anti-working-mother than pro-stay-at-home-mother (see Chapter 6). Meanwhile, many grandparents and their contemporaries look at their children's parenting with a lack of comprehension that often seems (and sometimes is) critical.

> It's bad enough being always short of time for the kids without my mum implying that I'm wrong to be working the hours I am, that I shouldn't 'put the job first.' Why can't she see that I'm doing it for the kids, so they can have the things the others have? Mind you, I know why, really. If I was working to put food on the table, she'd be OK about it; she had to do that herself. But she doesn't think any of them ought to have all the clothes and CDs and stuff. So I'm a double failure as a mother. Neglectful and a lousy disciplinarian. 'Just tell them no,' she says. But it's not like it was when we were children.   —FCCC mother

CHILDREN'S CARE AND STATES' ROLES

When the expansion of day care began to accelerate in the 1970s, some nations of continental Europe were quick to recognize a new working-caring equation for families and to start balancing it with relatively generous maternal and parental leave and publicly funded care places for children. In North America, the United Kingdom, and Australia, though, looking after children too young for school continued to be idealized as a private family responsibility, and publicly funded child care places were provided only for those severely deprived children for whom all else (meaning families) had failed. In that social climate, demands for purchased nonparental child care were not seen primarily as a welcome sign of economic expansion but as an unwelcome sign of the burgeoning women's movement. Many people—perhaps especially men—regarded it as "feminist" (a term of insult at that time) and "unnatural" (likewise) for mothers to pay someone else to care for a child in order to go out to work or study. At that time, no help, even via tax benefits, was provided to parents paying for private child care. Margaret Thatcher, the United Kingdom's first (and only) female prime minister, famously fretted lest Britain raise a "crèche generation," while employing two nannies for her twins as she positioned herself to run the country. Even today, thirty years later, child care in the United Kingdom, despite the real efforts of the New Labour government, in power since 1997, is still less available, less affordable, and of less consistent quality than it is in much of continental Europe.

SOCIAL CAPITAL

Families and the social connections they forge, within and between generations, are the traditional foundation of our social capital, and a growing body of evidence from around the world shows its demonstrable, measurable value. Communities that have more social capital have lower crime rates and fewer teen pregnancies, better schools, and cleaner streets. The children in such communities are at less risk of child abuse or juvenile delinquency. And, of course, a beneficial circle operates because the citizens in high-social-capital communities are more likely to pay taxes and fulfill other civic obligations and therefore to enjoy more honest and efficient government. It is because what media call failing marriages and dwindling families seem to eat away at that capital that divorce, cohabitation, and single parenting cause such disquiet, such moral outrage.

In America especially, but in Europe also, to a lesser degree, social capital as it has usually been defined is dwindling. People are less and less likely to participate in any form of local politics, or community activism. And compared to even two or three generations ago, people today are less likely to know their neighbors or to spend time informally with them. Since the mid-twentieth century, industrialized nations, with the honorable exception of Scandinavia, have experienced—and are still experiencing—declining membership in political parties and trade unions, and in almost all established democracies, turnout at elections, national as well as local or state, is down, often to embarrassing levels. Across Europe, church attendance has been nearly halved since 1970, while in the United States the authority of established Protestant institutions and hierarchies has declined, not because of the nation's religious diversity but in the face of different evangelicals celebrating individual religious experience via mass media and many small churches seeking to build local faith communities.

Robert Putnam, Malkin Professor of Public Policy at Harvard University, argued during an invited speech at a Downing Street seminar in 2001 that earlier periods of rapid social change, notably the Industrial Revolution, also brought loss of social capital, which was reversed in later decades and can be reversed again:

The last time many countries faced a social-capital crisis of this magnitude was in the Industrial Revolution's aftermath. In the U.S. at the end of the nineteenth century (and earlier in the U.K.), as people migrated from villages to factory towns, they left friends and community ties behind. The result was a weakening of community bonds, a social-capital deficit. But then, in a burst of social creativity, a remarkable generation of social reformers invented new forms of social connection that fitted the way we had come to live. The U.K., first to experience the social dislocation of the Industrial Revolution, was the first to begin to develop new forms of social capital. Many of the institutions invented by mid-Victorian social reformers to restore community bonds—the Salvation Army, unions, settlement houses, friendly societies—were then eagerly adopted a few decades later by U.S. social entrepreneurs to address our own developing social-capital crisis.

This time around, the social-capital crisis seems to be hitting America earlier and harder, probably because some of the underlying causes of the decline—suburbanization, two-career families—emerged in our country several decades earlier than in the U.K. and continental Europe.

Government decision-making should be pushed downward. Strategies that devolve real decision-making to the neighborhood level have proven effective. "Smart growth" strategies to curtail suburban sprawl not only reduce air pollution, but also enable workers to spend more time with family and friends.

Since the decline in civic engagement is particularly marked in the younger generation, we need to take more seriously our obligation to educate youth in civic responsibilities. We already know some educational policies that will work. Smaller schools, more extracurricular activities, enlivened civic education and community service requirements have all been shown to encourage broader civic engagement by young people.

Finally, we need greater workplace flexibility to allow employees to reconcile the conflicting demands of work, family and community. In a world in which virtually all adults work outside the home, we have drastically "downsized" the unpaid caring sector of our society. Both mums and dads need flexibility in their work life, so that family and community obligations do not go unmet. Smart firms will adopt flexible policies to attract top talent. Europe is ahead of the U.S. in this area and we should learn from your innovations.

Perhaps formal child care itself, brought into focus by changes in traditional family care of children, will prove to be one of the twenty-first century's sources of social capital. In the United Kingdom, new developments in family day care (childminding) (see Chapter 10) and the government's commitment to provide children's centers (see Chapter 12) in every community during the next two decades make that seem possible, if not probable.

2. The Issues

Other-than-mother care is an integral and growing part of twenty-first-century childhood; indeed, some such care in the (ever-fewer) years before school is now the norm for Western children, even those under two. Mothers (yes, still mostly them rather than fathers) have to find a way of life that is as nearly right as they can get it for themselves, for their partners, for the children in question, and, sometimes, for other children, too. That inevitably includes making decisions about staying at home with or without paid work; about going out to paid work full-time or part-time; and about studying, or putting in willing overtime and commitment for future work. The decisions would be less difficult and the lifestyle results more satisfactory if it was more generally realized that neither "women" nor "mothers" form homogenous groups. Different women grow up wanting different lifestyles—some primarily concerned with family, some with work, and many with finding a balance between the two—so the fact that some nonmaternal, nonparental, even nonfamilial care is part of the status quo is more welcome to some than to others.

The basic issues in nonmaternal child care are relatively simple and obvious, but because it is such a headline-grabbing and personally gut-wrenching topic, it is easy to lose sight of them. The "top ten," each of which is dealt with fully in other chapters, are signposted here.

ISSUE 1. FITTING CHILDREN'S UNCHANGED NEEDS FOR CARE INTO CHANGED SOCIETAL DEMANDS AND ADULT LIFESTYLES

Every baby and young child must have adult care all the time. Mothers in Western societies traditionally provided most of that care, not as the full-time "job" motherhood became in the brief period after the Second World War but at the same time as they did everything else they had to do. When they could not combine a particular day's work with a particular child's needs, other family members—importantly, including older children—took over the caring. Much the same is true in parts of developing countries today. In the postindustrial world, though, a large part of the "everything else" women have to do is work outside the home to earn money and status. Rather little of what it is necessary or fulfilling or interesting to do can be done with a baby on the back or a toddler underfoot. Furthermore, few women have older children who can be expected to care for younger ones routinely, and while a few do still share their homes with relatives, most of those who are physically and mentally capable of caring for children are in paid employment themselves. Child care by other family members is still what makes it possible for many mothers to work or study while their children are infants, and men in the family (children's own fathers or their mothers' partners) are making an increasingly important contribution. But it is rare for a father, grandparent, or other relative to be able to add child care responsibilities into the daily work they were going to undertake anyway. Unless they have retired from paid work, they, like mothers, have to sacrifice—or at least reorganize and limit— employment in order to undertake child care.

Issue 2. Swapping Child Care for Paid Work

Some women want to go out of their homes to other kinds of work, and others want to stay at home to look after small children. It sounds as if a straight swap between the two groups would solve all the problems. Unfortunately, it is not nearly as simple as it sounds. Modern societies are materialistic and profit motivated. If a woman wants to work at a job outside her home, the child care she buys has to cost less than she earns. The difference doesn't always have to be large; many mothers of children under school age work for little or no current profit as a holding operation and an investment for the future (see Chapter 4). But the need for some difference makes it uncomfortably likely that whatever a particular woman's level of education, qualification, and remuneration, she will employ someone less privileged to take care of her child and will pay her less than she herself makes. That alone makes it difficult to find, motivate, and keep private caregivers (why should they work hard taking care of children whose mothers opt to earn more doing something else?), and it makes many of the parents who directly or indirectly employ them feel uneasy, even guilty, about their child care arrangements and therefore sometimes reluctant to demand high quality.

It is not only pay differentials that complicate direct role swaps. There are time and commitment differentials, too, between what parenting involves and the 8 a.m. to 6 p.m. five days a week that is all that can be expected of even the most highly paid caregiver. Looking after a baby or small child probably takes as many hours again between evenings, night wakings, and early mornings, even leaving weekends aside as family leisure time. With at least some housekeeping and a lot of organization added in, this means that "working mothers" are not only spending much of their earnings on child care but are also almost inevitably overworked all the same compared with everyone else (see Chapter 6). Having a participant partner helps, of course—single parents or those with nonpartici-pant partners are even worse off—but however fairly fathers may share child care responsibilities, mothers almost always carry a disproportionate share of domestic responsibility and chores (see Chapter 7).

ISSUE 3. PAYING FOR CHILD CARE

The affordability of different types of child care in different places is central to all discussions of child care but is often wrongly framed. The real issue is not so much what child care costs but how those costs are to be met. Only the most highly paid parents in any partic-ular society can meet the whole cost of formal child care out of their taxed income (see Chapter 4). Every country recognizes this and offers less affluent parents at least some financial help, but only a few countries in continental Europe dispense with parental ability to pay as a consideration in child care policy, planning, or practice. To do so, they give child care parity with education or health care, financed by supply-side funding (from taxation) with a varying, but strictly limited, parental contribution.

In Scandinavian countries, for example, the care of young children is seen as a shared responsibility of parents and the state. All children are entitled to publicly supported child care with a means-tested parental contribution of around 30 percent of its costs. The expansion of publicly supported child care is justified not only as a parental entitlement that enables mothers (as well as fathers) to be employed but also as a right for children, with important educational, social, and developmental benefits. In the English-speaking world, however, child care funding is all demand-side: parents who want it must pay for it directly, with or without means-tested subsidies, tax breaks, and complicated ranges of programs for the poor such as Head Start and Early Head Start in the United States and Sure Start in the United Kingdom.

The full up-front costs of formal child care keep it out of the reach of low-income parents, especially single parents, on both sides of the Atlantic, but reducing those costs by means of subsidies and tax breaks is neither as simple nor as effective as it looks. Though each country's arrangements are different in detail, Canada's Dryden 2004 day care plan stands as a general example. However, due to a change of government, it was never passed. It was proposed that a Child Care Expense Deduction of income tax should be allowed to facilitate the lower-income parent in a two-parent family, or a single parent, taking a paid job or undertaking studies that would lead to a paid job. Yet a requirement that all claimed child care must be receipted effectively excluded most informal care, as many babysitters are reluctant to declare the income for their own taxation and many grandparents do not charge. Even where receipts for child care can be provided, such tax breaks are heavily biased toward center or nursery care; they may even exclude nannies. And since child care centers and nurseries are not often open 24/7, it also effectively excludes the many women—especially low-paid women—who work unsocial hours, that is, hours before 8 a.m. or after 6 p.m. Finally, to the fury of its many critics, the Dryden Plan not only excluded from benefit all parents who chose to care for their own children but also allowed women who were entitled to claim expenses for child care while they were working to claim for *all* for the hours of child care they used, including those that enabled them to go shopping or to the gym. When the Harper government came to power, the plan was dropped in favor of a $100-per-month Child Benefit to offset day care costs. Unfortunately, $1,200 per year scarcely covers a single month's fees at many child care centers.

In the United Kingdom, means-tested help with child care costs is similarly available through the tax credit system, and many parents can now also get tax relief through their employer. The Childcare Tax Credit introduced by the government in 2005 now (2008) contributes a maximum of 70 percent of child care costs to a maximum of £175 (approximately $280) per week for one child and £300 ($485) for two children. As in the Canadian plan, parents are eligible only if they use registered nurseries or childminders, not if they make informal arrangements to pay relatives to look after their children (as many impoverished single mothers do) or pay nannies to care for children in their own homes, as many better-off parents would like to do.

In England, the cost of a typical full-time nursery place has increased by 50 percent in a single year, according to a large survey published in February 2008. The rise outstrips inflation by nearly 20 percent; few parents' pay raises will equal that. A maximum-time nursery place for a child under two in the United Kingdom now costs £159 (roughly $255) a week, over £8,000 (nearly $13,000) a year. Parents living in London or the southeast of England and pay-

"Parents in the U.K. pay the bulk of the costs of childcare. But calls to our information line show that many parents struggle to find services that they can afford and many are missing out on the benefits for their children, as well as being unable to work or train.

"The Government has worked hard to make many more childcare places available for parents. But now we urgently need a review of the funding system for childcare to ensure that all children have access to good quality services, regardless of their family income. We need to invest more now for the future of our country."

Christine Walton, chief executive of Daycare Trust, 2006

ing the highest costs revealed in the survey could be paying almost £21,000 ($34,000) a year for a full-time place.

A full-time childminding (family day care) place is slightly less expensive at around £144 ($233) a week and up to £163 ($263) a week in inner London. The average annual salary of a daily nanny is around £16,000 (nearly $26,000). For school-aged children, fifteen hours per week at an after-school club typically costs £43 (about $70) across the United Kingdom. All those figures have to be compared with parents' average earnings, which were £457 ($738) a week by the end of 2007. All in all, parents in the United Kingdom pay around 75 percent of the costs of child care compared with other European parents, who pay around 30 percent of their child care costs.

The Childcare Bill, passed into British law in the summer of 2006, placed a new duty on local authorities to provide "sufficient childcare" in their areas for all working families who want it by 2008, and the number of available places are increasing. However, it does not address ways in which the care will be paid for.

On the other side of the Atlantic, however, finding and paying for child care may be even tougher for parents. According to researchers, America's "dramatic increase in the number of children in non-parental childcare over the past three decades has occurred in the absence of any comprehensive national system for increasing childcare, providing financial backing for families or facilities, or monitoring childcare quality."

There are more than ninety different government child care and early childhood education programs in the United States, and they are managed by eleven different federal agencies and twenty different offices. In Canada, similarly, there are fourteen separate child care jurisdictions—ten provinces, three territories, and the federal government—each with a number of different programs for care and education, as well as programs specifically intended to ameliorate poverty and/or support parents. So great is the variability of provision from province to province that nationwide figures can be only approximate. North American parents everywhere, however, bear the brunt of child care costs, averaging in 2003 $4,000 to $6,000 dollars, between 7 percent of the budgets of middle-income

> *"The dilemma is the majority of parents can't pay for care now, or they have a hard time paying for care. The child care community can't afford to provide the level of care that children need."*
>
> Carol Hunt, director, Project Child Care (now
> Resource Connection for Kids), Manatee County, Florida

families and 20 percent of the budgets of poor families. At the time of writing, the scarce good urban child care centers in the United States cost more than tuition at most public universities, and adequate care for two children in a child care center costs at least $12,000 a year, considerably more than a full-time minimum-wage worker can earn.

There are measures that are well designed to help, but they are not adequately funded. The Child Care and Development Block Grant, created to help low-income parents pay for child care, can serve only one in ten of the children who are theoretically eligible and provides inadequate funds even for them. Both Head Start and pre-K programs are fully subsidized at no cost to the mother. In most parts of the country, though, such programs are tragically few and far between. Likewise, while some state initiatives, such as Kentucky's Family Resource and Youth Services Centers, Georgia's universal access to prekindergarten program for four-year-olds, North Carolina's Smart Start, and Ohio's Families and Children First initiative, are making crucial contributions in their own areas and could be pathfinders for the nation, no state comes even close to providing the amount of affordable high-quality child care that is needed.

Even the most cogent criticisms of well-intentioned national plans do not fully convey the cobbled-together, chaotic arrangements and the resulting constant stress with which many poor American mothers struggle. Ajay Chaudry, in his book *Putting Children First*, beautifully conveys the painful struggles of New York mothers to arrange child care that will enable them to hold down a job and the knife edge they often must walk to keep the two in financial balance.

The woman Chaudry quotes below had worked at a store full-

> *"My opinion is that we need a greater investment in childcare for all children. I think childcare should be a public responsibility."*
>
> Kathleen McCartney, senior researcher, NICHD

time for three months when her schedule was changed to include evening and weekend hours. She spoke with her supervisor about regular daytime hours but was told that she "had to work according to the store's rules." Those rules meant that she had to use two care providers in addition to her daughter's subsidized pre-K program and to continually adjust her time with each at minimal notice:

> I had her grandmother—the father's mother—watch Flores on Saturdays and Sundays. I would pay her $50 for two days. Then I had this lady charging me $7 per hour to pick up my daughter and for the hours that she was staying with her. Sometimes when I was working late, like to ten o'clock, I would sit there and calculate how much I was paying. She picks her up like at 5:45, and I don't get there like until ten o'clock—that was another $50 or $60, 'cause those hours add up.

ISSUE 4. ECONOMIES OF SCALE IN RELATION TO ADULT-CHILD RATIOS AND CHILD CARE QUALITY

Since individual child care is difficult both to arrange and to pay for, group care, in nurseries or day care centers, seems the obvious economic solution irrespective of educational or social considerations for the children themselves. Such care often (though not always) offers economies of scale compared with care by a paid individual in the child's own home. However, while individual nanny care for a first child is almost certain to be more expensive than a place in a good center, adding in a second child may increase but certainly will not double the nanny's wages yet will double the bill from the center.

Even for single children, though, there is a fine balance between the economy of scale that comes from sharing one caregiver among several children, especially infants, and the quality of the care they receive. A central fact about child care, as widely known as it is widely ignored, is that what matters most to children's current happiness and ongoing development is warm and intimate personal

"While Project Child Care provides state-mandated training for all local child-care workers, it is very basic training. Most day cares can't afford to pay the salaries trained and certified teachers command, so they are forced to train unqualified staff members and have a higher ratio of children to adults just to break even."   Carol Hunt

relationships with their caregivers. Having more children to care for does not automatically preclude a caregiver from such relationships, but it certainly makes them less likely. The lower the ratio of children to adults, especially in the first three years, the more likely it is that the quality of care will be high. Unfortunately, of course, the lower the ratio, the higher the costs of the care. Attempts to hold down costs by reducing the number of caregivers in charge of a given number of children, and, often, the age and education (and therefore the pay) of the caregivers who are employed, are responsible for a great deal of poor-quality care.

ISSUE 5. ATTACHMENT AND SEPARATION; OR, "IS NONMATERNAL CARE BAD FOR BABIES?"

It is difficult to overstate the importance to babies of secure attachment to parents and/or people who consistently stand in for them, but it is very easy to overstate the relevance of child care to it. There has been—and in some quarters still is—confusion about what is meant by attachment, and consequently widespread expectation that physical separation of child and mother during working hours is likely to threaten its security.

"Attachment," used in the context of infant development, is a technical term, referring to the formation and security of babies' crucial first loving relationships with mothers or mother figures, as assessed by the repeatedly and internationally validated "Strange Situation."

Those first loving relationships are important forever. Babies' need for passionate personal attention that is sensitive and responsive to their feelings and states is just as real and legitimate as their need for physical care in the sense that they cannot thrive without either. Every time a baby's very existence is celebrated in another spontaneous hug; every time the adult who is caring for her notices her sounds, facial expressions, and body language and answers her; realizes that she is becoming distressed and acts to put things right for her, the foundations of that baby's future self-esteem and self-confidence, self-control, and social competence are strengthened. It is knowing and feeling that she is loved that helps a baby to become lovable and loving. It is through their first love relationships that babies learn about themselves, other people, and the world; experience emotions and learn to cope with them. And it is through baby love that they become capable of more grown-up kinds, capable, one far-distant day, of giving children of their own the kind of devotion they now need for themselves. Taking these relationships seriously is not just a matter of being nice to babies and parents; secure attachment in the first year of life plays a large part in the kind of person a baby will become, in the development not only of personality but also of his or her brain.

Newborn humans are programmed to focus their attention on an

Attachment figures

- Serve as a secure base from which a child feels it safe to explore

- Are available as a safe haven when danger threatens

- Recognize and help the child to understand social experiences and to identify and organize emotional responses

- Give the child the security of knowing that someone will always "be there for him/her" when necessary

Secure attachment remains valuable throughout life because:

- Without it, children are vulnerable to emotional problems.

- It ensures a more positive "working model" of relationships with other people in which both self and others are valued.

- It facilitates styles of interaction with other people that brings more opportunities for learning and loving.

- It enables greater understanding of emotional states in self and others.

"*The attention that we receive as babies impacts on our brain structures. If we find ourselves cared for by people who love us, and who are highly sensitive to our unique personalities, the pleasure of those relationships will help to trigger the development of the "social brain." In the simplest terms, the pre-frontal cortex (and in particular its orbitofrontal area) plays a major role in managing our emotional lives: it picks up on social cues, the non-verbal messages that other people transmit, it enables us to empathise, as well as playing an important part in restraining our primitive emotional impulses.*"

Sue Gerhardt, psychotherapist and author of *Why Love Matters*

intimately caring adult for the next stages of their development, just as newborn marsupials are programmed to seek the mother's pouch for the next stages of theirs. That first "attachment figure" is usually the person who is biologically set up for it—the mother—but usually does not mean invariably, and first does not mean only, certainly not only forever.

If they have sufficient opportunity, babies form parallel attachments to fathers (and sometimes to other relatives or caregivers). Recent studies following babies and both parents through childhood suggest that attachments to fathers are not secondary to, but distinct from, attachments to mothers. A child may, for example, have a "disorganized attachment" to one parent and a "secure attachment" to the other. Furthermore, different attachments "teach" different lessons. Mothers teach inner-world emotional lessons about the understanding of complex feelings, including the ability to acknowledge distress in others and the capacity to generate a flexible coping strategy, while fathers teach more outer-world social lessons about functioning in peer relationships.

An infant's first attachment is a two-way process: it's about both loving and being loved. Starting for many mothers (and perhaps their babies) before birth, it continues to strengthen through at least the first year, irrespective of whether the mother is with the baby all the time or some of it, whether she cares for the baby exclusively or shares that care. A mother does not have to be physically with the baby every moment in order to love her, "bear her in mind," and be sensitive to her, and that baby can and will love her whether she is physically present or not. Decisions about going back to work and seeking some other care for a baby are important in a lot of ways, and the intimate, personal quality of that care and of a caregiver to whom the baby can form a secondary attachment is vital, but the risk that leaving her with somebody else during adult working hours may in itself damage her primary attachment is not one of them.

Several misunderstandings seem to fuel that peculiarly parental anxiety. The first is over the actual meaning of the word "separation." Used as a technical term in attachment theory, "separation" means mother and baby not being together enough for the two of them to bond with each other in the first place, and/or being together too little and too unpredictably for the baby to hold on to an image of the mother as available and responsive to him, or even not being together at all. This is not the same as separation in an everyday sense, which might include mother and baby being apart from each other for a few hours at a time.

The second misunderstanding concerns the circumstances under which the absence of mother (or father) is likely to be traumatic. Not having a loving parent available only condemns a baby to drowning in a sea of abandonment and despair if he has no one else who, as well as taking care of his immediate physical needs, can serve as a secondary attachment figure, an emotional life raft on which he can float until his parents return. The truly tragic outcomes of "maternal deprivation," mainly reported from institutions for abandoned or orphaned children, most recently in Romania and China, result not solely from babies not having their mothers but from them not having anybody with whom to share an ongoing intimate, personal relationship.

> *"The attachment literature does not demand exclusive parental care. There will be a hierarchy of attachments, with number one sometimes changing faces (a childminder, father or grandparent may be preferred at some point)."* Sebastian Kraemer, child psychiatrist

Third, it is not always understood that while nobody can specify the exact age stages at which it is acceptable for children in general—or any one child in particular—to be apart from parents for a given number of hours under a given set of circumstances, there is no doubt that each baby-parent pair needs enough predictable time together to form those attachment bonds and that the benefits of those earliest relationships consolidate over time. Toddlers may be very unhappy when first separated from their parents, but the one who built up a secure attachment during his first year will be less vulnerable to any ill effects and more likely to be readily able to forge a relationship with a new caregiver.

Finally, even the words of the father of attachment theory, John Bowlby, are sometimes incompletely understood. Contrary to what many people have believed during the intervening half century, Bowlby did not say that babies and young children need their mothers to be with them for every minute of every day. His famous statement that "the infant and young child should experience a warm, intimate and continuous relationship with his mother" has been used (and misused) to emphasize the importance of mother-child bonds and the risks of separation. However, there was an important second half of that sentence that is usually omitted: "or permanent mother-substitute in which both find satisfaction and enjoyment." A baby can have a warm and intimate relationship with his mother that counts as "continuous" even if she is away from him for some hours each day, provided somebody loving stands in for her.

In an even less well known paper written in 1949, Bowlby seemed to foresee today's arguments about whether a mother who wants to pursue her adult profession may actually be a better mother for doing so although she is not with her baby all the time. Bowlby stressed that "a negative maternal attitude"—beautifully described in terms of "minor pinpricks of dislike" and "odd works of impatience and bad temper"—was as likely to have lasting ill effects on a young child as maternal separation.

So, rather than saying that a baby's mental health depends on having his biological mother with him all the time, Bowlby said that infant mental health depends on babies having a continuous and mutually enjoyed relationship with a caregiver. Being a child of a time when most mothers were at home, he would have described that caregiver as a "mother or mother substitute," but he knew that babies need to be with people who enjoy being with them and that exclusive mother care may not meet that need.

Three-quarters of a century later, Sebastian Kraemer, one of Britain's most eminent child psychiatrists, goes further:

> The point is that more than one caregiver is necessary. No one can care for a child alone. The lone parent is surely [only] a problem if she [or he] is really alone without confiding friends, lover, or family, and poor. This is likely to lead to depression—which is as much a social as a mental state, solitary and hopeless—[and then] the caregiver cannot respond to the baby's varying states of mind and body, so the brain gets wired up to manage without. Unlike all other mammals, most of the growth of the human brain is postnatal, and continues for several years.

Anxiety over the possible negative impact of nonmaternal care on relationships between mothers and young children, specifically the security of their attachment, has been raised repeatedly during the last half century by researchers and politicians, parents and policy makers. Indeed, it was the reemergence in the 1980s of suggestions that infant day care might contribute to insecure attachments between babies and their mothers that led to the funding of the world's largest study of day care: the NICHD Early Child Care Research Network study in the United States, much cited in this book.

Specifically designed to examine the relationship between infant child care and security of attachment, the NICHD study found that the amount, type, or quality of child care had no direct effect on attachment security unless a mother was extremely insensitive to her baby and the child care was of extremely poor quality. In that study and in subsequent research, by far the most important predictor of the security of an infant's attachment to his mother is her sensitivity to him. Beside that maternal sensitivity, child care is unimportant, as one of the principal investigators, Alison Clarke-Stewart, made clear: "We need to talk about quality of both home care and child care in making generalizations about what is best for children's development."

ISSUE 6. AGGRESSION AND BEHAVIOR PROBLEMS; OR, "IS NONMATERNAL CARE BAD FOR TODDLERS?"

Concerns of the 1970s and 1980s about possible ill effects of early nonmaternal care on babies' attachments to their mothers have been substantially allayed by research, but new concerns have arisen, specifically about whether children who have extensive early nonmaternal child care are more likely to display behavior problems at the time and later.

Some research studies have asked if experience in child care increases the likelihood of some children being more aggressive and uncooperative; others have asked if the extra social experience children get in child care makes them likely to be more sociable both with other children and with nonfamily adults.

Most recently published reports from the NICHD study suggest that children who had spent more time in child care with other children were more aggressive and unsociable in child care when they were two years of age and that children who had spent more hours per week in care over the whole period from three months to four and a half years old were more likely to be destructive, to have a lot of temper tantrums and fights with other children, and to argue and talk back to teachers as well as being highly attention seeking. These differences did not disappear when children left child care and went to school: kindergarten and first-grade teachers also noted more aggressive and disobedient behavior.

We are brought up to respect scientists as people who make objective inquiries after some kind of truth, and therefore to believe that if a body of scientific research is accepted for publication by other specialists in its field ("peer reviewed"), then it should be taken seriously, probably even "believed" by the rest of us. Unfortunately, it's not that simple. Even the best-funded and most extensive study, carefully designed, conducted, directed, and analyzed by respected researchers, can leave some question marks, even contradictions. That has certainly happened here. Some researchers accept the accuracy of those NICHD findings but interpret them differently. For example, NICHD researchers have themselves pointed out that the proportion of children who had spent a lot of time in day care showing behavioral problems was

17 percent, which is the same rate recorded (using the same measures) in the general population of American children. Among four-year-olds who had stayed at home with their mothers and had no day care, the comparable rate of aggression was only 5 percent. This might suggest that rather than child care having made children more likely to be aggressive, being at home with their mothers until age four had made home-care children less likely to be so. Other studies that have looked at social development in relation to child care over the last twenty years have reported that it is not child care itself that increases the likelihood of behavior problems but poor-quality child care. Some have found that child care of high quality has positive effects on children's socioemotional development.

Issue 7. The Quality of Child Care

Quality is probably the most important issue in child care. It increasingly dominates child care research and, of course, the concerns of parents, providers, and policy makers. We all want more child care and affordable child care, but we also want *good* child care, difficult though it is to agree on definitions or measurements of what that is precisely. Quality crosscuts so many other issues that discussion of it takes up many pages of this book, and it is therefore merely mentioned here.

The three things we know most certainly about child care quality are: (1) It matters enormously to children. Researchers have shown repeatedly that children who have better-quality care tend to have better cognitive and language development and more advanced social skills, while the reverse is true for children in poor-quality care, especially among children who are already at risk for poor outcomes. (2) Child care quality varies widely throughout the English-speaking world, from excellent to pretty terrible, both within one type—nurseries, say—or across types: nurseries, childminders, nannies. (3) As important as child care quality undoubtedly is, in terms not only of current happiness but also of its eventual outcomes for children, its long-term impact is not as great as that of poverty on the one hand or the closeness of the relationship between child and mother on the other.

ISSUE 8. INTERNATIONAL, NATIONAL, STATE, AND LOCAL DIFFERENCES

Until the last decade, most of the world's high-quality, large-scale child care research was carried out in the United States and, faute de mieux, other countries applied American findings to their own populations. More recently, child care researchers have begun to question the universality and generalizabilty of child care findings and to conduct studies in the light of national or state contexts and perspectives. All American child care settings differ markedly from European equivalents, and European countries differ from one another. The clearest example is family day care (see Chapter 10), which is very different in the United States from the United Kingdom, where it is called "childminding" and has higher rates of registration and training, as well as more stringent regulation and inspection, than in most American states. Scandinavian family day care is different again, with caregivers mostly employed and paid by local authorities or by charitable organizations rather than being self-employed and paid directly by parents.

Societal differences, as in the overall standards of child care, are important also, sometimes affecting the robustness of research findings. In North America, for example, children's attachment security is unaffected, even by care that is of poor quality by American standards. But that does not mean that attachment security is always immune to child care quality. If poor-quality care is bad enough (as it is—or was—in Israel), children's attachments may indeed be less secure. So quality of care matters everywhere, but the worse it is, the more damaging.

Early entry into nonparental child care is sometimes considered a cause for concern, but the age of entry depends on parents' work and leave arrangements, and the nature of the concern varies with the point of view. In the United States, lacking any federally mandated paid maternity leave, three months after the birth is regarded as a long time to stay at home with a new baby. In the United Kingdom, although more parents are seeking care for younger and younger infants, the thirty-nine weeks' leave, paid by salary for some weeks and by maternity allowance thereafter, that is available to all, with a further unpaid thirteen weeks, makes three months seem a very short time indeed. And in the European Union countries, where child care is paid for largely out of public funds, the relatively generous provision for over-ones that is the envy of the English-speaking world is possible only because most parents are expected, and enabled by relatively generous paid leave arrangements, to care for their own babies at home during at least the first year, when public provision of child care is so expensive.

ISSUE 9. CHOICE FOR PARENTS

If measures to raise the quality of child care as a whole are to be effective, they have to be planned and undertaken in the context of what individual parents want and what works for them and their particular children. It is useless for experts to feel that they know best for children and to make policies accordingly, if they do not have the agreement and support of parents. Children's ability to fulfill their own developmental potential depends crucially on their relationships with their mothers and fathers (or the people who take on those roles), so anything that undermines or damages that relationship is going to be bad for a child, and anything that supports or enhances it is going to be good.

As an example, consider policies concerning whether and when mothers should work outside their homes. However strongly a group of experts feels that it is good for a child to have a parent at home, pressuring a mother to stay at home full-time when she needs the money, companionship, or career continuity of outside employment is liable to take the shine off her time with her child. So policies that make it difficult for such a woman to work—for example, failing to provide acceptable, affordable child care and/or sufficiently flexible jobs—are likely to damage the relationship between child and mother. On the other hand, however sure policy makers are that parents' paid work is the way to lift children out of poverty, cutting back on benefits or making them conditional on employment so that a mother who would prefer to be at home with her child is forced to leave her with somebody else, is equally liable to take the shine off her feelings about being a mother.

How people feel about being parents makes a difference to how their children turn out; the overall contentment—even joy—of the adults doing the caring affects the development of the small people they're caring for. So parents, the people we hold responsible for the community's children, should get to choose how to meet that responsibility. Child care policies that may appear to be geared toward parents' (usually mothers') preferences, however, are often based on superficial assumptions about those preferences drawn more from employment statistics than consultation. In the United Kingdom, for example, the treasury currently invests heavily in child care because more and more mothers of young children are going out to work, and policy makers (concerned about child poverty) want all mothers to do so. Because many mothers are at work, it is assumed that they *want* to work. And whether they start out reflecting the wishes of a majority or a minority, assumptions about what mothers want have their own momentum. If women think "all mothers" want to be (or are) employed, more of them will come to feel not just that they want to be but that they ought to be at work, too.

> I hate the thought of him in a nursery and we're both having a good time just hanging out together, but I'll have to find a job soon 'cause two-year-olds just don't spend all day with mummy.
>
> —FCCC mother of twenty-month-old boy

Since mothers who are not employed often cite lack of suitable child care as an explanation, it is assumed that more child care will assist them. But when women are actually consulted, not only in the United Kingdom but in other European and North American countries, surveys find that substantial numbers of mothers would prefer to have one parent home-based while their children are under one or two years old, and then to work shorter hours than they do currently. Home care allowances, paid to women in several countries, including France, Finland, and Norway, specifically for the work of bringing up children in their own homes, have proved

> "The current system where the state subsidises anyone but the mother to care for a child makes no sense: choice is all."
>
> Polly Toynbee, *The Guardian*, 2001

runaway winners, being claimed by 100 percent of those entitled within a year or two of first being announced.

ISSUE 10. WHO IS CHILD CARE (AND EARLY YEARS EDUCATION) *FOR?*

Child care sounds like care for children, but to what extent is it for children's benefit or for the benefit of parents and the world of employment?

High-quality early education and child care certainly benefits almost all children over three and may benefit many younger children, especially those with deprived home relationships and circumstances (see Chapter 15). Research demonstrates developmental benefits such as better language and intellectual development, while greater experience of peer interaction improves children's social skills. These are some of the key benefits of the expansion of preschool provisions. Such facilities have become increasingly important with the general reduction in family size, increased mobility of families, and other factors that have led to the increased isolation of families with young children and consequently a reduction in other opportunities for peer play among young children.

The outcomes of early child care and education programs for the children of underprivileged families, tracked by various long-term studies in the United States, have been so outstanding that the Committee for Economic Development called for investments in such programs in these words:

> Education is an investment, not an expense. If we can ensure that all children are born healthy and develop the skills and knowledge they need to be productive, self-supporting adults, whatever is spent on their development and education will be returned many times over in higher productivity, incomes, and taxes, and in lower costs for welfare, health care, crime, and myriad other economic and social problems.
>
> The bottom line: investments in quality child development and after-school programs are money-savers, not budget-busters.

However, beneath their enthusiasm for early childhood services, what is notable about this statement and those in the following boxes is that they refer to high-quality child care as a worthwhile

> "*The question is not whether we can afford these programs, it is whether we can afford to jeopardize the safety of millions of Americans and saddle future generations with the cost of failing to make these proven investments today. When child care and after-school programs save dollars and cut crime, why shouldn't our federal and state governments provide the funding that will enable communities to get the job done?*"
>
> Elliot L. Richardson, former U.S. attorney general and
> secretary of Health, Education, and Welfare

investment in the future of the national economy: an investment in children for adults' sakes rather than for their own. Furthermore, not all child care is of high quality. In fact, much of it is of very low quality. While desperate parents may believe that the child care so vital to their lives is also good for their children, there is no research to suggest that poor child care is good enough.

The extreme pressures parents feel to work and earn money can lead not only to incorrect assumptions about the child care they want but also, insidiously, to policies that are not ideal for their children. A decade or so ago in the United States, for example, pressure on mothers to keep quiet about their child care responsibilities if they wanted to compete with all the other adults at work led to the establishment of "sick child day cares." The idea was that if your child was too ill to go to his ordinary day care and familiar caregiver, you took him instead to a special day care (often surplus hospital provision) to be cared for by strangers who were better qualified to understand his earache and fever than his feelings. It would be nice to think that the idea did not catch on in the United States or spread widely in Europe because everyone realized it was emotionally crass, but it is probably more realistic to think of it as falling victim to its own high prices and high insurance costs. Today, fewer parents who need to stay home with a child who is sick (far more often

> "*Investing in early childhood education provides government and society with estimated rates of return that would make a venture capitalist envious.*"
> Isabel Sawhill, The Brookings Institution

mothers than fathers) feel they have to tell their managers or col-leagues that they themselves are ill, but children's winter colds and flu and ear infections are still difficult to cope with. As one FCCC mother put it, "We're doing well if we can both go to work every day of a two-week period."

Even more difficult for many parents right now is the issue of night shifts. Apart from essential service personnel, like doctors, nurses, police, paramedics, and fire officers, it is those earning the most (executives) and those earning the least (cleaners, security guards, supermarket staff) who tend to work the most unsocial and unpredictable hours. The first group can usually buy solutions, but many shift workers have to work when their managers tell them to work irrespective of the hours they had planned for and for which they had made child care arrangements. There is a widespread assumption that children's needs for care should not interfere in any way with adult working patterns and that parents do not want them to. If that assumption is growing, it will not be surprising if late-evening, Sunday, and overnight child care grows as well.

3. How Much Child Care? What Kinds and Where?

As more women with young children stay in or return to the workplace, more children need nonmaternal care. But how many need it or get it? It is surprisingly difficult to tell. Sometimes media imply that only a small minority of mothers stay at home once any available maternity leave ends, but on other occasions they suggest that "working mothers," especially those of children under school age, are in the minority. These different accounts of the prevalence of nonmaternal care suit different social agendas. The "all mothers work" story tends to rise to the top when single mothers are being pressured to find work rather than rely on benefits. The "working mothers are a minority" story gets told and retold whenever "latch-key children" or unsupervised teenagers are in the news. Media are not entirely to blame for this confusion, however, because child care figures are very different across countries, and even within countries the availability of child care places varies widely across communities. Figures derived from academic research vary, too. Many stem from studies carried out ten or more years ago, making them of uncertain relevance to today, and very few are based on representative national samples.

Recent national (or representative) statistics show surprising agreement for the English-speaking nations. They show that approximately half of all children born since 2001 are regularly cared for by someone other than a parent before their first birthday. About a quarter of these are cared for by relatives, often grandmothers. Very few (less than one child in ten) are in nurseries or day care centers. Those are very broad figures, however, and they are difficult to interpret. A lot of assumptions are made that may not be accurate. A 2005 overview of Canada's Early Childhood Education and Care (ECEC), for example, says that "most of the over 70% of children with both parents (or a single parent) in the paid labour force were presumed to be in child care that was not regulated. . . . The range, quality and access to ECEC services vary enormously by region and circumstances." The U.S. Child Care Bureau, which oversees the Child Care and Development Fund (CCDF), admits that its "national statistics" do not represent the whole picture for the United States: the fund "serves a higher proportion of infants and toddlers in center care than the national average" (49 percent and 55 percent, respectively). Furthermore, "CCDF data do not distinguish between relatives and nonrelatives caring for children in their own homes or in family child care homes." In Australia, a government survey of child-rearing practices published in 2006 states that only 7 percent of infants under one year of age and only 21 percent of all children attend "formal care," including after-school care. However, these figures are not as startlingly low as they appear because care that is classified as "not formal" includes all forms of home-based care: nannies and babysitters as well as fathers, grandmothers, and other relatives.

If overall figures are opaque, though, it is clear that the use of nonparental care has risen very rapidly over the last few years in all countries and that the trend is toward greater use of group (center or nursery) care. Official figures for England published by the inspection body OFSTED dramatically illustrate this with substantial changes over a mere three months of 2005. During this very brief period, the total number of child care places being provided went up by twelve thousand, but numbers of family day care places increased by only five hundred while numbers of nursery places increased by more than ten thousand. Sessional places—mornings or afternoons one to five days per week—in nursery schools and playgroups actually dropped.

Although they can take the form of mind-bogglingly complex statistics, answers to the question "How much child care?" are important to all who are involved in child care issues, and, like it or not (and many people do not), that is almost everyone. The answers most clearly matter to policy makers, to child care providers, and to those who provide the infrastructure of child care: staff training, regulation, and inspection; financial investment and management. We need to know how much nonmaternal, nonparental, or nonfamilial child care is taking place in a given community before we can frame any of the other fundamental questions about child care— what kind of care, where, by whom, for which children, from what age, for what hours, paid for by whom, and with what results?—let alone answer them accurately. The relevance to individual families and their employers is less obvious but still real. A parent with a difficult decision to make about working and caregiving needs to know not only his or her range of choices but also what other people in similar circumstances do: how phrases such as "family friendly" or "flexible work hours" are interpreted by most firms in their line of business; and, perhaps above all, whether the pattern of daily care that's being considered for his or her child is commonplace for a child his age in their particular community.

> The idea of handing Claudia over to a nursery nurse in a baby room seemed completely absurd: incredible really, until I realised that that's what the other parents in our postnatal group were doing and that at 8 months she'd had longer full time at home than any of them.
> —FCCC mother

It is because these figures matter and trustworthy ones are scarce or difficult to compare that this book relies heavily on two major follow-up studies of child care, one American and the other English, each involving more than one thousand families, and on two very large surveys, one American and one English, for transatlantic comparisons.

The NICHD Study of Early Child Care and Youth Development (hereafter NICHD), carried out by the NICHD Early Child Care Research Network, followed 1,364 American infants born in 1991 in ten sites across the United States and is still ongoing. The Families, Children and Child Care study (hereafter FCCC) followed 1,201 English infants born in 1998–99 in two sites in southern England from birth to four and a half years. Neither of these samples is nationally representative.

BABIES IN CHILD CARE

Infant child care is a phenomenon of the English-speaking world rather than of continental Europe. The family policies adopted by the Organisation for Economic Co-operation and Development (OECD) nations and in Scandinavia vary widely, but all combine government funding of child care services with paid maternity, paternity, and parental leave. Most families can, if they wish and are prepared to accept the lowered income, have a parent at home with a child for one to three years, and many choose to do so for at least the first year.

In North America, the United Kingdom, and Australia, it is among mothers with babies under a year old that the clearest increases in employment and use of child care have been seen over the last two decades. The rise has been steepest in the United States, where more babies start child care earlier than ever before, and earlier than in other countries. About 70 percent of North American babies are in regular nonmaternal (though often paternal) care before the age of four months as compared with around 9 percent of British babies. Half are in regular *nonparental* care at the age of nine months, and by the end of their first year, 82 percent of infants in the United States are regularly cared for by someone other than their mothers (72 percent by a nonparent) as compared with 48 percent in Britain.

Although child care and parental, especially maternal, work are

SUMMARY COMPARISON AMONG UNIVERSAL MATERNAL ENTITLEMENTS IN SWEDEN, THE UNITED KINGDOM, AND THE UNITED STATES

	Time off work	Equivalent pay	Right to part-time work?
Sweden	480 days (60 days must be taken by father)	80% of monthly wage for 390 days, then £15 ($24) per day	Yes—at 80% of normal wage until child is 8
United Kingdom	365 days	90% of monthly wage for 42 days, £117 ($189) per week for 270 days, then no payment	Only to request (and have request taken seriously)
United States	None (sick leave only)	None	No

---

*Nonparental care for children of U.S. mothers
employed full- and part-time*

Mothers working full-time are more likely to use nonparental care: In the NICHD study 49 percent of babies of full-time working mothers had nonparental care, versus 24 percent of infants whose mothers worked part-time. In national data collected by the Early Childhood Longitudinal Study Birth Cohort (ECLS-B), 42 percent of preschoolers with full-time working mothers had nonparental care versus 24 percent of preschoolers whose mothers worked part-time.

Conversely, father care is more than twice as prevalent among children of part-time employed mothers as full-time, 35 percent versus 17 percent in the NICHD study; 24 percent versus 11 percent in national data (ECLS-B).

---

closely linked, a surprisingly large number of parents use child care when they are not working but want time away from the baby—more than one hundred thousand in Australia in 2006, for example. An equally surprising (and much larger) number do not use child care whether they are working or not. In the United States, for example, while around 70 percent of children under age five in nonparental care have employed mothers, 30 percent do not. Their mothers may of course be absent from the family, physically or mentally ill, or doing unpaid work such as caring for elderly relatives.

Some parents—almost exclusively women—take children to their workplace. Some of the growing number of parents who work at home—mostly women—manage to combine work and child care, often by doing the work during babies' nap times and at night. But a much larger group than both of these put together consists of couples who arrange flextime, shift work, and unsocial hours so that one parent can always be at home while the other is at work.

Such informal in-family arrangements speak to the ingenuity of parents trying to cope but bedevil child care statistics. If there are thousands more women at work who are known to have babies than there are places for babies in registered child care, it is often assumed that those babies are in some informal or unofficial child care and that the numbers of those babies can be taken as a measure of unmet need for child care. The assumption may be wrong, though. A report of the unusually detailed survey from the Australian Bureau of Statistics shows that in 2006 almost two-thirds of Australian families did not need or want formal child care because the parents preferred to care for their children themselves or with informal help from family members. In that same year, only 61 percent of under-threes in the United Kingdom were receiving either formal or informal child care, and in Canada 80 percent of families preferred parent care according to the report of a national survey. If parental care was not an option, the next choice was relative-based care, followed (a long way behind) by family day care, and only 7 percent endorsed for-profit center care. These Australian and Canadian figures cannot be directly compared, though, as the latter figures relate to what parents say they prefer rather than to what they actually do.

The possibility of sharing child care between two working parents obviously depends on the number of hours that each parent works and on their schedules. Parents who work outside the home are unlikely to be able to provide enough child care to allow their partners to work full-time unless their own hours, including travel time, are limited. Even then the timing usually works out only if at least one parent works part-time and comparatively close to home.

Despite all these exceptions, the majority of children in child care do have employed or student mothers. And this is certainly what most of their governments intend. Outside Scandinavia, tax breaks and subsidies to pay for child care are not given because treasury departments want mothers to have downtime or children to have stimulation but because they want mothers, like almost all adults, to take paid employment. And governments and economists not only want mothers to earn so that they will not draw benefits; they also want them (as well as everybody else) to earn money so that they will *spend* it: on paying other people, such as caregivers, dry cleaners, and other service personnel; on buying more clothing, fares, convenience foods, and other consumer goods; and above all on *paying income tax.*

Considerable transatlantic differences in the number of young children in nonmaternal care certainly relate to differences in maternity rights legislation. In the United Kingdom, the nine months of paid maternity leave plus three months of unpaid leave to

> *Provision of maternity leave by American employers*
>
> • 26 percent of employers provide four to six weeks of paid maternity leave.
>
> • 24 percent provide a maximum of four weeks of paid maternity leave.
>
> • 48 percent provide no paid maternity leave.
>
> • Paid family leave is available to only 14 percent of professional or managerial-level employees.
>
> • Paid family leave is very rarely available to employees earning less than fifteen dollars per hour.
>
> • The federal government provides no paid maternity or family leave: employees must use sick days or take unpaid time off.
>
> Institute for Women's Policy Research, 2007

which every employed woman is entitled is expected to rise to a full year of paid leave during the next parliament (2010). In the United States, there is no official paid maternity leave; only California has a policy providing for it. Of course, various states and various corporations offer some women a range of opportunities, but not as a universal right and usually without pay.

Furthermore, although both nations have "welfare to work" policies, the pressure on American mothers to find work and put children in child care so as to come off (or avoid going on) welfare is far greater than it is for British mothers. In both countries, single mothers are encouraged to find work as their only route out of poverty. But in the United Kingdom, the encouragement so far is largely positive; in the United States, it can be punitive.

Many other aspects of the work world also contribute to transatlantic differences. In the United States, the bulk of the available part-time work has long been mainly in blue-collar or service-sector jobs. Higher-status jobs, especially in the professions, have mostly been full-time. Although that is changing, and increasing numbers of American men and women hold down service-sector, white-collar, and professional jobs on a part-time or partly home-based basis, the U.K. job market is still more "family friendly" than that of

How Much Child Care? What Kinds and Where?

49

CHILD CARE IN THE FIRST YEAR OF LIFE:
NICHD AND FCCC SAMPLES APPROXIMATELY COMPARED

	Type of care at 3 months		Type of care at 12 months	
	U.S.	U.K.	U.S.	U.K.
Mother	children in mother care not included	92%	children in mother care not included	53%
Father (or partner)	25%	2.5%	23%	7%
Grandparent (or relative)	23%	3%	21%	14%
Family day care	24%	1%	27%	11%
Nanny, au pair, sitter	12%	0.8%	12%	4%
Child care center/nursery	12%	0.4%	17%	10%

NICHD percentages are for children receiving nonmaternal care; FDCC percentages are for all children, whether receiving nonmaternal care or not

the United States, with 44 percent of all employed women working part-time and an increase in part-time women employees holding down professional or managerial jobs from 25 percent to 33 percent over ten years.

In the United Kingdom, the proportion of women in paid work eight to eleven months after childbirth has risen from around a quarter in 1979 to around half in 2004. That's a huge increase, shifting nonemployment from the norm to being evenly divided with employment, in a single generation. However, it still leaves half of all babies' mothers home based for at least a year, and only a small minority of those who work during the first year do so full-time. Extending paid maternity leave to cover the first year after childbirth will acknowledge and ease an existing reality.

As the table above demonstrates, public discussions that focus on formal, purchased types of child care, giving the impression that these are what most families use, are misleading. In the first year in particular, that is far from the truth. Many mothers feel able to work while their babies are so young only if their own mothers or their partners provide child care. Arrangements in which mothers and fathers work complementary hours or shifts to ensure that one is always home to take care of the baby are not exclusive to intact families. In the United States, around 2 percent of all preschool children of single mothers are cared for by their fathers while their mothers work, as compared to 20 percent of children of married or cohabiting mothers. The contribution of biological fathers, especially black fathers, to the care and upbringing of babies in single-mother households, while seldom discussed, is very real.

The age at which babies begin to spend time in the care of someone other than their mothers is only part of the infant child care story. The next important questions are how much time, with whom, and where?

The phrase "infant day care" conjures up a vision of babies spending all day in rows of identical cribs in big nurseries, but this is clearly not the experience of most of the babies on either side of the Atlantic who are in nonmaternal child care while their mothers are at work. The average weekly hours initially spent in nonmaternal care was similar in the American NICHD and English FCCC samples—around thirty hours—but there was a wide range around that average. The figure changed very little during the first year. However, according to the Early Childhood Longitudinal Study Birth Cohort (ECLS-B), nine-month-old American babies who were cared for by relatives were more likely than babies in other settings to be in care for ten or fewer hours per week, while babies who were in centers at that age were more likely to be in care for forty or more hours per week.

Although thirty hours each week is a long time for a baby and mother to be apart, having a baby cared for by someone else for that average length of time does not, in itself, enable a mother to hold down a full-time job even if her travel time is minimal. A very large majority of mothers (especially mothers in the United Kingdom) work part-time, but that thirty-hour average includes some babies who spend far more hours in child care—as many as sixty in some cases of grandparent or nanny care.

Although media sometimes imply that babies who spend less time in a center or in family day care spend more time at home with their mothers, that is not necessarily true. A baby who spends forty hours each week in child care may actually spend more hours with his or her mother than the baby who is only recorded as spending half that time in child care. Many families rely on extra bits and pieces of help, such as a friend picking up a child from the center and "watching" him until a parent gets home, which seldom get reported, recorded, and counted. For many families, especially poor families, child care is something of a jigsaw puzzle that must be put together day by day to cover the needed hours. Some of the pieces are too small to be recorded in research studies, which usually define "child care" according to a bottom limit; this was ten hours per week in the NICHD study and twelve hours per week in the FCCC study.

Information about the hours infants spend in different types of care also needs to be read and compared in light of how those types were recorded and grouped. Types of child care can be studied in many different ways, and the method will often reflect particular values. For instance, if an analysis divides types of care into "parental" and "nonparental" or "familial" and "nonfamilial," the classification itself suggests that a blood relationship between caring adult and cared-for child is expected to be important. However, if types of care are divided up according to whether the child is more or less one-on-one with the caregiver or is part of a group, available adult attention is being treated as more important than family ties; and if the classification distinguishes between "in the family home" or "outside the family home" or between informal or formal care, the emphases are different again. Some purchased care may be one-on-one or nearly so—a nanny or U.K. childminder, for example—while care provided in a center will be in a group setting. Some care in the family home may be one-on-one, relatively expensive, and highly professional—a trained nanny, for example. But the care of a relative who comes to the family home or of a trained family day care provider in her home will be very different both from each other and from the care of a nanny.

TODDLERS AND PRESCHOOL CHILDREN IN CHILD CARE

As children grow past babyhood, fewer are cared for primarily by their mothers, and as they grow through toddlerhood, more move from informal to formal care. This is well illustrated by national data from the U.K. Childcare and Early Years Provision (CEYP) study. Similar trends can be found in the detailed findings available from the FCCC study in Britain and the NICHD study in the United States. In Britain, while 53 percent of the FCCC mothers

AMERICAN CHILD CARE TYPES: YEARS 1 THROUGH 3 (2000)

Type	15 months	24 months	36 months
Nonparental care at home	16%	13%	10%
Father	18%	14%	12%
Grandparent	13%	11%	9%
Family day care	33%	33%	25%
Center/nursery	21%	29%	44%

cared for their one-year-olds without any child care, only 48 percent were still doing so when those children were eighteen months old, and the proportion continued to drop, reaching 40 percent at three years. Furthermore, those who were using any child care were increasingly using formal out-of-home care rather than care by fathers and grandparents in the child's home. In the United States, NICHD researchers similarly found that among children having some nonmaternal child care, the percentage cared for in their own homes—whether by nannies, babysitters, or relatives other than fathers or grandmothers—dropped steadily from the first to the third year, while attendance at child care centers rose.

There are several probable reasons for such a change at this age, one being that personally and financially demanding options, such as father or nanny care, are regarded as less essential, and another that the relationship between parents and grandparents or other elderly relatives who are providing child care often begins to sour as a child's first year ends (see Chapter 8). Many grandparents find caring for a toddler far more demanding than looking after a baby. And as if the child's growing activity level and sense of self were not problematic enough, parents often come to feel that the quiet, home-based daily routine that a grandparent has provided and they have welcomed for their infant may not be sufficiently stimulating for a two-year-old. Some worry, with considerable reason, that the child does not have enough opportunities to mix with others, play-group style; some worry that she is not acquiring the skills they see displayed by children who attend Gymboree or music or dance classes. So just when elderly caregivers feel the child is beginning to demand too much of them, parents want them to give even more.

However, things do not have to go wrong with informal care arrangements for parents to decide that this is the time for a group setting with more formal educational content. Parents in every country are affected by the increasing international recognition of the value of preschool education and the resulting pressure for places for three- to five-year-olds. As the age at which children begin formal schooling has dropped, so has the age at which direct preparation for school is considered appropriate. Two generations ago, American children went to kindergarten at five to prepare to enter first grade in "real school" when they were six. Now there is pre-K before kindergarten, and preparations for that start by age three or four with attendance at preschool—in a child care center, a formal nursery school, or a playgroup. In the United Kingdom, part-time (fifteen hours per week) preschool education places for three- and four-year-olds are free of charge to all families (as are places for many disadvantaged two-year-olds). Even in Australia, where the number of babies and toddlers in formal child care is relatively small, fewer than five preschool children in every hundred remain in exclusively informal (or parental) care; almost all spend twelve to fifteen hours each week in some kind of school setting.

There is good evidence that such preparation "works," in that children who attend educationally oriented groups before they reach school age have higher scores on cognitive tests and on various measures of school readiness. From the Second World War onward, three years has been the age at which it was thought appropriate for children to start part-time attendance at what was then called "nursery school." Modern research has not yet shown whether the outcomes for children are even better if they start earlier—at age two, say—but a major European study carried out in the United Kingdom has made it clear that almost every child benefits from attendance by three years, provided that the quality of the child care is good.

SCHOOL-AGE CHILD CARE

In the English-speaking world, changes in the ages at which children start school have changed the landscape of later child care also, making "wraparound care"—before and after school and during school holidays—central to it. In the past, the youngest children in school were at least five and often six years old, and many families managed without child care on school days, relying on an older child to see the youngest into school and home again. Now children start school at the age of four or perhaps younger, and even if there are older siblings, few parents feel comfortable making them responsible. So, while some children in third grade upward receive no nonparental care during school terms, even if both their parents work outside the home, there is increasing pressure on parents to make arrangements for most of them and for almost all children in kindergarten and grades 1 and 2. Some are picked up from school and cared for by relatives during nonschool hours when their parents are not available, but a range of other types of care, formal and informal, continues from preschool into school life.

Nevertheless, many children arrive home before any adult and spend the intervening time unsupervised. Approximately 6.8 million American children, 15 percent of those between the ages of five and fourteen, come home to an empty house and spend an average of six hours per week alone there. They are often called "latchkey children," a term that probably originated in a 1944 NBC documentary and refers to children who return to an empty home after school and have the door key either on a string around their necks or hidden.

For some families, self-care for schoolchildren is a choice, but for others it is a necessity. Parents who cannot afford to pay for supervision, or who live in communities where supervised care by relatives or friends is not available, have no recourse but to leave their children alone or give up or radically revise their own employment. The decision to give up all or most of a job or career is difficult enough for those with children below school age to care for; it must seem even less attractive when it is the care of school-age children that is at issue.

In the United States, concern about this situation has stimulated some action from the federal government (through the Dependent Care Grants Program) and at the state level. However, it is non-profit agencies and local corporations in their home communities that are doing most to provide after-school and vacation care. In the United Kingdom, after-school and holiday care and activities for all under-fourteens are planned as part of the "extended schools" program (see Chapter 12).

It is clear that many American children are currently in self-care, though the exact number is not known, perhaps in part because this is such a sensitive issue for some family members that they cannot be completely candid about it. There is currently much concern about the effects of self-care on children of different ages, including loneliness, boredom, and fear in younger children, and more susceptibility to peer pressure and therefore to smoking, drinking, drug-taking, and inappropriate sexual relationships among teenagers. Some studies do cite positive effects, however, including greater self-reliance and independence. Furthermore, children who have experienced after-school care in a poor facility or have been supervised by a neighbor who they felt was intrusive or too restrictive or by a bullying older sibling may prefer being on their own. All in all, research is inconclusive, and the issue of latchkey children in the United States continues to be a sensitive one.

Child care for school-age children, when available, is offered in a wide range of settings, including day care centers, family day care homes, public and private schools, and religious institutions. Programs are also offered by park and recreation departments, youth groups (such as Ys, scouts, boys and girls clubs, cooperative extensions), and in the summer by youth camps. All school-age child care programs provide adult supervision and age-appropriate activities in the hours before and after school, but only a minority serve the needs of working parents by also providing care during school holidays and vacations. Perhaps the best-known school vacation care in the world is that provided in North American summer camps, of which there are approximately twelve thousand in the United States, offering anything from an eight-week stay at considerable cost to free or subsidized daily attendance for a week for disadvantaged children in inner cities.

In the United Kingdom, the current situation is rather different and is changing more rapidly. The present government's imminent target is for full-day, all-year child care to be made available for every child up to the age of fourteen. Currently about half of all school-age children receive child care outside school hours, and this is fairly evenly divided between formal and informal care. Although childminding is generally thought of as infant, toddler, and pre-school care, childminders look after many children before and after school and during school vacations. A survey in 2005 showed that a quarter of the children registered with childminders were five to seven years old and almost another quarter (22 percent) were eight years old or older. Almost all these caregivers offered up to ten hours per day of care during the school vacations as well as care before and after school. A few also cared for children on weekends. In 2008, few school-age children in the United Kingdom attended nurseries or child care centers, but as the planned integrated children's centers open up and more primary schools become "extended schools," this is likely to change (see Chapter 12).

In some European countries, integrated centers are already a reality, and school, after-school child care, and vacation activities are themselves integrated. The following is an edited description of Swedish school-age child care as experienced by one non-Swedish family:

> Farrah is currently in her first year of compulsory schooling and attends the local school (*grundskola*) situated a short walk from her home. The school is a whole-day school, which is open from 7 a.m. to 5 p.m. and combines a preschool class, compulsory schooling and school-age childcare. Her class has 25 pupils. . . . There is a team of adults in the classroom, including two teachers who job-share and a free-time pedagogue (a worker specialising in school-age childcare and more informal education) who works in the classroom at certain times as well as being responsible for school-age childcare provision in the school. There are also often student teachers on practice placement. . . .
>
> . . . Children can arrive from 7 a.m., but the school day itself starts at 8:15 a.m. with a quiet time, when most of the class read books of their choice or play quietly. After this formal teaching begins. . . . At 12:30 p.m. the children have lunch, which is provided free of charge. After compulsory school has finished at 1:15 p.m., Farrah and her friends make their way to the rooms set aside for the leisure-time centre (*fritidshem*)—the school-age childcare service. These are on the school grounds and are laid out specifically for leisure activities, although they are used during the school day as workshops or for one-to-one work with children. This type of school-age childcare service is used by the majority of Swedish children from six years old (when they start school on a voluntary basis) up to and including nine years old: Indeed children of this age are entitled to a place. . . .

Children in school-age childcare are supervised by free-time pedagogues but do not have to do their homework or study. Instead Farrah
spends some of her time in activities planned by the pedagogues and
the rest in free play; she often plays outside, for example, climbing
trees or tobogganing. Around 40 children attend this centre along
with three staff, all of whom have trained as free-time pedagogues by
completing a three-year higher education course.

Elsewhere, many parents still experience appalling difficulty in
arranging adequate and reliable care and transportation for young
schoolchildren on school days, together with safe and enjoyable
vacation coverage. On both sides of the Atlantic, this is forcing
changes in traditional patterns of school hours and terms, bringing
them closer to adult working hours. In many American communities, schools are trying extended days, with homework or sports
clubs outside school teaching hours. In the United Kingdom, plans
for extended schools providing wraparound child care for all ages as
well as preschool and traditional education are being implemented.
Meanwhile, North America's traditional long summer vacation is
being worn away, and Britain's Easter and Christmas holiday breaks
have been reduced from almost four weeks each to little more than
two. Even the centuries-old three-term (semester) school year in
the United Kingdom, with a week's (half-term) break in the middle
of each, is gradually being transformed into a school year of six
short terms and six short holidays. There is no clearer reminder that
for many families school is child care as well as education, though
many traditionally qualified teachers still resent it being so.

4. Parents and Child Care

How and why do parents make decisions about child care? This chapter is not about how individual parents can make the best choices for their children (that's in Chapter 16), but about what research can tell us about parents and child care in general.

Nothing about child care choices is simple or obvious, not even why people use nonparental child care at all. It is widely assumed that when parents look for child care, it's because both of them (or the only available one) need to go out to work to earn money. That's obviously part of the story, and there is considerable evidence, especially from Scandinavian countries, that cash benefits to parents to reduce their financial need to work while their children are very young reduce the demand for infant child care. But the idea that parents work because they need money and they use child care to free them to go to work is overly simple. On both sides of the Atlantic there are many parents who do indeed need money and would like to work to earn some, but who cannot afford the child care that would make that possible. And, as we have seen, a surprisingly large minority of the children who spend some time each week in nonparental child care have mothers who are neither employed outside the home nor studying. When a woman says she is "desperate for child care," it may be for a range of reasons that have little to do with employment. Some of those mothers are committed to kinds of work that economists tend to disregard, such as voluntary work or caring obligations; some want child-free time for themselves or want one child looked after so that they can have some one-on-one time with the other(s); and some mothers, especially those who feel least confident in their parenting, want non-parental care for their children's sake rather than for their own, to give them more and different kinds of stimulation, the experience of spending time away from home and family, and especially opportunities to play with other children. As we shall see, wanting children to socialize with their peers becomes an increasingly common reason for seeking child care, especially group child care, as children approach the age for nursery school or pre-K. However, there are parents who believe that if early education with a group of other children is a good thing, the earlier it starts the better—and playdates don't count.

> Six months was a good age for him to start nursery. He wasn't clingy and it's really important for him to have that interaction with other kids.
> —FCCC mother

WHY PARENTS USE ONE TYPE OF CHILD CARE RATHER THAN ANOTHER

Child care choices are often discussed as if parents made them the same way as they make any other consumer choice: by balancing (high) quality and (low) price. However, choosing child care is not like choosing a refrigerator. When parents are faced with making real-life child care decisions that they are planning to implement immediately, particular details of what they need from child care may weigh even more heavily than what it will cost. In the FCCC study, mothers who worked unsocial or irregular hours, for instance, focused intensely on the flexibility that different types of care could offer; of these, many of the wealthiest opted for a live-in nanny while others sought an arrangement with a grandmother that included overnight stays:

> My work is fairly demanding and often makes last-minute demands. I need to be able to give 100% when I'm at work. You know, we've had two days when the nanny has been sick and that's quite difficult to handle at work, but being tied to a rigid pick-up time would be even worse.

The availability and location of various kinds of care may also make a crucial difference. In communities where one car per family is the norm, child care that is not on the parents' route to work or close to their transportation to work may mean they must buy a second car and travel separately. Even in North America, where each parent is likely to have a car, the child care choice of a family living in a rural location may be effectively nonexistent.

The number of children in a family and the spacing of their births often affects child care choices, too. When the financial costs of nursery (center) care or family day care (childminding) are discussed, either by individuals or government bodies, the fact that a second child doubles them is often ignored. Furthermore, it is not at all remarkable to have three children under school age in a family, but three in purchased child care is formidably costly. Families that considered the possibility of a nanny for the first child and rejected it as too expensive may see it as possible once a second child arrives, even allowing for a hike in the nanny's salary to cover the care of two children, and positively economical if there is a third.

As usual, though, costs are not the only issue related to the number of children in the family. Mothers who have more than one child under school age are often faced with children's conflicting needs and caregivers' unwillingness or inability to meet them:

> I was trying to find a childminder . . . who could take one of them to nursery and pick up, and look after a baby at the same time. I only found two people that were physically able to do that combination of duties.   —FCCC mother

Higher income may help families buy their way out of this kind of child care difficulty, but if neither a nanny nor the requisite number of places in a nursery or in family day care are affordable, parents may seek informal child care only to encounter a new set of difficulties. It is often far more difficult to arrange care for two (let alone three) children than for just one. If care is needed not only for a toddler but for a baby as well, an arrangement with a family member that was becoming shaky often disintegrates altogether. Other ad hoc arrangements become more difficult, too: parents who can take one child to work with them (at least in child care emergencies) are unlikely to be able to take two, and women who have somehow managed to fit in working at home around one child's naps and bedtimes often find it impossible once there are two. Some mothers who have gone to great lengths to keep working while they have one child decide to stay at home once a second is born. In the FCCC study, for example, first children were twice as likely as others to be in nonparental child care during their first year. With hindsight, some of their mothers actually regretted ever having gone back:

> If I'd known I wasn't going to be able to keep going with a second baby, I'd have settled into being an at-home mother from the beginning. As it is Jon [the first baby] spent more time in the nursery than was good for him and I spent more time in tears. And for what?

For some parents, a baby's characteristics may also play a part in decisions about child care, although research on this topic is sparse and contradictory. A mother who regards her baby as fussy and "difficult" may be more (or less) inclined to use any or any particular type of child care, as one of the FCCC mothers suggested:

> The type of baby she is, very easygoing and happy, makes me feel happier about using child care. If she was crying a lot or ill in the first few months . . . my instinct would have been to give up work. Her temperament makes things easier for us.

Several mentioned that their baby separated easily from them and didn't appear to object to being left:

> He is a very good baby. If things had been different I can see that I might not have gone back as quickly but I could see he'd do well with the Family Day Care lady; he's extremely easy to leave with anybody. He just sort of gets on with it.

FAMILY CHARACTERISTICS THAT AFFECT CHILD CARE CHOICES

Although much is written about choosing child care, the type of child care a family uses is often not a matter of choice in the normal sense but determined by many different factors working together. Some of these factors are obvious. The costs of care and parents' income and education are part of it; parents' personal situations, such as marital status and quality, job history, and entitlement to maternity leave, make a difference, as do parents' individual characteristics, such as mental health and attitudes to work. However, these and some other family circumstances influence child care choices in ways that are not obvious, single parenthood being one example. Apart from questions of poverty, single mothers' arrangements are often dependent on their own mothers or other closely involved relatives living nearby. A willing grandmother, who is not only inexpensive (often cost-free) but also can be counted upon because of her relationship with the child, is ideal, but other extended family members undertake child care also, and, as we have seen, some ex-partners remain participant fathers. A single parent who has none of that support may have no alternative caregivers or security-blanket backups available, and that can make the whole work–and–child care equation seem impossible to solve. If a child must stay home because of illness, these parents have to take time off work. Worse, if weather or traffic dramas delay them on the journey home from work, there is nobody else who can pick up the child. In addition to the child's unhappiness, these parents may have to face disapproval, even sanctions, from nurseries or family day cares, some of which are (understandably) strict about children being picked up on time. There is no doubt that some single parents who give up work and stay at home despite their urgent need for income do so less because they cannot find or afford child care than because suitable child care seems so difficult, so exhausting, to arrange and to manage.

In most countries and communities, parents' race and ethnicity have a considerable bearing on their child care choices, although it is not always easy to separate the influence of ethnicity itself from other influences that may or may not be associated with it, including parenting practices and beliefs and language issues. An Australian study of child care used by indigenous, Somali, and Vietnamese families illustrates the difficulty of interpreting research findings and the risk of misinterpreting them. All three groups chose family day care, but they chose it for entirely different reasons. The indigenous Australian families chose family day care because it offered more individualized care than could be expected in a group setting. Neither the Somali nor the Vietnamese families were at all concerned with the issue of individualized care; their concern was that their children be cared for in a setting where the family's original values and beliefs were reflected: in chosen households rather than in day care centers with their mix of staff and families.

Whatever the dominant reasons for their choices, different racial or ethnic groups have been shown to choose different types of child care in almost every study. In the American study of ten thousand babies born in 2001, for example, almost two-thirds of black children were in nonparental care when they were nine months old, as compared with just under half of white, Hispanic, and Asian children. There were differences in the types of care at that age, too. Of all babies who were in nonparental care, black children were more likely than others to be in a day care center. In the English FCCC sample, Asian mothers were twice as likely as white mothers to be using child care at ten months and to use it for longer hours.

WHO CAN AFFORD WHICH TYPE OF CHILD CARE?

If the cost of child care is not always the overwhelming issue in parental choice, as is sometimes suggested, it is certainly *an* issue. However, the relationship between family income and the child care that can be afforded is not straightforward. Parents with two high incomes, for example, might be seen as free to choose any type of child care, but while such a couple can certainly afford any child care setting or provider that is locally available, that does not mean that they are free to choose any type of child care they wish because they may not be able to afford to care for the child or children themselves. Home care by a stay-at-home mother or father, or by the two parents sharing, would mean that the family had to forgo one income or part of one or both incomes. It could be argued that the higher the salaries these parents earn—and the more expensive the lifestyle they support—the more difficult it is to sustain the loss of income. The financial question such couples face is which will cost them more (and can they afford that cost): paying for expensive child care—a nanny, say—or ceasing to bring in one parent's income in the present and the loss of an unknown percentage of future earnings.

When families of any income level decide that parent care is affordable, or perhaps essential, many still take it for granted that the mother will be the one to stay home. But on both sides of the Atlantic there are a few families (and the number is growing) in which the father is the principal caregiver, not because he and his partner have separated but because they asked themselves "Which of us should work and which of us stay home?" and answered the question pragmatically. If she earns more than he does (and perhaps enjoys her work more), then he may be the one who gives up paid employment and stays home with the children.

In families where it is still assumed that mothers are primarily responsible for caring for the children, it may be the mother's income rather than that of the whole family that dictates what kind of child care is affordable. In those circumstances, a mother who chooses to work and use child care will often be expected to meet the full cost of that care out of her earnings. If she cannot earn enough to cover the amount of child care her job requires, or the type of child care she and her partner both want, she may feel under pressure to give up her job and stay at home to care for the children herself.

> [I went back because] I actually enjoy work. There's no financial gain of going back to work other than perhaps my own sanity and to keep my career going. . . . If I take everything into account . . . travel, child-care, absolutely everything, I might just break even but it would be pennies.   —FCCC mother

> I still don't earn enough money to pay anything in the house. . . . I just pay the childminder and for my petrol and that's all, so my husband thinks it's a bit silly to do that.   —FCCC mother

Whatever the different choices, decisions, and practices of individual families, the affordability of child care and the difference between purchasing it and other consumer goods is profoundly affected by national policies and practices. Both the provision and the financing of child care are different in different countries. In some European countries, notably Finland, child care and early years education, like mainstream schooling, is provided by the state and paid for almost entirely out of taxation. In the United Kingdom there is an uneasy blend of public and private provision, with tax breaks rapidly changing the affordability profile. In the United

States, provision is fundamentally private, and, according to the Child Care Action Campaign, a national not-for-profit child advocacy organization, in 2001 parents nationwide paid an average of $3,500 per year. There are tax breaks, and there are complex schemes and subsidies for poor families, especially for single mothers, but the supply of child care places is inadequate to meet the demand, so even those families who meet criteria for subsidy that would make a place affordable are rather unlikely to find one.

On both sides of the Atlantic, public provisions made, for example, by Head Start and Early Head Start in the United States and Sure Start in the United Kingdom tend to be trailblazers and centers of excellence. Ironically, though, well-to-do parents who are not eligible for financial aid may not easily be able to afford the excellent child care that such programs provide cost free or heavily subsidized for much less privileged families. In many parts of the United States, there is a curvilinear relationship between wealth and child care, with center-based care affordable only by the rich and by poor families who have access to subsidies; for middle-income families, center care—particularly for a second child—is unaffordable. A national survey of ten thousand American families in 2001 (ECLS-B) showed that among under-threes with employed mothers, it was those from the highest- and lowest-earning families who were more likely to be in centers or family day care. Children with employed mothers from average- to low-income families were more likely to be in the informal care of relatives.

The cost of any child care can be a tough barrier for parents who want to work or train for work, and in English-speaking countries, single parents in particular find that rising costs prevent them from getting jobs and staying in paid work. In the United Kingdom, two-thirds of all nonworking mothers (and an even higher proportion of

"Quality is a concern to many parents, but here, money drives their decisions about child care. You can hear the frustration in the voice of parents who know what type of child care they want. When we tell them how much it will cost, they sacrifice quality for less money."

Rosa Trahan-Wise, resource director,
Project Child Care, Manatee County, Florida

nonworking single mothers) said they would prefer to go out to work or study with a view to working, if they had access to good-quality, convenient, reliable, and affordable child care. Research suggests that in London, where child care is most scarce and expensive, this is certainly true for at least some women, as the employment rate for those with dependent children is more than ten percentage points below the national average. However, it is impossible to know, and difficult to guess, how many women who say that it is only lack of suitable child care that prevents them from choosing to go out to work would actually make that choice if more and/or better child care were made available. There is a great deal of evidence, especially from North America, to suggest that most stay-at-home mothers choose not to work and that many working mothers would prefer to work less or not at all while their children are young.

RELATIONSHIPS BETWEEN IDEAL AND ACTUAL TYPES OF CHILD CARE

Even before they have any children, many parents, especially women, can describe the child care arrangements they think would be ideal. Those abstract ideals are usually based less on practical knowledge of types of child care or of children's needs than on the individual woman's feelings and beliefs about families and about women's and men's roles. Family and gender are complex and much-researched topics, but two clusters of beliefs, briefly described below, seem to dominate.

The "traditional" cluster is characterized by the belief that a woman's fundamental role is to be a mother while a man's is to provide protection and economic support to his wife and children. At the other extreme, the "egalitarian" cluster is characterized by the belief that parenthood is no more fundamental for women than for men, and that women and men alike should pursue both familial and nonfamilial roles. Women with traditional views of family roles are more inclined to opt for staying home with young children than women with more egalitarian views.

Such beliefs about child rearing and attitudes toward maternal employment and its impact on children are powerful influences on parents' behavior, although they themselves may be unaware of them. In both the NICHD and the FCCC studies, mothers who believed children benefited if mothers were employed tended to put their children in child care earlier than others and to use child care for more hours. In contrast, mothers who believed that maternal employment carried high risks for children tended to use child care for fewer hours. In the American study, they were also especially likely to rely on the child's father for care.

When it is time to move on from theory to practice, parents who have a range of choices available to them may try, consciously or unconsciously, to match the two up: to make child care arrangements that fit their personal ideals. But if parents' child care choices are limited, it may not be possible to find a good fit. A mother who has grown up with a set of attitudes that incline her to believe she should be at home with her child but finds that she cannot stay at home because of work or career commitments may feel sharply conflicted. Many women adapt their career plans and lifestyles so as to be able to care for their children in ways that feel comfortable to them, but some women find ways of adapting their ideals to bring them into line with the child care they need to use. One FCCC mother said, "I used to think I'd stay home once I had kids, but I guess that was my mother speaking rather than me. Nobody does that any more do they?"

Even leaving aside the "option" of full-time mother care, the relationships between the types of child care parents say they would prefer and the types they actually use are not straightforward or easy to understand, especially as the information on which an "ideal" judgment is based can range from careful research or personal experience (such as having a mother who worked in child care), through attention to the experiences of friends with children, to nothing more than media child care stories. In the FCCC study, for example, some mothers did not differentiate between a registered professional family day care provider (childminder) and a babysitter. And some parents said that care by au pairs was ideal because they give the same service as live-in nannies but for much less money.

Sometimes a decision to use a particular care facility, even though it is quite different from an existing ideal, is made opportunistically, perhaps because an unexpected offer of care is made or financial

help for a particular care setting is offered as a job perk. Among the
FCCC mothers who used types of child care quite different from
the types they had said would be ideal, the main reason was not that
they could not find or afford what they wanted but that when the
time came for real-life child care many of them did not go looking
for it. Instead of making a deliberate search for the child care that
best fit either their ideals or their present circumstances and preferences, many of these mothers had waited until the need for child
care was urgent and then taken whatever was offered. One mother
was clearly aware of this and sought to rationalize her situation by
blaming her lack of choice rather than her failure to exercise any
other options:

> I was in a bit of a panic by the time I found her [childminder] 'cause I'd
> only got a couple of days left. . . . It's not what I'd have chosen. I wish
> there were other options open to me quite honestly; I'm annoyed that
> there isn't any real choice. I think more should be done to help. Just
> because you work it doesn't mean that you're financially able to afford
> what you'd like.

It is difficult to assess how important achieving child care ideals is to
families' feelings about child care and their work-home balance.
Recent data suggest that while mothers who end up using the kind
of care they had originally wanted are not likely to be more satisfied
with it overall, they are likely to use child care for more hours than
other mothers.

What proportion of mothers actually get to use their personal
ideal of child care? It is difficult to generalize, because when parents
tell researchers that they would have preferred a different type of
child care to the one they are using, hindsight often confuses the
issue. Mothers of toddlers who are currently being looked after by
relatives or are in family day care often say they would prefer them
to be in a nursery or day care center. But how many of them would
have made that choice if they had had the opportunity a year or
more ago? It is difficult for the mother, let alone the researcher, to
be sure. "Prospective studies," in which parents are asked about
their child care ideals well in advance of any need for child care and
then followed up months later when child care has begun, give a
more accurate picture. As part of the FCCC study, almost one thou-

sand mothers who were still on maternity leave and whose babies were around three months old were asked to pick their ideal child care arrangements for the future from a list, assuming that all types of care were equally available and affordable. Then, toward the end of the first year, the mothers were asked about the type(s) of child care they were currently using so that a comparison could be made. As can be seen from the table below, fewer than half the mothers were using child care that matched their earlier-stated ideals, although two-thirds of the mothers who had said they wanted to stay at home and care for the baby themselves were doing so.

Why were mothers whose ideal was full-time mother care more likely to get the kind of child care they wanted? Like many interesting questions, this one can be answered only speculatively. It may be that, more than other choices, the ideal of staying at home with a baby reflects attitudes and beliefs that come from women's own upbringing and are likely to bring them personal social support from partners and extended families. It may also be because, out of all the types of child care that are theoretically available, mother care is the type that is most within a woman's own control. Although life can be—and is often made—extremely hard for a woman who is determined to stay home with children, nobody can actually prevent her from doing so unless her refusal to go into the workplace leads to such extreme poverty that it is deemed neglect of the child.

COMPARISON BETWEEN TYPE OF CHILD CARE STATED AS IDEAL DURING MATERNITY LEAVE (BABY THREE MONTHS OLD) AND CHILD CARE IN USE WHEN BABY WAS TEN MONTHS OLD

Child care type	Specified as ideal at 3 months	Use at 10 months	Percent at 10 months achieving ideal	
Mother	476 (48.4%)	542 (55.1%)	317 /476	(66.6%)
Mother and father	65 (6.6%)	27 (2.7%)	12/65	(18.5%)
Father	6 (0.6%)	18 (1.8%)	2/6	(33.3%)
Grandparent	101 (10.3%)	87 (8.8%)	18/101	(17.8%)
Relative	17 (1.7%)	20 (2.0%)	1/17	(6.0%)
Friend	4 (0.4%)	9 (0.9%)	1/4	(25.0%)
Childminder	40 (4.1%)	87 (8.8%)	12/40	(30.0%)
Nanny	60 (6.1%)	35 (3.6%)	16/60	(26.7%)
Centre/nursery	107 (10.9%)	94 (9.6%)	31/107	(29.0%)
Combination	108 (11.0%)	65 (6.6%)	13/108	(12.0%)

In contrast, a woman whose ideal is to leave her baby with her own mother can be foiled by her mother's illness or unanticipated refusal, while a mother whose ideal is nursery care may find that there is no affordable setting within reach that has a vacancy.

CHOOSING PARTICULAR CARE SETTINGS AND CAREGIVERS

Reasons for settling a child into a particular facility or the care of a particular individual are not necessarily the same as reasons for choosing a type of care.

When FCCC mothers talked about their actual caregivers or care settings, few described themselves as having been guided by earlier ideals or having searched systematically. Some seemed to "fall into" a child care arrangement because a vacancy unexpectedly became available in a conveniently placed nursery, but often an instant decision was made because care was offered by grandparents or other relatives, close friends, or sometimes their friends' daughters.

In the first year of their babies' lives, by far the most important issue for almost all mothers on both sides of the Atlantic was feeling able to trust the care provider. This accounts for the strong preference for care by a family member, especially the mother's own mother.

> I wouldn't leave him with anyone but his Grandma. I don't trust anyone. If my Mum hadn't have had him I wouldn't have worked. They're all meant to be fine I know but you hear all these stories on the telly.
> —FCCC mother

> Trust was the big thing. It was my mum or nobody. If my mum hadn't had her I'd not have gone out to work.   —FCCC mother

If care by a relative was not available, many American and English mothers sought family day care, often choosing a caregiver they had known previously, someone who had cared for their own older child, perhaps, or for the children of friends. If they did not know a prospective care provider themselves, they took verbal recommendations very seriously. Some mothers chose to use an unregistered caregiver when a registered individual was available because the former was somebody they knew or knew of, while the registered caregiver was "a stranger." If no individual who is known to the family is available, however, some parents feel more comfortable going to the other extreme: leaving their child in a formal group situation.

> I think we all have more confidence in big establishments for some reason . . . it's inherently there in most people that if it's a big establishment it's vetted by social services and they are going to have strict guidelines and they're going to watch each other. You just feel more safe than you do with someone working all on her own—you don't know what's happening behind closed doors.   —FCCC mother

Anxiety about the trustworthiness of care providers in general is widespread among parents and often fanned by alarming media stories. The Louise Woodward case worried American parents for many months, and during the same period there was widespread, media-induced anxiety in the United Kingdom about mistreatment in group care because of a BBC TV documentary about nurseries. Surprisingly, though, once the FCCC mothers had found possible care for their babies—a childminder, for instance—very few of them visited others for comparison, and even fewer checked individuals' formal references. In a very few instances, mothers employed au pairs from other countries on the strength of nothing more than a telephone call facilitated by an interpreter. Furthermore, once a care arrangement has begun, there seems to be very little checking back to make sure it is satisfactory or up to expectations. Unannounced visits by parents to nurseries or family day care homes, for example, are rare. Perhaps mothers feel that they would know by the baby's reactions if she was not happy with the care provider, perhaps they feel that checking up might be seen as spying and cause ill feeling, or perhaps they are simply busy integrating work back into their lives.

For most mothers, trusting a care provider was not only a matter of trusting her provider to keep the baby physically safe or to protect him or her from abuse or neglect; it was also about the way the care provider fitted the family's values.

> She [childminder] might be very good at her job, but how do I know what she thinks that job *is*? When the baby's with my Auntie I know

she's being brought up about the way I'd bring her up myself; we're family and that's how we do things. A stranger might have quite different ideas and even if they were *good* ideas I wouldn't want that.

—FCCC mother

Parents who are not using a family member or someone personally known or recommended to them to care for their child have to find a stranger whom they feel they can trust. That feeling, and the consequent decision to leave a baby with a particular caregiver, is usually based on the kind of person she appears to be and the way she interacts with their child or with children already in her care. The individual characteristic that matters most to parents everywhere is "warmth."

> The woman in charge of the baby room took an immediate interest in who she would be maybe caring for; asked to pick her up and then chatted to her and walked her around—the others I saw didn't do that so much.   —FCCC mother who chose a nursery

> I think personality is very important—and this nanny is one of life's happy, loving people.   —FCCC mother who chose a nanny

A care provider being "warm and loving" is important to almost all parents and overwhelmingly important to many. In American studies, a majority of mothers have said that "a warm and loving caregiver" was not just important but the most important feature in any care setting they might be considering, sometimes outweighing issues of affordability and convenience. When mothers in a recent large-scale Canadian study were offered a wider range of provider characteristics to choose from, they still endorsed warmth but also added the care provider's personality, experience, and the confidence she inspired in them regarding her trustworthiness and reliability.

The English FCCC study provided an opportunity to discuss mothers' reasons for making child care choices and their feelings about them during face-to-face interviews. These interviews confirmed what might have been predicted from the studies discussed earlier, and when FCCC mothers who were using child care at ten months were asked to pick the three caregiver characteristics that were most important to them from a list of nine, nearly nine out of ten put "provide a loving and understanding environment" first. Two-thirds of the mothers selected "provide a safe physical environment" as another of their three preferences, and almost half selected "provide worry-free child care."

Parents of children less than one year old are usually reported to be more interested in their own, very personal and subjective, assessments of care providers as people than with the education, training, or specialized experience on which they could have assessed them as professionals. Despite the widespread awareness of the value of early years education and the pressures on English parents to ensure that toddlers achieved preacademic milestones formerly expected of older preschool children, most FCCC mothers seemed to feel that the educational aspect of child care was not relevant until children were around three years old. Even at that age, many mothers felt that "education" came more from a classroom setting with planned activities and a formal program than from children's interaction with individual teachers. The few mothers who did give educational activities priority from the first year onward tended to seek an educationally structured care environment— a nursery or center—rather than an educationally qualified individual childminder/family day care provider or nanny.

Irrespective of their concern with education, families in English-

---

Caregiver characteristics from which mothers in the FCCC study selected the three that were most important to them

- provide professional child care
- provide substitute for mother care
- teach babies new things
- provide adequate outdoor space and toys
- provide a safe physical environment
- provide dependable care
- provide adequate indoor space and toys
- provide a loving and understanding environment
- provide worry-free child care

REASONS FOR CHOOSING A TYPE OF FORMAL CHILD CARE

	Age 0–1 %	Age 2–3 %	Age 4–5 %	Total %
I could trust this person/these people.	33	19	11	20
I wanted my child to be educated while being looked after.	5	16	22	15
I wanted my child to mix with other children.	13	14	9	13
It had a good reputation.	6	12	19	12
I wanted someone properly trained to look after my child.	7	8	5	6
It is easy to get to.	1	5	9	7
It was recommended to me.	7	6	4	5
His/her brother(s)/sister(s) went there.	4	6	7	5
I knew they would bring up my child the same way I would.	3	2	1	2
It was low-cost.	2	2	1	2
It fitted in with my/my husband's/ wife's/hours.	2	3	1	2
I wanted reliable arrangements.	5	2	1	2
I could not afford to pay for formal child care.	1	1	2	1
I wanted my child to be looked after at home.	3	1	1	1
I wanted someone who would show my child affection.	2	1	1	1
No other choices available to me.	3	1	4	2
Other reason(s)	4	4	4	4
Unweighted base	*176*	*1,084*	*295*	*1,555*

Base: All families with a preschool-age "selected" child who mainly used only a formal provider (including nannies and babysitters) for this child in the last week.

speaking nations tend to choose different types of care for older and younger children. Mothers of under-threes, and especially of under-ones, are more likely than mothers of older children to prefer family day care or in-home care and less likely to prefer center care. However, lucky-chance experiences of good care for a first child sometimes overrides age-related preferences for a second and may lead to the deliberate choice of similar care for a second child at a much earlier age:

> With Laurie my choice of nursery from the beginning was really 'cause of experience with my older one. Lucy was at Nursery, you know, so I knew that could work well.
> —FCCC mother

Sources of Information About Child Care Used by U.K. Parents

	% using each source
Word of mouth (e.g., friends or relatives)	43
School	21
Local advertising	11
Local authority	10
Health visitor/clinic	9
Children's Information Services	7
Child care provider	7
Local library	5
Internet	5
Jobcentre, Jobcentre Plus Office, or Benefits Office	4
Your employer	4
Doctor's surgery	4
ChildcareLink (the national helpline and Web site)	3
Yellow Pages	3
Local community centre	2
Church or religious organisation	4
National organisation(s)	1
Other	1
None of these	33

As children reach preschool age, the extent of educational activities offered by child care settings and the specialized training of the staff increasingly influence parents' choices, while the issue of trust becomes less important. For example, the table on page 74 shows that whereas a third of British parents of babies using formal child care said that trust was their main reason for choosing a particular setting (and only 5 percent mentioned education), almost a quarter of parents of children ages four or five said that they had chosen a particular setting because they wanted the child educated as well as cared for and/or because it had a good reputation, while only a tenth mentioned trust.

Where Parents Look for Child Care Information and Advice

Many parents feel that not enough information is brought to their attention either about the child care that is available in their areas or about how best to choose one type of care or one setting over another. Accordingly, a recent study in the United Kingdom reported on the sources of information used by 5,344 families whose children

SOURCES OF INFORMATION AND ADVICE ABOUT CHILD CARE
USED BY FCCC MOTHERS

Sources of information	N (%)	Discussion	N (%)	Influenced final selection	N (%)
Health visitor	18 (32)	Partner	49 (86)	Availability	39 (68)
Leaflets	17 (30)	Own mother	29 (51)	Location	36 (63)
Print media	15 (26)	Friends	22 (39)	Partner's views	28 (49)
Friends	13 (23)	Relatives	21 (38)	Cost	26 (46)
Help line	10 (18)	Other mothers	17 (30)	Recommendation	23 (40)
Mother/baby group	10 (18)	Work colleagues	13 (23)	Facilities in own home	14 (25)
Family	7 (12)	Health professional	10 (18)	Stories in media	13 (23)
Television	6 (11)			Work child care provision	4 (7)
Prenatal class	4 (7)				

FCCC mothers of infants; alternatives in each column are not mutually exclusive.

had been in nonparental child care during the week before the survey took place. (See table on page 75.)

Apart from word of mouth, there were many more parents who had not used any of the suggested sources of information than parents who had used a specific one. Only about one in ten parents who used any or all of the first six sources of information found them "very" or "quite" helpful. More detailed information—but for a much smaller sample—was collected during the FCCC study. The table above gives not only the sources of information about child care that mothers had used but also the individuals with whom they had discussed child care issues, and who and what had influenced their actual decisions about what child care to use.

Although health professionals, prenatal classes, and postnatal groups had been used as sources of information about child care, few mothers had chosen to discuss it with any of them. Furthermore, although most had discussed their situation with their own mothers, the generation gap yawned so widely that none felt that their mothers had influenced their child care decisions.

No, I didn't discuss it with my mother; she only worked part-time when we were children and it was different for her.

The discussions mothers found most useful were with friends, colleagues, or neighbors, peers who themselves were involved with child care.

> I discussed it with my next-door neighbour 'cause she uses a childminder. What was useful was knowing the going rate of pay, what you were expected to do as far as a contract was concerned . . . really what it involves to employ somebody.

> I discussed the pros and cons of various methods that friends had chosen . . . people like us.

Collection of information from this group of FCCC mothers was completed by 2002, so it is perhaps not surprising that none of them mentioned the Internet as a source of information. As I write, in 2008, the Internet is the first port of call for most people seeking information about anything; it is widely used by parents both for making supportive contact with one another and for gathering information about child care from experts and retailers alike. In the United Kingdom, a site has been established that not only provides child care information but also a secure means for parents who need childminders or nannies to make contact with those in their home areas who have vacancies.

Television, mentioned as a source of information by only 11 percent of those surveyed, clearly had a powerful and sometimes a direct influence on mothers' choices:

> And also there was the, you know, Louise Woodward stuff on the TV which does make you pause and think about leaving your child with, you know, one person at home.

Some of those who were considering child care for the first time were influenced—alarmed—not only by specific media stories but also by a generally anti–child care zeitgeist:

> You hear so many stories . . . about nannies abusing babies and that. That's why I wouldn't leave her with anyone else. . . . I'd rather just have my sister.

Part Two

TYPES OF CHILD CARE

Introduction: Family Care, the Baseline

Most children around the world are cared for primarily by their parents, just as they always have been. This apparently obvious point sometimes gets lost in the disproportionate amount of attention, especially media attention, given to nonparental care when mothers and fathers work outside their homes. Child care in general is of enormous economic and political concern, and it is of great importance to parents as well as to children, because the quality of care a child experiences will have an impact on her development. But no matter how many hours she spends in child care, the care she gets the rest of the time from one or both of her parents is the most important, almost always and almost everywhere.

Mother care is the first to be experienced and the only kind common to almost every child. Newborn babies start out in full-time mother care, and almost every baby and most toddlers and children, too, go on spending more time in the care of a biological or adoptive mother than in anyone else's. So mother care is universal, background to all types of child care rather than one type in its own right.

Nevertheless, when people talk about "full-time mothers" or "stay-at-home mothers" (and talk about them they do), they refer to women whose mothering takes a particular form: those who care for their own babies or children (with or without the help of partners or family members) to the exclusion of paid employment and without regularly using any other type of child care. Of course, such a mother may write a novel at night—and eventually make a high income from it. And, of course, caring for a baby full-time doesn't mean that she never leaves him with her mother while she goes to the gym. Still, if caring for a child is the reason a woman is not employed outside her home, her mother care is an alternative to other kinds of child care and should be considered alongside them. After all, being at home with children is at least as demanding as any other kind of work, though unpaid. Choosing to "stay home" is at least as big a decision as choosing any other child care arrangement. It costs money (in the form of loss of earnings or potential earnings), just as a nursery does, and in some countries, the choice is contrary to government social policy and carries punitive tax implications.

Father care is not universal, of course, men being dependent on women to tell them that they have fathered a child. A review of ethnographic reports from 156 cultures concludes that only one-fifth of them promote men's close relationships with their babies and even fewer with young children. Furthermore, worldwide, many children miss out altogether on being fathered, because the relationship between their parents breaks down or is never solidified, or because the father dies or is away at war or in migrant employment.

Nevertheless, father care is very much more important than is generally realized, and in the West, despite sometimes misleading headlines about rising rates of separation and divorce, it is growing. Fathers' input to their young children's care and development is still very small compared with that of mothers, but it has increased rapidly over the past ten years and is still increasing, as is society's understanding of fathers' particular importance. In the United Kingdom, this importance was formally acknowledged in 2003 with the introduction of one to two weeks' paternity leave for all fathers, paid (to those who had been with their employer for six months or more) at the same (inadequate) rate as maternity leave, currently £117.18 (about $189) per week.

---

*Percentage of childhood years spent without
the biological father (but with the mother)*

Botswana 36%	Kenya 27%
Brazil 9%	Mali 8%
Colombia 13%	Peru 9%
Dominican Republic 14%	Senegal 16%
Ecuador 7%	Trinidad and Tobago 30%
Ghana 29%	Zimbabwe 30%

Along with increasing recognition of fathers' importance goes increasing awareness of their difference from mothers. We have learned, for example, that contrary to earlier assumptions children's relationships with fathers are not built on or a reflection of their relationships with mothers but are separate and different, even in early infancy. Specifically, recent research into attachment has shown that children not only form attachments to each available parent separately but also develop different emotional skills from attachment to mothers and to fathers.

While there is a general call in the English-speaking world and in some European countries for more men to be more involved in child care, it is not always clear whether men are being exhorted to take a larger share of the care of their own children or of other people's through work as family care providers (childminders), nursery workers, or play leaders. In either case, men are deterred from getting involved by the overwhelmingly female image and expectations of child care environments. It is not so much that men think child care is a female role (almost all fathers know how important fathers are, and many men recognize the need for more male workers in child care) as that they think only (or almost only) females do it, and so they will feel out of place. It's clear that men are more likely to get involved in the care of young children—their own or others'—if they can see that there are men already involved. The Pre-School Learning Alliance (a playgroup movement in the United Kingdom) published research in 2005 showing that fathers are more likely to take their children to toddler groups or classes and other early years activities if there are men on the staff; once there are one or two fathers attending, others are likely to follow. It recommended that all such groups make special efforts both to recruit men to work in them and to be "father friendly" to those using the service. The two probably do go together, and there is certainly room for improvement in both. In Britain, the current male occupancy of jobs in nurseries, playgroups, and preschools is around 1 percent. In the United States, there are even fewer men in nurseries, although the few more who work with older children in after-school and vacation care brings the total percentage up to the British level. In contrast, in Denmark, where the inclusion of men in all aspects of child care has been steadily increasing for two generations, 5 percent of child care jobs are held by men.

While it is certainly easier for men to follow other men into what used to be a female preserve, whether that is their child's daily routine or his classroom, the barriers that prevent men from working in child care are seldom the same as the barriers to their full participation as parents. Very few men work in child care because—outside a few countries in northern Europe, notably Sweden, Denmark, and Finland—such work currently requires minimal qualifications, is paid minimum wages, and carries no prestige. Women with few career options may take these jobs for their emotional rewards, but men who are going to work for minimum wages are likely to seek more "masculine" jobs. In the United Kingdom, despite strenuous ongoing efforts to achieve integration of staffing, a young man who wants to work with children may still find a clearer career path if he trains as a teacher than as a child care worker.

It is not easy to estimate the contribution fathers make to child care while mothers work or study. Since most fathers of young children share a home with them and with their mother, the lines between "father care" and "joint (parental) care," and between child care and family life, are often blurred. If a father bathes his young children and puts them to bed while his employed partner makes the family's weekly trip to the supermarket, which role is he filling? Participant fathers take part in every aspect of family life, but sometimes the need for mutually exclusive categories in research studies distorts this fact. However, just as "stay-at-home mothers" are recognized as a category of mothers, so fathers who are their children's principal caregivers are recognized as a particular category of fathers.

5. Shared Care by Mothers and Fathers

Shared child care or joint parenting is neither new nor as simple as it sounds. It is difficult to define as well as difficult to practice. Does "shared" mean equal hours, fifty-fifty down the line, or can it be contributory, with one parent doing a quarter to the other's three-quarters? There is some evidence that what has been termed "the British pragmatic solution" but is now also recommended by American commentators—a 1.5 dual-earning couple, usually with the mother working part-time—serves to protect children's well-being, especially in the first eighteen months of life, but at a cost to women's careers and economic advancement. The number of hours each parent works is not the only consideration. *Which* hours they work also matters. To count as "equal parenting," must both parents cover the hours that are difficult (i.e., the hours when most adults are at places of employment) as well as the less difficult hours (evenings, weekends)? And does only sole charge of a child who is awake count as "care," or can being available to him or her as backup for an au pair also count? Or being the parent the school will call if a child is taken ill? Or being responsible for a sleeping child overnight? Mothers and fathers tend to differ in what they think shared care or joint parenting actually is, and it is hard to imagine a shared household in which parents do *not* share the care of their children to some degree. However, joint parenting or shared care is recognized as something different. Reports suggest that more men than women say they want joint parenting and that they have achieved it. Clearly some women do not recognize the share of children's care that fathers claim.

There are families in every Western country in which the equal provision of child care by mother and father is a matter of principle,

"The man who is to gain a living by his labour must be drawn away from home, or at least from the cradle side, to perform that labour; but this will not, if he be made of good stuff, prevent him from doing his share of the duty due to his children."   William Cobbett, 1830

sometimes in the name of gender equality (especially equal access to the workplace), sometimes to ensure 100 percent family care for the children. By willing if complicated negotiation, couples find ways and means to continue their employment while caring for the children between them. Sometimes the conundrum is solved by both partners reducing their working hours. Sometimes parents rebalance work and family within the context of running their own business, working freelance or from home, or carefully combining or dovetailing social and unsocial hours. Such couples are often discussed in the media and are therefore opinion leaders among parents, but there are actually very few of them, far fewer than some 2003 statistics from the United Kingdom's Equal Opportunities Commission (EOC) might seem to suggest. Commenting on findings from European, North American, and Australian studies showing that this generation of fathers spends far more time with their children than did the last, the EOC report says, "Overall, time spent by fathers accounts for one-third of all total parental childcare time." This has led commentators to suggest that "one-third of active parental child care is already carried out by fathers," which perpetuates the confusion between child care and parenting. The figure of one-third is certainly not a measure of fathers' hours of child care as defined in this book. Much more of the time men spend on child care is in a helping role rather than in sole charge so that mothers can pursue other activities, such as paid work. Time-use diaries from a study called *Growing Up in Australia*, for example, show that Australian "fathers of infants spend less than an hour a day in sole care of their child."

The hours quoted in different studies and from different countries vary widely, but they are all measures of men's hours of attention to or interaction with their children rather than their hours in charge of child care. Furthermore, there is widespread agreement

that most of those hours are on weekends and that most of the interaction centers on play activities, as this American mother explained
to me: "I would say he is a bit of a weekend dad. I mean he is fantas-
tic on the weekends . . . but during the week he is never here. . . .
He probably spends less than five minutes with them during the
week, per day." An American commentator suggests that "weekends
are emerging as special times for many working families, providing
opportunities for parents and children to sustain family relationships, often in the face of increasing working hours."

Some groups of fathers are far more hands-on than others, and
which is which is not always predictable. Time-use studies in the
United Kingdom, for example, suggest that in full-time dual-
earning couples, fathers spend up to three-quarters as much time
with their children as the mothers do. And a national study of
twelve thousand children in the west of England indicated that
father involvement in the first year of life—often meaning father
care—can compensate babies for their mothers' absence. If that is
the case, babies of single mothers who are working full-time in the
first year clearly need support to compensate for the fathers'
absence. Fathers who do not live with their children, especially
those in underprivileged areas and reliant on state benefits, may
spend unexpectedly large amounts of time with their children, most
of it in sole charge.

If fathers still spend far less time with children than mothers,
their relative participation in domestic tasks is even more unbal-
anced. In all countries where research has been undertaken, it is
clear that fathers participate in their children's lives far more than
they participate in running their households. International time-use
diary comparisons show this to be equally the case in the United
States and the United Kingdom. In Australia, fathers of children
under five have been shown to do exactly the same amount of
housework as married men who are childless, while fathers of children over five do even less. A majority of Australian men take on
extra hours of paid work when they have children rather than trying
to spend more hours at home.

The barriers to men's equal participation in the care of their own
children are largely attitudinal. In North America and Australia,
though less so in the United Kingdom and continental Europe,

Fathers and flexible working hours

"[Since 2003 U.K.] fathers of young children (under six) or of disabled children will get the right, like mothers, to request that they work flexibly. [It's a] law that could change everything: if fathers take up their right to work flexibly, it will benefit us all. It will be fascinating to see what happens. . . . It will affect the quiet revolution in parenting we need if, first, fathers grab the chance to ask for more family-friendly hours, and employers let them have them. . . . Will company managers be able to accept that bringing up children matters to the whole of society? It could be the wettest of damp squibs or it could be genuinely revolutionary. . . . In the end this isn't about 'working practices.' It's about civilisation."

Jackie Ashley, *The Guardian*, March 27, 2003

many mothers and fathers still have a traditional view of family roles, seeing women as gatekeepers where the care of children is concerned, primary caregivers whom fathers should assist but not replace. In many families, the breadwinner role is an exact mirror image of the mothering one: a role belonging primarily to men in which women should assist but not replace them. These attitudes are not, of course, confined to individuals or families; they also pervade much of the corporate and political world, even governments. So the couple that plans to share parental responsibility equally will be lucky if the father can take more than a week at home after a birth to get to know a new baby. Later on, he may find that it is far more difficult for him than for his partner to stay at home because a child is ill or to leave early to attend a meeting at school, because he faces not just the disapproval (and faint sense of guilt) that besets her but amazement and derision as well. Many managers (of both sexes) feel that it is bad enough that mothers have to be allowed these "privileges," but *fathers* . . . Even more than women, men may find that attempts to rebalance work and home are dangerous to their careers, yet failing to do so endangers their partnerships.

Things may be changing, though. In what workplace specialists are calling "The Daddy Wars," men are going to the U.S. Equal Employment Opportunities Commission with complaints of discrimination against employers who will not allow fathers the same benefits allowed to mothers, such as using accrued sick leave for paid time off when a baby is born. In a 2007 survey, Monster.com found that 71 percent of fathers with a child under five had taken paternity leave when it was offered by their employers.

It is because it is made so difficult for fathers to behave "like mothers" that the fight for gender equality in this particular arena is so important. The more employers find themselves forced to make inconvenient family-friendly arrangements for women who are mothers, the more inclined some are to limit their employment of women. In the United States, feminist groups report more and more "maternal profiling," with women who have or might one day have children being excluded from jobs or promotions and from top rates of pay. In the United Kingdom, law on gender equality does not allow an employer to ask a prospective employee about her family responsibilities, but just being a female of childbearing age may

---

U.K. Equal Opportunities Commission, 2004, key findings

- The breadwinning role remains crucial for many fathers. Many also emphasize "being there" for their children, and aspirations for more involved fatherhood are high.

- Most fathers play a support role within the family—they often have minimal involvement with their children during the week but put weekends aside for family life.

- Some fathers' support role is extensive. About one-third of active parental child care is already carried out by fathers.

- The gap in pay between men's and women's wages and the high cost of child care are among the factors affecting fathers' level of involvement.

- Fathers are more involved in child care when their partner has a relatively high income and is working full-time.

- The increase in fathers' participation in child care is greater than the increase in their participation in household tasks.

- Fathers often regard balancing family and work as a personal responsibility and use informal arrangements with managers.

- Fathers' expectations and use of specific family-friendly policies and practices are low despite high demand from parents for an improved balance between work and family.

keep her from being selected for an interview. Many women now face not only a glass ceiling but also a motherhood crash barrier. Establishing the same rights for men who are fathers can effectively force employers to regard all employees with children as parents who need flexibility at work.

6. Care by Full-Time Mothers

It is more difficult to describe and generalize about full-time mother care than about other kinds of care, even when a full-time mother has been defined as one who cares for her own children without regularly using any other type of child care and to the exclusion of paid employment. Families and homes are even more diverse than centers or family day cares. There are small children who do not go to child care because their mothers are home full-time but who see rather little of those mothers and rather a lot of the mall, the golf club child care room, and perhaps daytime TV. On the other hand, some "stay-at-home" mothers really are almost full-time and seldom away from their children; but some of those mothers are depressed and resentful or bored and isolated, while others are enjoying the home-based lifestyle, with a circle of friends and a range of local activities.

> I was going along to mother and toddlers group and just spending the day with Mary, we'd go out in the park or whatever and then meeting up with my friends from antenatal class and I'd go swimming to our local school pool at lunchtime. . . . Every day there was something we could do and I just thoroughly enjoyed myself. —FCCC mother

We know woefully little about any of these home-based lifestyles because recent research has focused on mothers who are working or seeking to work almost to the exclusion of mothers who are not. We do not even know how many full-time mothers there are, internationally or nationwide, because, incredible though it may seem to anyone who is actually involved with children and their care, national censuses do not identify them. "We don't specifically track stay-at-home moms because they aren't relevant to the labor force," said an official in the U.S. Census Bureau. And in Canada, an activist full-time mother was almost arrested for refusing to check the box on her form that said she was a housewife, because being a full-time mother is not the same. The omission of this simple information, differentiating women who are not employed outside their homes because they are caring for children within them from all those who are not employed for other reasons—including their own health, caring for someone else, involvement in voluntary work, or some other non-commercial endeavor—is astonishing. Censuses are intended as snapshots of societies to inform public funding, political policy, consumer marketing, and so forth. The U.S. federal government, for example, uses census data to allocate funds for economically disadvantaged individuals, job training, public assistance programs, and other services. The private sector uses it in product development as well as in advertising and marketing, and legislative bodies use it for community planning. Without census data, none of these vital planning and policy bodies can pay due regard to full-time mothers—or, indeed, full-time fathers. No wonder home-based women sometimes feel invisible.

Very rough estimates of the numbers of stay-at-home mothers can be gleaned from child care figures on the grounds that if a child is not in any other kind of care, he or she must be with a parent. It is not exactly science, but it's the best information we have. As we have seen, recent research studies suggest that in the English-speaking world, almost half of all one-year-olds and perhaps one-quarter of three-year-olds are *not* in regular child care of any kind, formal or informal, and therefore can be assumed to be in the care of their mothers and/or fathers at home.

With so little information about how many mothers are at home, it is difficult to discover their reasons for being there. How many are at home because they choose to be there (and why do they make that choice), and how many are there because they cannot find available, affordable, acceptable child care and/or a suitable job? Once again, national statistics cannot tell us much, because the sparse available information focuses mostly on why women seek (or return to) employment, not on why they become or remain full-time mothers.

Making the most of patchy statistics, however, it seems clear that lack of affordable child care plays a part in mothers' decisions to stay at home, but probably not as large a part as has been assumed by some governments, which are eager to get women back to work. Many individual mothers tell researchers that they would take a job if high-quality nonparental child care was more widely available and less expensive, and some of them undoubtedly would. However, we know that many would not. Major improvements in child care provisions have only marginal effects on mothers' employment statistics nationally, even where buoyant economies mean that jobs are reasonably available. In Australia, for example, where there is no state-funded maternity leave or tax help for stay-at-home parents, thousands of government-funded child care places have been provided since the early 1990s, and thousands more private child care facilities have been opened to federal subsidy. As a result, child care is probably more readily and affordably available in urban Australia than anywhere else except in the northern European countries. Yet rather than becoming a society in which almost all mothers work and use nonfamilial child care, two out of five of Australia's 1.4 million children under school age, spanning all levels of advantage and disadvantage, are at home with a parent.

Countries that have coupled the carrot of subsidized child care with various economic sticks have seen dramatic increases in the numbers of mothers working while children are young, but there are still a great many remaining out of the workforce and even more working part-time. The United States' welfare-to-work policies, designed to use the leverage of benefit cuts to force women, especially single mothers, into jobs, are not 100 percent effective. The Canadian government's refusal to give equal tax breaks to those doing their own child care as to those paying someone else to do it has not driven all mothers out to work. And although the New Labour government announced to the United Kingdom soon after it was elected in 1997 for its first term that it had "nailed its colours to the mast of supporting the working women" (Labour deputy leader Harriet Harman's words), it faced at least as much pressure for longer maternity (and paternity) leave as for more child care places. Clearly, there are a great many parents in many different countries who, for a period at least, prefer to be able to care for their children without child care from outside the family. The phrase "for a period" is important: today's full-time mother may be tomorrow's full-time executive.

Talking with mothers about care in the first year of life

So you think the very best kind of care for babies in their first year, the ideal, is to be at home with their full-time mothers?

Yes I do.

Is that ALL babies and mothers?

Well, yes . . . what do you mean?

I mean do you think every mother who's at home full-time can give her baby ideal care?

Maybe some can't. I mean, some mothers get depressed, don't they?

OK, so that ideal care is "at home with their full-time mothers who aren't depressed"?

Yes, I guess so. Aren't depressed or too lonely. I mean it can be tough being at home with a baby if you're on your own and maybe at the top of a high-rise.

Right. So the ideal care is really "at home with mothers who aren't depressed and aren't lonely or isolated or unhappy." What would make that difference?

Well, having grown-up company around I suppose—other mums and babies maybe, your own family. And getting some support from your husband. Living in a reasonable place and not being too short of money helps, too.

So to make being at home with full-time mothers into ideal care for all babies, we'd have to change the whole of society pretty much, wouldn't we? In the meantime, what about all the mothers who aren't in that position: Should they feel guilty about making different arrange-ments—maybe some paid work for themselves and child care for their baby?

Not guilty. Of course not . . . I suppose what I really mean is that "in an ideal world" happy babies would be home with happy moms. In the real world maybe we can only do the best we can.

Mother Care in the First Year of Life

Choices of child care, especially the choice for a parent to stay at home, very much depend on children's ages. Maternal (or parental) care in the first year of life is so usual that it should perhaps be regarded more as a stage in child care than as a type. The demands of mothers' recovery from birth almost guarantees a period of full-time mother care for newborn babies everywhere. After that, the length of time mothers stay at home is often controlled by their entitlement to maternity leave. In the Scandinavian countries, well-known for universally available and affordable high-quality child care for working parents, less-known paid maternity, paternity, and parental leave entitlements mean that a large majority of babies are at home and in parental care throughout their first year.

None of the English-speaking nations is generous in comparison with many European nations, although legislation passed in November 2006 brought the United Kingdom more into line with the continental countries. A substantial research study published in 2005 and covering eighteen countries and more than ten years showed how wide the differences in paid maternity leaves are between countries, and how isolated the United States and Australia are in providing none. This study does not detail the financial arrangements and size of the leave payments made in each country, only their presence or absence. Some payments are calculated as percentages of mothers' previous earnings; some are a flat-rate allowance. Several countries combine the two. In the United Kingdom, for instance, where every woman is now entitled to a full year's leave, the first six weeks of maternity leave is paid at 90 percent of the woman's average earnings over the previous year, and the next thirty-three weeks at a rate of Statutory Maternity pay set annually by Parliament and currently standing at £117.18 (about $189) per week. The final thirteen weeks is unpaid.

Research suggests that where job-protected leave is available but unpaid, only a very small minority of women take advantage of it. However, where paid maternity leave is available, almost every mother takes her full allowance, regardless of the size of the sum paid. In the United Kingdom, for example, most of the women who

WEEKS OF JOB-PROTECTED, PAID LEAVE (MATERNITY, PARENTAL, ADOPTIVE, FAMILY) IN THE YEAR 2000

Country	Weeks of Job-Protected Paid Leave	Country	Weeks of Job-Protected Paid Leave
Australia	0	The Netherlands	16
Austria	16	Norway	52
Belgium	15	Portugal	26
Denmark	52	Spain	16
Finland	39	Sweden	68
France	16–48	Switzerland	16
Germany	14	United Kingdom	18
Greece	17	United States	0
Japan	14		

were part of the FCCC study stayed out of work for exactly as long as their paid leave (then eighteen weeks) and any paid vacation time lasted. Of the few who returned to work earlier, most did so for reasons other than money.

> I wanted to go back because I like my job and I missed being with people and being part of a team and everything.   —FCCC mother

> The main reason I went back at three months was 'cause I'd said I would. I'd got my new job, accepted it and everything and then found out I was pregnant. So it was a case of just really having to go back.
>   —FCCC mother

The multination study referred to above, whose importance does not seem to have been appropriately acknowledged publicly, suggests that job-protected, paid maternity leave has a previously little-known impact on infant health. Every additional ten weeks of such leave has been found to reduce mortality in babies between the ages of one and twelve months by more than 4 percent. The reasons are not yet fully understood, but it is thought that women who can confidently anticipate long maternity leave are not only more likely to breast-feed but are also more likely to feel able to take leave during the last few weeks of pregnancy and that this may minimize the numbers of babies who are born prematurely and/or smaller than would be expected from their time in the womb. As well as having enormous implications for parents' and siblings' emotional and mental health, any reduction in infant morbidity and mortality lessens the demand for special hospital care for infants and has a major impact on health economics.

THE END OF MATERNITY LEAVE: WOMEN FROM THE FCCC STUDY

Whatever the conditions or the length of their maternity leave, not all women go back to work because they want to, and even fewer go back to work at a particular moment in time because that feels like the right time to them. Most of the mothers in the FCCC study would have liked at least a few more weeks or months at home first.

> I'd have liked another couple of weeks at home because when I went back it was only a couple of weeks since I started to feel on top of things . . . confident; myself again; normal. I'd really started to enjoy my time with her and I'd have liked a bit more.

What drove women back to work was some combination of the end of maternity leave, work pressure and responsibilities, anxiety about job security, and finding that child care was available.

> Why did I go back right then? The responsibility and the investment in my career as a professional . . . and we can't really afford for me not to work.

> Staying off longer might have meant that I'd have lost my post. I wouldn't have lost my position in the company—they have to keep that for you—but my base would have changed. . . . They could have posted me anywhere they wanted, basically.

> Financial reasons and job security mainly. Career progression also because I've been there for quite a while now so to start all over again somewhere else wouldn't be good. I've been working my way up in Pensions.

Not all the mothers wanted to stay at home beyond their maternity leave, though, even for a further brief period.

I had to keep up with my career: it's something I've always wanted, to teach, I've always enjoyed teaching, and being in the classroom, etc. I couldn't ever see myself sitting down and not working. I couldn't do it.

I'd reached a point where I needed to go out into the big world again because it was just me and E and I wasn't seeing anybody or doing anything constructive.

For some women, there was a clear, and clearly important, distinction between socializing in an adult-and-baby world and in an adults-only world. When stay-at-home mothers are unhappy with their role, it is often assumed that they are lonely and socially isolated. However, some women experience the same camaraderie in home- and child-based life that others find so enjoyable, but nevertheless find it tedious or demeaning.

I needed to have contact with other people; grown-up people. People who don't have babies.

Part-time work was the preference of almost all these mothers and the practice of more than half. Even more would have liked to work part-time hours but were not able to. One father said, "We thought long and hard about ways that we could afford for Janet to go part-time if we couldn't afford for her to leave altogether."

Some of the women who worked part-time preferred to do so even though they were aware that there was little if any net gain to the household income, especially if they were paying for child care. Not all of them saw half a job as a half-empty cup. To others it was half full:

I don't exactly work for *money* this way 'cause I don't earn much. But I cover the costs—child care and transportation—and get to keep my hand in at work as well as at home. So who's grumbling?

Staying Home After Maternity Leave: Becoming a Stay-at-Home Mother

Women who are at home with their babies during maternity leave are not, perhaps, "stay-at-home mothers" as we have defined them, since they have not left (or stayed out of) employment but have taken a leave from an ongoing job. However, the divide between the two is not nearly as clear and complete as is suggested by terms such as "working mothers" and "stay-at-home mothers" and by media reports in the United States of something close to enmity between the two.

"The Mommy Wars"

"It's 37 years since I first became a mother and what passes for public discussion about that role still resembles a food fight more than breakfast in bed.

"I've been an embedded correspondent in the mommy wars between stay-at-home and go-to-work mothers for at least 20 of those years. My daughter is now a mother and the combat has engaged a second generation, as if it were something new.

"In real life, the mothers I have known commuted back and forth across those battle lines without even passing a checkpoint. Some had husbands who lost their jobs. Others just lost their husbands. Kids entered the nest and left the nest. One family needed health care benefits. Another had a sick child at home. One woman couldn't take the stress of juggling, and another couldn't take the stress of bills. They performed the Improv that's called life.

"Were many of us ambivalent? Of course. But on the war front, the commanders and recruitment officers divide ambivalence into opposing armies of true believers. They regularly rev up the mommy wars like some ancient religious conflict.

"This year, there was the furor over whether or not professional women were 'opting out.' Then there was the firefight over some sociologists' suggestion that housewives were happier.

"On the literary front, Leslie Morgan Steiner's collection of testimonials, a fine-tuned orchestra of ambivalence, was originally going to be named 'Ending the Mommy Wars.' But it came out of the publishing house packaged as 'Mommy Wars.'

"Now the current star of mommy-war lit is Caitlin Flanagan, full of retro-hip confusion about being a full-time mom with a full-time nanny. In her book, 'To Hell With All That,' she tips her hat to mixed feelings but delivers punch lines aimed directly at the 'enemy' jaw.

"She asks herself, for example, what did her boys gain from having her at home? Her answer: 'an immersion in the most powerful force on earth: mother love.' Whammo. Don't the kids of working moms get mother love?"   Ellen Goodman, *Washington Post* Writers Group, May 12, 2006

A large majority of stay-at-home mothers in all countries have children under two—in fact, the younger a child is the more likely he is to have a mother at home full-time—and most of those have babies under one year so that they overlap with the maternity leave group. Those who are at home with older preschool or even school-age children commonly have a younger one (or more) as well and may have stayed out of employment for longer than they originally intended because of the sequence and timing of births. For example, women who take maternity leave with one baby and then find themselves pregnant again often stay home.

Research into why women stay at home from child to child is sparse. Reasons women give during informal conversations include:

- Their own health—e.g., pregnancy sickness toward the end of the first maternity leave or exhaustion anticipated later in the pregnancy.

- Their older child's well-being—e.g., instead of being in child care up to and after the new baby's birth, the toddler is at home with mother and can remain at home through the new baby's leave entitlement.

- Costs—if child care for one child is only just manageable, child care for two may be unaffordable.

Many of these mothers, even those who are unpaid for several years while having two or three children, see being at home as a temporary break from their employment: extended maternity or family leave that is self-financed if they happen to live on one side of the Atlantic but might be state-supported if they live on the other. Such mothers seldom planned for their first baby to reach school (or perhaps nursery school) age without ever having any nonparental care. They stayed out of the workplace as long as they did because of circumstance rather than conviction. They are mothers who are currently at home with their children but not necessarily women who are making a point about the importance of every mother doing so; relatively few join advocacy organizations such as Full Time Mothers (FTM) in the United Kingdom or the United States.

STAYING AT HOME WITH TODDLERS AND OLDER CHILDREN

Without census data, estimates of the numbers of women who remain stay-at-home mothers after their youngest child passes babyhood and all maternity leave has been exhausted have to depend on employment statistics. This is obviously unsatisfactory. Working mother and stay-at-home mother are not the only possibilities. Children certainly make a difference in women's employment rates, but an unemployed woman who happens to have children is not necessarily a full-time mother.

Differences between employed and nonemployed mothers

Most of the research comparing stay-at-home with employed mothers is more than ten years old and, given the rate of change in post-industrial societies, may be out-of-date. It is possible that being at home, at least for a period, or taking advantage of increasing opportunities to work at or from home with the help of more and more sophisticated information technology, are seen as good options by some women. There are indications that the have-it-all culture of the 1990s is softening in the face of different approaches to balancing work and family. Furthermore, increasing (if still small) numbers of women see being at home as something much more positive than simply not being at work. The number of mothers who are home-schooling children, for example, is very small but has doubled in the United Kingdom since 1999 (from twelve thousand to twenty-one thousand), while one in twenty children in the United States is said to be homeschooled.

The bulk of twenty-five years of research with different samples in various countries, however, has found higher morale among employed mothers irrespective of their social class or personal circumstances. Some investigators found no significant differences, but none, to my knowledge, found that the mental health or sense of well-being of full-time homemakers was actually higher than those of women in employment. Wage-earning women tend to have higher levels of satisfaction with their lives and lifestyles and to score lower on assessments of psychosomatic symptoms, measures of depression, and various stress indicators. Employment has also been shown to be a source of psychological support in times of family difficulties. Most of this research has been conducted with samples of middle-class women whose employment is usually assumed to be personally satisfying and relatively well paid. Furthermore, the jobs that seem to be most beneficial to mothers and their children are those that are complex, challenging, and allow considerable autonomy—all qualities that seem more likely to be associated with professional or managerial employment than with unskilled jobs. However, satisfaction with work and the mental health advantages associated with it are not peculiar to middle-class women. On the contrary, when samples of working-class mothers have been studied, their employment, however routine it may appear, has even more consistent mental health advantages. It may be that there are different kinds of satisfaction to be derived from different kinds of employment. Perhaps women doing semiskilled jobs that don't sound very interesting or challenging to outsiders get their satisfaction from the increased social support and stimulation provided by coworkers, the marked advantages that their wages bring to their families, and the increased sense of control they feel over their lives, rather than from their actual tasks. It may also be that the alternative to employment—being a full-time mother, housewife, or perhaps caregiver to elderly relatives—is a less attractive option to many working-class women than to middle-class women. Higher levels of depression among working-class homemakers highlight the advantages of employment for working-class mothers.

These differences between employed mothers and mothers at home are not dramatic; not every employed mother is happy, healthy, and full of enthusiasm, and not every stay-at-home mother is miserable. Much depends on the mother's attitude toward her job, the stability of child care arrangements, the availability of support from family (especially grandparents) and friends, and, above all, the father's participation in child care. Indeed, some research findings suggest that women who are currently married experience the higher morale that typically goes with employment only if their husbands help with child care.

Effects of mothers' employment on roles and relationships in the family
When married mothers go out to work, their husbands take more part in running the family. Although we cannot assume that moth-

ers' employment is the cause and husbands' participation the effect—it might be that fathers who are more involved with their families encourage their partners to take employment—couples themselves report that it is. Of course, there are active and participant fathers in families where mothers are at home as well as in families where mothers are at work, but that paternal participation shows itself in different ways. If the mother is at home, more-active fathers participate by spending more time with their children but are not as likely to take part in child care and household tasks. If the mother is at work, on the other hand, a merging of roles is more common. It is in dual-wage families, especially where the mother is employed full-time, there is more than one child, and there are no older children (especially older daughters) in the family, that fathers take on more of the family tasks traditionally carried out by mothers. Fathers' participation is extremely important to mothers' happiness and well-being, but possibly more for emotional reasons than for the practical reasons often cited. It is said that participant fathers lessen working mothers' overload from their dual role. But even if fathers' participation doubles when their partners take outside employment, the base from which their involvement starts is so small that the actual hours fathers spend on child care or family work remain very few and the relief offered minimal. Working mothers' double burden remains.

Differences in child rearing of stay-at-home and employed mothers

Research comparing the child-rearing behavior of full-time mothers with those who are employed is sparse and most of the available findings somewhat obvious. Stay-at-home mothers tend to have more traditional and gender-differentiated views of family and child rearing than employed mothers, which is not surprising, since it is mothers with more traditional views who are more likely to want to stay at home. Stay-at-home mothers are also more authoritarian than others—which goes with traditionalism—demanding more respect and obedience from their children. Stay-at-home mothers (less predictably, working-class stay-at-home mothers in particular) are better at supervising sons.

Hardly surprisingly, employed mothers regard household chores as less important than do stay-at-home mothers and take a more easygoing approach to many aspects of child care. They expect greater involvement from fathers.

Employed and nonemployed mothers tend to describe themselves as undertaking the same activities at home (though for different hours), and their answers to a questionnaire about "what most mothers do" were indistinguishable, except that "yard work" (i.e., gardening) and playing with the child were seen as optional extras that were often squeezed out of the daily lives of the employed women.

Outcomes for children of stay-at-home mothers

Mothers—and fathers—who decide that one parent should be full-time at home usually believe that this will be better for the children. Studies among children in general comparing the development and accomplishments of those who have employed mothers with those who have stay-at-home mothers do not find significant differences beyond the ones dictated by the home situation. For example, sons and daughters of employed mothers in all social groups have less traditional sex-role ideologies and participate more, at an earlier age, in household tasks and self-care, such as cleaning their own rooms. However, studies that make comparisons between children of employed and stay-at-home mothers within subgroups of children—especially by age, gender, and social class—do show some consistent differences. Patterns that have been demonstrated over the years include the following:

- In the first year of life, neither having a mother at home nor spending time in child care is simply associated with babies' development. The "quality" of mothering, measured by women's sensitivity and responsiveness to their babies, is critically important to the relationship, the secure attachment, between them. If that relationship is established and mothering is of high quality, being in child care will not damage it—or the infant's development. However, the development of a baby who receives poor mothering is at risk, and in that case, spending many hours in child care, or time in child care that is of poor quality or unstable, greatly increases the disadvantage.

- Although the results of early child care are affected by its nature and quality, many studies suggest that negative effects from the first year last well into the school years, with seven- to eleven-year-olds who were cared for away from their mothers more likely than those whose mothers were at home to be described by teachers as aggressive, uncooperative, and lacking frustration tolerance and described by other children as "mean."

• Boys are more likely than girls to be negatively affected by mothers' early and current employment, especially boys in working-class families. A few studies have found that sons of middle-class mothers who stayed home showed higher school performance and higher IQ scores during the grade-school (primary school) years.

• Girls, on the other hand, seem more likely than boys to benefit academically from having working mothers. Daughters of employed mothers have higher academic achievement, greater career success, more nontraditional career choices, and greater occupational commitment than daughters of stay-at-home mothers.

• Studies of children in poverty, in both two-parent and single-mother families, found that those with employed mothers scored higher than the rest both on measures of cognitive abilities and on social-emotional development.

• Nonacademic differences between children with employed and non-employed mothers have been found in other groups also, but with less consistency. For example, daughters of employed mothers may be more independent, particularly in interaction with their peers in a school setting, while results for sons have been mixed, varying with social class, preschool experience, and age at testing.

These relationships between mothers working outside the home and aspects of children's development are more complex—and possibly less direct—than they may seem. It may be that children are not directly affected by their mothers working but by the higher morale mothers have when employed. We know that mothers' good mental health is vital for effective parenting and that effective parenting enhances children's emotional adjustment, cognitive development, and school performance. Since we also know that employed mothers tend to have better mental health, it is likely, though not yet proven, that mothers' employment status, parenting styles, and child outcomes are all mediated by mothers' mental health or sense of well-being. That speculation is supported by another body of research suggesting that what is important is not employment per se but mothers' satisfaction with their roles, whether as full-time or as employed mothers. There is a powerful argument for mothers' right to choose their work-home balance.

7. Fathers as Principal Care Providers

Care by fathers becomes "child care" within the meaning adopted by this book when fathers take care of their children for regular pre-arranged hours specifically in order to free the mothers to go out to work or to study. This occurs in a very small group of families and has been little researched, but their numbers and interest in them are increasing. A 2006 University of Texas study indicated that the number of full-time stay-at-home dads had risen 300 percent since 1996 and stood at 159,000, with a possible 2 million fathers undertaking substantial but part-time hours of child care.

In every country studied, fathers are more likely to be the caregivers for babies than for older children, especially for babies who are still very young when their mothers return to work outside the home. Hence, while the Equal Opportunities Commission has estimated that U.K. fathers provide about 2 percent of nonmaternal care for children across all age groups, American fathers provide a bigger proportion than this, partly because American babies start nonmaternal care much earlier than British babies. In the NICHD study of early child care, the average age at which babies entered nonmaternal care was three months, and a quarter of them were cared for by their fathers while their mothers were at work. In the FCCC study, only 8 percent of babies that age were in nonmaternal care, and a quarter of them were cared for by their fathers. By the time both samples of babies reached one year, fathers were the main providers of nonmaternal child care for 23 percent of the American infants whose mothers were working compared with 15 percent of the English infants. By the time the infants reached three years, 12 percent of American fathers were the principal caregivers while mothers worked, as compared with only 8 percent of English fathers.

Although the image of fathers who are the principal caregivers for their children portrayed in the popular press is of "new men" partnered with professional women, the reality is rather different. Father care, on both sides of the Atlantic, mostly correlates with youth and poverty, and sometimes with ethnic background. This is a further explanation for there being more father care in the United States than in the United Kingdom: young fatherhood is more common in the United States, particularly among black men, who are especially likely to be poor. In the United Kingdom, 34 percent of all men have their first child before they reach the age of twenty-five, while in the United States, the corresponding figures in 2005 were 41 percent of white men, 47 percent of Hispanic men, and 61 percent of black men. In the NICHD study, men who took on more child care responsibilities tended to be younger fathers with positive personalities, who had intimate marriages with women who were also young and worked long hours. These fathers contributed a lower proportion of the family income than others and were employed for fewer hours. They took on more caregiving responsibilities for sons than for daughters.

Father involvement in all aspects of child care is popularly regarded as a good thing, and it is generally assumed that almost every mother would welcome it in her own family, if only fathers would cooperate. Yet findings from the FCCC study, one of the few large-scale child care studies that has considered this issue, suggest otherwise.

When 1,201 mothers of three-month-old babies in the FCCC study were asked to select their ideal type of child care from a list, assuming that all types were available and affordable, only six mothers (less than half of 1 percent) chose care by the father. And while almost half of the mothers (48 percent) said that their ideal was their own care, only forty-nine (7 percent) chose care by the mother and father together. In contrast, more than one hundred (10 percent) chose a grandparent or a nursery, forty-nine (7 percent) chose a nanny, and twenty-six (4 percent) a childminder.

When a group of these mothers who had returned to work in the first seven months of their babies' lives were asked how they had chosen the child care they were using, only two volunteered that discussion with partners/fathers had played a part in their decision, and when they were asked directly about the father's part, most talked about it as a matter of him confirming their choice rather than putting forward his own views:

> We did talk about it but he wouldn't have an overriding opinion one way or the other.

> He's happy to go with whatever I say. . . . he's happy to accept my judgment.

Some women may have perceived these compliant-sounding fathers as supportive, but others made it clear that they deliberately excluded or ignored the men's input regarding child care decisions:

> His [now ex-husband's] views didn't come into it at all.

> He wanted his mum to look after the baby. If I hadn't liked his mum it wouldn't have made any difference (well, we probably would have got a divorce!). But I like Cindy so that's made it easy.

Presumably fathers are fully involved when child care decision making leads to them undertaking the role of principal caregiver. However, since families in which mothers rely on children's fathers to provide child care while they work tend to be poor and short of choices, it is not surprising that some of the fathers who take on the role of caregiver at the expense of the role of provider do so reluctantly.

> Mr. Mom? Um . . . yeah . . . it's kinda rewarding, but it's also very frustrating. The way things are for us right now it makes sense for my wife to be working but, it's ah . . . it feels kinda funny and being with my son all day, it's fun and all that, but sometimes I need some adult time, you know what I mean?

Interestingly, when those same English mothers who were so unenthusiastic about the prospect of father care actually found themselves relying on it, most of them liked it. By the time the babies in the FCCC study were approaching one year, eighteen mothers (1.8 percent) were relying solely on their child's father to provide child care so that they could work. Those few mothers were more satisfied with that care than the mothers who were using any other type of nonmaternal child care (see Chapter 18).

Not all fathers who undertake the care of their children while the mothers work or study have to alter their own working patterns in order to do so, especially if the mothers work part-time and perhaps unconventional hours. Some fathers work shifts that allow them to be at home when their partners are at work. Some work for themselves, freelancing or running their own businesses, and can therefore arrange their own hours. At the other extreme, some have only casual employment that can be fitted in, when necessary, often with the help of child care from other family members. However, the decision to deploy a child's father as caregiver while the mother works is life-changing for two groups of families. One is the small but growing group in which both parents decide to reduce and reorganize their working hours so that they can manage the children's care between them. The other is the group that decides on what is still often thought of as a role swap or role reversal, in which the mother becomes the principal wage earner and the father becomes the principal caregiver. Some studies suggest that in the first year, at least, this may be a better option for the baby than both parents working long hours and using possibly poor-quality, nonparental child care. The large-scale national cohort study of twelve thousand children in the west of England (the Avon Longitudinal Study of Parents and Children, or ALSPAC study) showed that the relatively poor outcomes in social and emotional development often reported in babies whose mothers were employed during the first year were no longer observable when care was provided by fathers.

ROLE REVERSAL

"New men" are not as new as many people assume them to be. Father care while mothers worked was commonplace enough two centuries ago to be the subject of this nursery rhyme (ca. 1830):

> *Hush little baby, lie still with thy daddy,*
> *thy mammy has gone to the mill*

To grind thee some wheat to make thee some meat
Oh my dear baby lie still.

If fathers caring for their infants seems new now, it is because of
the relatively rigid separation of roles that followed two world wars.
That gender role assignment has come to be called "traditional,"
although apart from a very small minority of wealthy and aristo-
cratic families, it probably dominated no more than two generations. Some contemporary couples who have the economic freedom
to choose reverse those traditional parenting roles rather than simply sharing their children's care, because they see it as a way of giving their child parent care while giving themselves and each other
what they most want out of family life and what they believe each of
them is most suited to:

> Emmy always knew I wanted kids and that's really why she went along
> with having them. I've always known that she wouldn't be happy at
> home caring for them or even fitting her career around child care
> arrangements. But it suits me; I actually love taking care of them. Even
> the housework is a small price to pay.   —FCCC father of two

Most of the few studied couples who switched the conventional
roles, however, made the decision on pragmatic, usually largely
financial grounds. If a woman earns substantially more than her
partner, it may make sense that she should pursue her work outside
the home while he tailors or abandons his in favor of child care.
That position is rare, though, because all over the developed world
most women earn less than the men who are their partners, and
within parent couples, the gender gap in pay is exacerbated by a
huge gender gap in working hours. According to the Equal Opportunities Commission's study *Fathers: Balancing Work and Family*
(2003), 86 percent of fathers work full-time compared with 30 percent of mothers. In North America, as opposed to Europe, the decision as to which parent should remain in the workplace often
depends on which job carries health benefits for the family.

Dual-earner households in which women earn more than their
male partners are the ones where men tend to be most involved—
even equally involved—in both child care and housework. Even in

these households, though, the decision to move beyond shared parenting to an actual reversal of traditional parenting roles is not an easy one. One of the fathers who took part in the FCCC study contemplated leaving his own employment and assuming the role of principal caregiver; his words reflect the balancing act that many of the families were undertaking, weighing who could be the most productive breadwinner against who they felt was the more appropriate caregiver(s): "Part of me thinks I would happily give up work to look after Mark and to a certain extent that would make more sense because Janine earns more than I do but how well would I really cope compared with her?"

Detailed study, using video recordings, of one hundred of the fathers in the FCCC study, twenty-five of whom were principal caregivers to their one-year-olds, yields an unusually rich picture of contemporary father care. There were no overall differences in the attitudes to child rearing of the two groups of fathers: those who stayed at home were neither more nor less progressive or traditional than the rest. These couples seem to have made the decision to role swap on pragmatic grounds. Nevertheless, those progressive and traditional attitudes were as important in this group as they were among the American fathers studied by the NICHD. Whether they were principal caregivers or not, fathers with more traditional attitudes tended to be less responsive to their babies and to be observably less "happy" when playing with them.

OUTCOMES FOR CHILDREN

Although there are millions of fathers worldwide who are the principal caregivers for their children following divorce or the death of the mother, there are so few within intact couples that there is very little research concerning the outcomes for children of that particular parenting style. Powerful narratives collected in the study *Dads on Dads: Needs and Expectations at Home and at Work* describe it as positive for children and for caring fathers. Although we have no evidence that being cared for by a stay-at-home father while the mother works is better for a child than the conventional way around, we certainly have no reason to think it worse. There is a considerable amount of evidence that having one parent at home is valuable to babies and young toddlers (and some indications that it is often better than being in nonparental child care while both parents work outside the home). And an accumulation of findings suggest that all the things that go to make up good parenting (sensitivity, enthusiasm, affection, stimulation, patience), and that matter very much to a child, can come primarily from father or mother or both.

There may nevertheless be an important if indirect gain to children who are cared for by their fathers. Being a child's main caregiver, even for a few months, more or less guarantees that a father will remain closely involved with a child, and that is important. The *Dads on Dads* study suggests that all fathers broadly fit into one of the four categories described below. While all fathers, and therefore all four categories of fathers, are clearly enormously important to their children, specific outcomes are significantly better for those whose fathers are best described by group D—and to a lesser extent C—than A or even B.

A. *Enforcer dad* is not involved in the day-to-day care of children and sees the most important aspects of being a father as providing a role model and clear rules for the children. These fathers are usually older and tend to emphasize traditional sex roles.
B. *Entertainer dad* often entertains the children while mother does the household work, such as cooking and cleaning, but tends not to be involved in those tasks himself.
C. *Useful dad* also entertains the children but helps out with day-to-day child care and some household tasks. He still takes the lead from the mother about what needs doing and when.
D. *Fully involved dad* is as involved with running the home and family as his partner, at least some of the time, and parental roles are virtually interchangeable.

The outcomes that go with fathers' involvement last all through childhood and include higher educational attainment, better social and emotional adjustment, and less antisocial behavior such as truancy or crime. It has been known for many years that parental participation in children's education boosts their learning, but it has only recently become clear that when both parents involve themselves, the double dose of parental influence can be doubly powerful. When fathers in particular show greater interest in their children's educational attainment and confidently convey high expectations, children have higher expectations of their own progress, enjoy and behave better in school, and have higher scores on tests and examinations.

8. Grandparent Care

Despite all the talk of family breakdown, grandparents in many communities on both sides of the Atlantic are closely involved in the lives of their grandchildren. Although many people believe that if extended families exist at all they are scattered across states if not continents, there are many cities in North America and the United Kingdom in which at least one grandparent lives close enough to see at least one family of grandchildren as often as every week. And see them they do. As long as they have a good relationship with the parents (their own children or children-in-law), almost all grandparents who live within a few minutes' drive of the grandchildren's home visit at least weekly. About three-quarters of the grandparents who live farther away, even those who really do live in different states or on different continents, contact grandchildren several times each week, sometimes by phone or letter but increasingly by e-mail. In a recent U.K. magazine survey, three-quarters of grandparents claimed not only to be involved in their grandchildren's lives but also to contribute to their upbringing. This was confirmed by the academic study *Grandparenting in Britain:* one-fifth of grandparents cared for children under twelve for at least one day a week.

Much of grandparents' involvement with grandchildren and many of the contributions they make to grandchildren's upbringing have nothing to do with child care. Even when grandparents take physical charge of a child for periods, it is often difficult for researchers, or families themselves, to be certain which contacts are principally social and which are mainly useful. Does the child stay with his grandparents overnight each weekend for his and their pleasure, as babysitting to free his parents to go out together, or as child care to accommodate their weekend work shifts? Often, of course, it will be a bit of each. Grandparent care as this book defines it is providing care for children to facilitate their parents' working or studying, but that definition, strictly applied, probably underestimates grandparents' total contribution. Throughout the English-speaking world, more children who need care while parents are working get it from grandparents than from anyone else.

Grandparents' contribution to child care starts very early in children's lives; in fact, when mothers first leave babies in somebody else's care so as to go back to work, that person is equally likely to be a grandparent or the father. Once they had any regular care from anyone but the mother, around a quarter of the American babies in the NICHD study and a similar proportion of the English babies in the FCCC study were cared for by grandparents for an average of around thirty hours a week.

By the end of babies' first year, neither father care nor grandparent care is quite so predominant because other types of care are used more frequently. Grandparents continue to provide a large proportion of the total, however—often a larger proportion than is immediately obvious from statistical tables. When children are in more than one type of nonmaternal child care, the second or "extra" type is usually grandparent care. In the FCCC study, for example, when children were in what was termed "combination care"—family day care, say, plus something else—the something else was almost invariably care by a grandparent. And when grandparents' contribution to "combined care" was added to the category of "grandparent care," it became clear that grandparents were providing more child care than any other category of caregiver.

Grandparents are caring not only for infants and toddlers. In the United States, about one-third of children under six are cared for by their mothers and/or fathers; another third are in all types of purchased child care; while a final third are cared for by relatives, a large majority of whom are their grandparents. A very large survey of child care in the United Kingdom published in 2006 showed that almost one in five (19 percent) of all families using child care and/or early years education for a preschool child (up to age five) relied principally on care by a grandparent. And in Australia in 2002, more children under the age of twelve received informal care by a grandparent than any other kind of care, formal or informal.

Grandparent care does not necessarily end even when children reach the age of twelve years. The British Daycare Trust stated, in 2006, that each week a quarter of families with children under fifteen use a grandparent to provide child care for an average of sixteen hours per week, and many adolescents, who don't exactly *need* care and probably wouldn't be offered it from any other source, welcome grandparents' caring companionship when parents are not around.

The particular importance of grandparents' care for teenage grandchildren is highlighted in a study of communication in British families. During the survey period, more than one in five of the teenagers who had spent time with a grandparent while their parents were at work had talked to that grandparent about personal issues and problems, a higher proportion than had discussed such things with parents, teachers, or siblings.

Even when grandparents are not their grandchildren's principal or secondary caregivers, and even if they undertake no regular child care at all, many still make a large—if largely unrecorded and therefore hard to quantify—contribution to those children's care and well-being. Furthermore, they often make an incalculable contribution to the parents' ability to hold down a job. Grandparents who live within easy reach of the grandchildren's home often serve as backup caregivers who can be called upon to step in when regular arrangements go wrong. Even grandparents who live hours of traveling time away are sometimes called upon to come and stay with children who are too sick for their regular child care so that parents need not take time off from work.

Most grandparents who provide child care do so for love and family obligation rather than for money. The affordability of child care is an issue for most parents, as we have seen, so it is obvious that grandparent care saves many parents a great deal of money. Less obviously, perhaps, it also saves governments money that they would otherwise have to pay in subsidies to low-income working parents using formal care or in benefits to low-income parents unable to find jobs. A large survey in Britain found that 64 percent of parents were relying heavily on grandparent care, at an average savings of £2,685 (about $4,500) per year. The United Kingdom's Daycare Trust estimates the value to taxpayers of grandparents' informal services at over £1 billion ($1.6 billion) per year.

There is one group of people for whom grandparents' care is

often a cost and a burden, however, and that is grandparents themselves (and sometimes their spouses or dependent elderly relatives). Grandparents, such as those in a U.S. AARP study, incurred day-to-day costs when providing necessary items for the children, such as cribs and toys, in their homes, as well as the longer-term lifestyle costs common to caring grandparents in all countries. Some grandparents, especially grandmothers, retire earlier than they would have done had there not been grandchildren needing care; others put their own jobs in jeopardy or reduce their hours and wages so that their adult children need not do so.

Who Is a Grandparent?

Given the overwhelming importance of grandparents to many contemporary families, it is astonishing how little factual information we have about them. Even their identity is surrounded by question marks. It might seem that biology makes it perfectly clear who is and is not whose grandparent, but does it? If your child's grandmother is your husband's mother, she's your mother-in-law; if she's your mother, she's his mother-in-law, but what if she is his or your stepmother?

Relationships between today's parents and grandparents are often planted in yesterday's anxieties and misunderstandings, predating the birth of the first grandchild. A divorce puts "ex" in front of most of those relationship names, and a remarriage introduces the modern phenomenon of the stepgrandparent. And, of course, a divorce may be followed by a new partnership that isn't a marriage. Is the father of a parent's live-in lover her children's grandfather—and if he is not so regarded now, how long must the couple be together before he is? And what about the new partner of the grandfather himself? Is she—or he—your children's stepgrandmother or stepgrandfather even if the role has not been formalized by law and the original partner is still around?

When child care studies report on extended family care, they often fail to distinguish between grandparents and other relatives or to differentiate maternal from paternal grandparents or even grandmothers from grandfathers. While there are certainly aunts, cousins, and stepgrandfathers contributing to child care, the relatives who

"When grandfathers reported looking after grandchildren, only 4 percent of those interviewed said they took the main responsibility of care, while around half shared it with their partner or spouse and nearly half said their partner or spouse was solely responsible for the grandchildren. In contrast, more than half (54 percent) of the grandmothers reported taking the main responsibility of care for grandchildren, with just over one-third saying they shared the responsibility with their partner or spouse."

Christine Millward, *Family Relationship and
Intergenerational Exchange in Later Life*

are most relevant to child care in every country are maternal grandmothers: the mother's biological or adoptive mother or very occasionally her stepmother.

Grandfathers, especially maternal grandfathers, also take part in grandparent child care, especially if they have retired from work. Sometimes grandparent couples report that each of them spends similar amounts of time looking after a grandchild. While the time commitments may be the same, though, the levels of responsibility usually are not. Very few grandfathers take sole or even main responsibility for the care of a grandchild. At most the responsibility is shared.

Nevertheless, just as contemporary fathers have moved toward and into new roles, so their fathers and fathers-in-law have also embraced a more interested and more nurturing role, taking the time to be affectionate and loving. One grandfather, newly retired, expressed the sentiments of many when he said, "When my children were growing up, I was so busy making a living I had very little time for them. Now my biggest joy is being with my grandchildren. Maybe I'm trying to make up for what I didn't do before."

SOME PROS AND CONS OF GRANDPARENT CARE

Baby care by grandmothers is sometimes presented only as a cheap and easy option. In the United States, where relative (including grandmother) care is used most often by low-income mothers, especially those who are single, it is assumed that it is often used more out of necessity than choice. Conversations with parents, however, suggest that grandmother care is very much the first choice of many, and not only because it is (usually) free. In the FCCC study, more mothers selected care by their own mothers—the maternal grandmothers—as their ideal type of child care than picked any other type of care except their own, and several of those who returned to work before their babies were six months old had felt able to do so only because their mothers provided child care.

While all three generations often flourish with a grandparent in a caring role, that's not always the case. From the point of view of the grandparent, it is often difficult now and likely to become more difficult in the future. Grandparents (usually) want to help, but decreasing numbers can make themselves available, not only because of distance but also because more grandparents continue to work until later in life. Many grandparents already have to balance serving their own needs through employment with serving the needs of their adult children by caring for grandchildren; that conflict can only become more intense. At the same time, other pressures are building. The population is aging, and because increasing numbers of babies are being born to older parents, grandchildren are arriving later in people's lives. Grandparents face demands to undertake child care not only when they themselves are older but also when spouses and other relatives are aging. Responsibility for grandchild care may clash with caring responsibilities within grandparents' own generation.

While those practical problems are likely to arise in all countries, the emotional complications in grandparent child care that are currently reported are not the same in different English-speaking countries. The question of who grandparent care is really for and whose interests it serves, for example, shows clear differences between the United States and the United Kingdom. In surveys in Britain (and in Australia), parents tend to be the ones who encourage contact between grandparents and grandchildren and want to involve grandparents in their parenting, often more than the grandparents would choose. In the United Kingdom, although in most surveys nine out of ten grandparents describe their grandchildren as "very rewarding" and are happy with high levels of contact and closeness, many of those grandparents report feeling pressured to provide more care than they would choose to do, at the expense of work, volunteering, or retirement interests such as travel. In a recent Australian study, some grandparents expressed resentment at any assumption that they would take on the role of child care provider for their grandchildren and objected to this role being taken for granted either by their grown children or by the community at large. A majority would prefer to step back from active involvement: "One thing I've always said, even with my own daughter, I would never look after grandchildren during the day while they go to work. I don't agree with that. I've brought up my own children and I don't want to be tied down every day looking after grandchildren."

In North America, in contrast, surveys such as "What It Means to Be a Grandparent in the 21st Century," carried out for *Child* magazine by Penelope Leach in 2004 and described on www.parents.com, suggest that it is grandparents rather than their adult children who work hardest to maintain and enrich extended family relationships. No matter how much they get to see their grandchildren, grandparents would like to see them more, often far more than the parents choose. Some parents appeared to feel that grandparents were critical of their child-rearing practices, and some of the grandparents did indeed speak critically about them. Some parents were concerned about the grandparents' values and the example they might set for the grandchildren, while others were worried about either too much or not enough discipline. Some couples who lived too far from the grandparents for easy half-day visits said that this distance limited contact because they were not comfortable with grandparents having the children for sleepovers. Recent American reports of grandparents battling with their own children and children-in-law for visitation with grandchildren after divorces and family breakdown suggest a more combative relationship between the generations than is commonly reported in the United Kingdom.

How Much Child Care Do Grandparents Provide?

In all countries where surveys have been undertaken, grandparent care ranges from about one in five grandmothers providing child care once a week for mothers who work full-time to almost half of the grandmothers of young babies offering all-day child care during the first few months after the mother's return to work. A recent report on 8,752 English families found that 44 percent of the children were regularly cared for by a grandparent at ages eight, fifteen, and twenty-four months.

Those figures rise dramatically when routine parenting breaks down because of separation or illness. About three-quarters of maternal grandmothers care for their grandchildren if the father is no longer at home and the mother has a full-time job. This grandmother spoke for many of them, though: "I love *them* but God forgive me I don't love *this*. I thought I was done with bringing up kids. I thought Bill and I were done with being responsible for anyone but ourselves. And I get tired, tired out."

Grandmothers in multigenerational households often provide full-time child care while the parent works whether the household is made up of a grandparent living with her children and grandchildren or a single parent and his or her children living with grandparents. In the FCCC study, children who were in a multigenerational arrangement spent the most time in nonparental care per week. Sometimes it was clear that the grandmother looked after the child overnight as well as during daytime working hours; indeed one parent claimed to use grandparent care for her baby 168 hours per week.

On both sides of the Atlantic and in Australia, there are increasing numbers of households in which grandparents are responsible for their grandchildren around the clock in the absence of the parents. All authorities seem to agree that the number of "skip-generation" households is still rising rapidly not only due to increasing family breakdown, but also because where children are the victims of parental abuse or neglect, or parents are jailed (often for drug offenses), social workers in most countries and states now make strenuous efforts to place them with relatives rather than in foster or institutional care. This solution is usually better for the children and always much cheaper for the taxpayer. National figures are difficult to come by, but by the year 2000, there were around 4 million children in the United States being raised by grandparents and around 70,000 in Canada. In Australia in 2003, 22,500 families, or around 1 percent of all families with children under age seventeen, were in this situation.

OUTCOMES FOR CHILDREN

The reported outcomes for children receiving routine child care from grandparents are very variable. Some poor outcomes are to be expected since they correlate with poverty and disadvantage, and it is poor and disadvantaged families—especially young, single mothers—who are most likely to use grandparent care. However, the quality of grandparent care may be given unfairly low scores if it is measured using the same methods applied to nonrelative care. Predictors of high-quality care and good outcomes in a nursery or family day care home include measures that are not applicable to grandparents, such as training and interest in child care as a career. One major study in the United States, using a method designed to measure quality in regulated (family day care) homes, found lower-quality ratings in relative homes, with good quality care in only 1 percent, adequate care in 30 percent, and inadequate care in 69 percent. In contrast, the NICHD study, using a method designed for application across different settings, reported higher-quality care for babies in grandparent care than in any other care type.

The outcomes of grandparent care also vary with the ages of the children. While findings from the NICHD study suggest that many infants benefit from one-on-one care in a grandparent's home, a study of 1,519 single mothers reported at the World Congress of the Econometric Society in 2005 suggests that informal familial child care arrangements that continue past the first year have a detrimental effect on children's achievements.

The outcomes of grandparent care in skip-generation households in the United States are, sadly, poor. The children's academic performance tends to be lower than that of comparable children in parent-headed households, and the grandparents are at higher risk for physical and emotional health problems, although the U.S. Census Bureau reports that a third of custodial grandparents have excellent health and are employed outside their homes.

Many grandparent-headed households face family problems—including grief over and anger at absent parents—and poverty, which may be sufficient to account for the poor outcomes. If outcomes for children brought up by grandparents are not good, however, outcomes for children brought up in institutional or foster care are worse. Recent findings from Canada suggest that children whose parents cannot care for them do better in the care of grandparents than strangers and that the arrangement is often the best that can be managed not only for the children but for the grandparents as well.

9. Care by Nannies, Au Pairs, and Other In-Home Child Care Providers

Long regarded as the outrageously expensive preserve of the unreasonably rich, nannies have often been ignored as irrelevant in studies of child care. Research on nannies is difficult to find because they are the least studied (as well as least regulated) of all types of caregiver. Enter "nannies" in any Internet search engine, and there will be thousands of hits. Almost all of them, however, are employment-agency sites (with a few blogs from—usually disgruntled—parents). These sites are about individual nannies, not about nannying as a type of child care or as a profession.

Even when care by nannies has been included in research as one type of at-home child care, their relatively small numbers, along with the difficulty of defining what constitutes a nanny, pose such problems for statistical analysis that nannies soon vanish into combined care categories such as "in-home care provider" or "other." In the U.K. Department of Education and Skills (now called the Department for Children, Schools and Families) report on child care, for example, 2 percent of parents were using a nanny or an au pair as the main source of care for a child under five, and another 2 percent were using a "babysitter." These caregivers were not separately defined, and the analysis of the three together was not pursued as "the number of parents using these other providers were too small for separate analysis." A report by the U.S. Center for Economic and Policy Research revealed that 3.6 percent of American mothers were using "nanny/sitter care." Because they are defined together as "care by someone who is not a relative of the child in the child's own home," there is no certain way of differentiating these two very different groups or of excluding au pairs, who are not men-

Talking to parents about nannies

If you have enough space and money, a trained or experienced nanny who lives in may seem to offer the ultimate in freedom to come and go without anxiety.

There can be snags, though.

- Unless you can allocate her separate accommodation, she lives with you and will be there when you don't want her as well as when you do. By being there, she may alter the relationship you have with your child, not to mention with your spouse.

- Nannies often undertake nothing that isn't directly part of caring for the child or children, so you might end your workday cooking her supper and spend your weekends doing housework. Many nannies come daily, and some parents prefer this, especially if some evening babysitting is built into the arrangement.

- The all-day concentrated attention of a nanny with nothing else to do can be surprisingly boring for a toddler (and for the nanny). Unless your nanny can become part of a network of other toddlers and caregivers, you may need to find (and pay for) friendly, interesting places and activities where she can take your child.

tioned. However, the fact that the weekly cost for their services is greater than that of family day care and not much less than formal center care suggests that most of these were nannies. The NICHD study showed that 15 percent of infants were cared for by "in-home sitters," and, judging by their relatively low standard of education and their lack of experience in child care, most of these were not nannies. In the FCCC study, 3.6 percent of the mothers were employing a nanny toward the end of the babies' first year. These were definitely nannies rather than babysitters, au pairs, or housekeepers, and they were maintained as a discrete category throughout the study.

WHAT—OR WHO—IS A NANNY?

For some people, the word "nanny" still conjures up a Mary Poppins image: a uniformed, baby-carriage-pushing graduate of the world-famous Norland nanny college in the United Kingdom or somewhere similar; thoroughly trained, a little old-fashioned, and something of a status symbol. Such nannies still exist, and while they really are expensive rarities (many of them employed outside the English-speaking world), demand, according to the London *Times*, is increasing: "*Supernanny* and other reality television shows about how to bring up children have pushed overseas demand for British nannies to record levels." Nanny agencies report a 57 percent rise in demand and a sharp increase in salaries in the last year. Yet young parents' perception of a modern nanny and the contemporary nanny's perception of herself has changed almost beyond recognition. No uniform or exclusive college is needed, but real expertise in home child care is expected.

A woman (or it might be a man) does not need to have any training in child care (or in anything else, for that matter) to call herself a nanny and present herself as such to employers. To many employment agencies and the parents who consult them, experience is a qualification as good as, if not better than, formal training, and an untrained but experienced nanny almost always attracts a higher salary than a newly qualified one.

So What Makes a Nanny a Nanny?

Different countries and agencies have different ideas about what makes a nanny a nanny. The American Occupational Information Network describes a nanny's job thus: "to care for children in private households and provide support and expertise to parents in satisfying children's physical, emotional, intellectual and social needs. Duties may include meal planning and preparation, laundry and clothing care, organization of play activities and outings, discipline, intellectual stimulation, language activities and transportation." That's very close to the job description for U.K. nannies given by the agency that runs the voluntary registration program for nannies.

The U.S. Department of Labor, on the other hand, categorizes nannies as unskilled domestic workers. Its description of a nanny's role ends "they may also perform the duties of a general housekeeper, including general cleaning and laundry duties." In another subsection, the Department of Labor classifies home care workers and babysitters as "companionship" service providers and thereby exempts them from minimum wage or overtime protection. In June 2007, in a case brought by a home care worker, the U.S. Supreme Court ruled unanimously that this low pay was fair. On that basis, of course, a nanny cannot be distinguished from an old-fashioned "mother's helper" or an even more old-fashioned "maid." However, the following description, given by the U.K.'s National Childminding Association in 2004, probably comes closer to the public understanding of a nanny's role:

> Most nannies consider their job to be looking after every aspect of the child's well-being. This usually includes providing a safe, fun, and stimulating environment for the children, planning and preparing play and educational activities, doing school and nursery runs, taking them to appointments and activities, and organising and supervising play sessions with other children. It may also involve preparing the children's meals, cleaning their bedrooms, bathrooms and play areas, and doing their laundry and ironing.
>
> The nanny is not normally expected to do any household chores for other members of the household. But as there is no legal definition of a nanny's role and responsibilities, the nanny's tasks can vary with each family.

With a job description that usually excludes general household duties and a salary that tops every other category of household work except possibly that of a butler, a nanny is easily distinguished from other domestic workers, and in Britain, nannies are gradually becoming more accepted as child care professionals. A recently introduced "light-touch" (or somewhat halfhearted) voluntary approval program for nannies has been introduced, but it is nowhere near as stringent as the compulsory registration requirements for family day care providers. To gain approval, a nanny must have a pediatric first-aid certificate and an "enhanced" child-safety police check, and must either have a recognized child care qualification or attend a child care course. It is a step forward but not a large one, since the course lasts only about two days or twelve hours. Approval is given annually and costs the nanny £96 ($155) per year. The primary beneficiaries in the short term are not nannies themselves but their employers. Parents whose nanny is approved can, for the first time, claim the same tax benefits for in-home care as were previously available only to parents using nurseries or childminders. In the long run, though, widespread acceptance of this voluntary program will benefit U.K. nannies themselves, making them at once more recognizably professional and more widely affordable.

Although uniformed nannies can still be seen in Central Park in New York and in St. James's Park in London, as well as in capital cities in the Middle East, modern nannies have (mostly) abandoned not only uniforms but also the image of a Nanny McPhee as a full-time, live-in employee. Many nannies prefer to work daily, keeping their private lives separate from work and being paid a premium to offset their extra living expenses. That makes nannies a possible child care option for the many city-dwelling families who have more disposable income than space. Nanny-shares are also becoming commonplace. Some nannies take care of the children of two families simultaneously, sometimes in whichever house the parents agree on, sometimes alternating between the two. Other shared nannies work two or three days a week for each of two families in turn. And increasingly, nannies are offering the kind of flexible care that is sometimes badly needed but almost impossible to find. One parent explained: "We're both surgeons. Our daily nanny will not only stay late if we're late, she'll be 'on call' whenever we both are so that when that dread night comes when we're *both* called in the middle of the night, we only have to ring and she'll come."

The expense of a nanny still puts this type of child care beyond the reach of most families, of course, but then most families cannot afford an unsubsidized day care center either. If two families living in a high-cost city share a nanny, they can pay her well for the extra work involved in the sharing yet still save on what each would have had to pay for center care. And as soon as there are two, let alone

---

Talking to parents about daily in-home child care

Daily child care arrangements often work better than residential ones. It is easier to maintain mutual respect and dignity when you neither have to share private lives nor draw awkward lines between time "on duty" and time "as family." But parents need to remember to allow for the possibility that the caretaker will experience similar difficulties to their own while working, especially if she also has children, who will sometimes get sick.

three children in a family needing child care, a nanny may be the least expensive option for high-quality unsubsidized care.

Nannies are already more widely used than many people imagine, although, as we have seen, accurate figures are unobtainable. U.S. immigration laws make it impossible for non-American nannies to get work visas, but given that about 21 percent of the estimated 1.5 million child care workers in the United States work for private households, there are probably 300,000 legally employed American-born nannies. The number employed in the United Kingdom tops 100,000, while Statistics Canada has recently released figures showing that 5 percent of all Canadian children under five are cared for by a nanny.

AU PAIRS

The International Nanny Association describes an au pair as "a foreign national who resides in the United States for up to one year, lives as part of the host family, and receives a small stipend in exchange for babysitting and helping with housework. She may or may not have previous child care experience." The U.K. description is very similar except that "learning English" and being given the time to attend English classes are part of the arrangement.

Although the terms under which individuals may live "au pair" in a host country and family are carefully specified, they are widely ignored. For example, au pairs in America can be asked to undertake up to forty-five hours per week of child care as "part of their responsibility to the host family." In the United Kingdom, au pairs' working hours are supposed to be limited to twenty-five per week, though they often are not. Attendance at language classes is part of the agreement for au pairs in both countries, but even if classes and the transportation to get to them are available, it may be so difficult to fit classes in around those working hours that the agreement is not honored.

In both North America and the United Kingdom, and to a lesser extent in continental Europe, the rising level of mothers' employment is being underpinned by the low-paid work of women from elsewhere. About ten thousand young women from European countries visit the United States through cultural exchange pro-

> *"Some of us work hard for very little money in U.K. terms. . . . I've been paid £50 per week as an au pair. Now, though, I've moved out and I do two different nannying jobs that together bring in £300 a week. It's a fortune when you bear in mind that I'd be paid around £200 a month if I went home to Slovakia and got a job as a teacher."*   U.K. au pair, 2007

grams each year. They are technically and legally au pairs, but most will be expected to work as full-time nannies. If proposed new regulations are passed, however, agencies may only be permitted to make au pair arrangements with families who have children under two if the proposed au pair is more than twenty-one years old and has at least six months' experience looking after babies and toddlers.

An unknown number of young women travel to the United States on tourist visas and join the harder-to-estimate numbers of those who cross the border with no visa and take illegal employment looking after children.

In the United Kingdom, a large majority of au pairs now come from Eastern European countries. As countries such as Slovakia, Poland, and the Czech Republic entered the European Union, this labor force increased and is becoming more visible. Currently, the best estimate of numbers, derived from a Labour Force Survey carried out in 2003, is that about a quarter of all workers involved in "childminding and related occupations" come from Eastern European countries and that many of those are technically au pairs. That means they are paid perhaps £70 per week instead of the £250 that is the rock-bottom average for child care workers. The irony, of course, is that many of these exploited women are very happy with their live-in jobs. As long as they do not have to pay for accommodations and living expenses, wages that are well below U.K. or U.S. minimum-wage levels look attractive to women coming from countries that are still in transition to market economies, with high unemployment and low salaries. The temptation to exploit them is very real.

PROS AND CONS OF NANNY CARE

Nanny care has the potential to fulfill all the criteria for "positive care giving." However, because a nanny works largely alone and unsupervised, the quality of care she provides depends entirely on her individual qualities and skills. Good nannies can provide very high-quality child care, perhaps especially for babies, but a bad nanny can be truly terrible. Although the outcomes of nanny care for children have not been separately assessed, the FCCC's study of the quality offered to ten-month-old babies and eighteen-month-old toddlers in different types of care showed that nannies compared favorably with all other types of care. In particular, they offered a wide range of different activities to their charges at both ages, and they had higher levels of positive relationships with the children at eighteen months than either the other individual care-givers—grandparents and childminders—or the caregivers in nursery or day care center groups.

Nannies fulfill an increasingly important demand for flexibility in child care. With fewer people working a nine-to-five day and a standard week, the regular hours of operation for nurseries and centers and the time limits set by family day care homes often leave care gaps that are difficult to fill.

> There wasn't any real choice for me. I had to have a nanny. My work is fairly demanding and the hours are unpredictable. I need to be able to go to work whenever and give one hundred percent whenever I'm at work.   —FCCC mother

With no infrastructure dictating to them, nannies can work any hours or patterns that they choose and parents will pay for. "Niche nannying," a growing trend, includes "after-school" nannies (often nursery school teachers with a short working day), who will pick up children from school, make their snacks, and supervise their homework until a parent gets home. There are also "night nannies," who will take over sleepless babies so that sleep-deprived parents can catch up, and "weekend nannies" and "holiday nannies" for parents who don't want to cope when there's no school. Many extremely high-earning dual-career parents in the United Kingdom employ two nannies. As this mother explained, "We have to have two nannies. One comes at 7:30 a.m., so we can't ask her to work past 5 p.m. But neither of us is home by then, so the second nanny comes at 5 and works until midnight or until one of us is home."

Correspondence with a reader: Must shared care be shared love?

I resent the idea that if we're both at work full-time, we're necessarily sharing our small sons' upbringing. Even more, I resent your suggestion that the baby will—and should—get "attached" to anybody else. He's our child. The fact that we're out of the house eight to six five days a week doesn't change that.

I employ someone to take care of my children and I expect her to do as I tell her. I don't want her input to their values and personalities any more than I want advice on interior decorating from the person who cleans my house. I don't want the children diverting love that belongs to us to anyone else either, so I use au pairs on six-month contracts. The language difference makes sure that the boys are thrilled to see us each evening, and if an over-close relationship should form all the same, it ends before it can threaten the family.

A house and a child are not the same. A house is an object, so you can metaphorically put it on ice and it will just sit and wait until you're ready to use it again. A child is a person, so he goes on being and growing and changing when you're not there. Furthermore, very young people need to involve adults in those processes and will form relationships with whoever is around. Lack of a common language may hamper the adult, but the children will probably deal with it by using universals like gestures and beginning to learn whatever language she speaks to them. As for affecting their attitudes and behavior, the care provider you employ will not be able to help herself, even if she actually tries to obey your orders and serve your children rather than caring for them. Babies and toddlers use adult faces as mirrors, seeing their own behavior reflected in facial expressions. Even if she does not or cannot say a word, they will soon learn what she thinks of their eating or crying, their games and their squabbles. And they will care what she thinks, even if you don't.

I wish you could believe that your little boys would be just as thrilled to see you each evening if they'd spent the day with somebody who spoke fluent English and loved them both. They are indeed your children and spending the working days without you will do nothing to change their awareness of that or their feelings about you. Children's love for adults is not rationed or confined to particular channels. It cannot be used up or diverted. Indeed, the more people children have to love and feel loved by, the more lovable and loving they are likely to be. Don't project the threat that might be implicit in a close relationship between your husband and another sexual partner onto a close relationship between your children and another caregiver. You do not have to try to keep your children loveless through the working days in order to ensure your due measure at weekends.

Apart from the costs, most of the disadvantages of nanny care come from personality clashes between parents and nanny or between child and nanny, and from shared-home problems if nannies live in. Another problem sometimes occurs when nannies want to be close to their charges and respected by their families, but the parents fear competition for their children's affection. The correspondence in the box on page 133 is typical of many.

Introduction: "Formal Care"

When a child is to be cared for outside his own home by someone who is not part of the family and who is to be paid, the choice is between family day care and group care in a day care center or nursery. Together, these two types of care constitute the "formal child care sector," what people usually mean by "day care." Family day care and center care are different in almost every other respect, but that does not mean that they are easy to compare and contrast. The very same features that are regarded as advantages of family day care by one person will be regarded as disadvantages—and therefore reasons for preferring center care—by another, while the features that lead some parents to prefer group care are the very ones that lead other parents to reject it in favor of family day care.

The most basic difference between these types of care is that in family day care the child is in a domestic home (even if it has been enlarged or adapted), always cared for by the same person—or two people at the most—and sharing that care with perhaps one or two other children in his own age group and three or four other children of different ages. In a nursery or center, the child will be in relatively large purpose-built or adapted premises where a staff of providers cares for tens of children. Those children will be divided by age into relatively small groups (or "classrooms") so that she spends her time with perhaps five to fifteen children within a year of her own age. There will be two or more caregivers in her room, and she will probably be assigned a "key person" from among them. However, she will be cared for by other adults when that person is not on duty.

> I have looked at a couple of nurseries and I think they're great for two- and three-year-olds but for a baby I think they need a home environ-

ment and they also need peace and quiet sometimes. . . . Jean [child-minder] has a cot for Natasha that she puts in her bedroom. When Natasha wants to sleep she goes upstairs and goes to sleep. In a nursery they provide cots and a sleeping room but there are eight babies in one room and at any time one's bound to be crying.   —FCCC mother

I did go and see a family day care home but how could I send him there and go on working myself? I mean she was just an ordinary Mom like me. If sending him there was my only option I'd have to stay home— and I don't want to do that! At least in the day care he's learning stuff he couldn't get at home.   —American mother

If both are high quality of their type and all care providers are good at their jobs, is a domestic setting and one consistent caregiver better or worse than a group in a child care institution?

Advantages of domestic setting	Disadvantages of domestic setting
The child in family day care usually gets more variety of activity, place, and ages of playmates. He may join in the care provider's "real life" domestic activities—cooking, gardening, etc.—at home and be taken out and about in the local community. The child in a nursery may spend all day in the same setting (sometimes the same room) in a same-age group, sharing and competing for space, facilities, toys, and adult attention.	A child care home is likely to be less spacious and less well equipped than a nursery/center.
As in a family, siblings may be cared for together.	The child is less likely to be offered a formally planned educational program and may not receive much encouragement of richly creative play.
The child may have other familylike opportunities to relate to children of different ages and experience being both the older and the younger child.	Composition of the small group may mean that a particular child lacks playmates of the same age or gender, and much older or younger children may seem to get more attention.

Advantages of single care provider

A single care provider who is good at her job can offer children very high-quality care. Having only one or, if she has a working partner, two caregivers ensures that children have continuous, consistent care, all day and every day, with all its potential for a really close relationship. The child is likely to settle in relatively easily and to make friends with the small group of children.

Because the care provider knows the child so well, she is in a good position to notice if he is unwell or unhappy and to offer any special care he may need, such as support when there are problems at home—a parental separation, for example—or special care in guarding against food allergies.

Parents are able to choose and then get to know the caregiver as an individual and be sure that the person they chose when they visited will be the one who greets the child when the arrangement starts. They can also be fairly confident that the same person will stay in the job for the indefinite future, whereas the person that they meet when they visit a nursery may have left by the time their child starts, or she may move on soon after.

Children can usually remain with the same caregiver not only from infancy to school age but for as long as they need wraparound and vacation care. Many enjoy the small social group and especially enjoy the opportunity to play with older and younger children rather than being confined to their own age group.

The care provider may be more accessible to the parent than a nursery caregiver can be on a daily basis, and friendships are not uncommon. She may also be able to offer more flexibility as to hours and days than a nursery can manage. Some family day cares offer occasional overnight and weekend care to parents who work unsocial hours, and most are relatively tolerant of dramas and delayed pickups.

Disadvantages of single care provider

A single care provider who is not good at her job can offer children care that is of poor quality or even neglectful. When a caregiver works alone, some parents worry about what goes on behind closed doors. In a group care setting, members of staff monitor and support each other.

Some parents worry about their child having a close relationship with the caregiver, fearing that it might compete with the child's relationship with the parents or that he will look forward to "day care days" more than "home days."

Continuous care by one person may be a disadvantage if a sole care provider and child do not like each other, or if the caregiver and the parents do not get along well.

A single caregiver will close for vacations and may have no backup to cover her own illness or emergencies.

Parents may resent having to devote time and effort to maintaining a supportive personal relationship with the caregiver.

10. Family Day Care

Most children in the English-speaking world who are not being cared for by their families are with family child care providers, but family child care, varies in different countries and is known by other names. In the United States and New Zealand, it may be called family day care, and in Australia it always is. Different terminology in various European countries complicates matters further. In the United Kingdom, family child care is called childminding and is provided by childminders, while a childminder in France is known as an *assistante maternelle*, mother's assistant. Moreover, the generic term "family child care" can cause confusion because, of course, the care is "familylike" rather than familial. For simplicity, the terms "family day care" and "family day care provider" are used in this chapter.

What Is Family Day Care?

Family day care providers are women (and a few men, mostly working with a partner) who take children into their own homes and look after them there while the parents are at work. Generally speaking, family day care providers are self-employed, small-business entrepreneurs rather than employees of the parents whose children they care for (as a nanny usually is), or of a corporation or local government, charitable foundation, or community organization, as staff in child care centers (nurseries) are.

Family day care is usually less expensive than center care because it is provided on a smaller scale with fewer expenses. Some owners may add a playroom or downstairs bathroom for the children to use, but there is no need for a special building or a complex administrative structure, and in some American states less training is required and there are fewer regulations. The lower fees for family day care, however, make it difficult for providers to ensure high quality or to invest in improvements. As June Statham and Ann Mooney have written in the introduction to their 2003 volume *Family Day Care*, in many countries, the nature and organization of family day care makes it vulnerable to tensions:

> [There can be] conflict between the affective, caring aspects of the work and being paid to care. This love/money dilemma is especially acute where day care providers are self-employed and subject to market forces, since they are in effect running small businesses. They have to find customers, charge enough to make a living without pricing themselves out of the market, and engage in financial and contractual negotiations with parents. These circumstances can create tensions in the relationship between providers and parents, which usually do not occur in other forms of childcare provision.

THE DEVELOPMENT OF FAMILY DAY CARE IN DIFFERENT PARTS OF THE WORLD

For many generations, parents have been paying other people to provide child care (originally including wet nursing) in the caregiver's home rather than the child's. From the time of the Industrial Revolution, large numbers of infants were cared for—if such a phrase can be used to describe circumstances in which so many died—by wet nurses while their mothers (usually single or widowed) were in paid employment. In France, childminders continued to be known as *nourrices* (wet nurses) until 1976. But although generations of individuals everywhere have arranged child care with nonrelative providers, family day care as a formal service has developed in different ways and at different points in time around the world.

WHY FAMILY DAY CARE IS OFTEN REGARDED AS A LOW-STATUS OPTION

In many countries, family day care has had an unfortunate history, from the notorious "baby farms" of the nineteenth century to the untrained, unlicensed "babyminders" of the twentieth century, recognizable in every poor neighborhood by the crowd of strollers parked around the door. Even in contemporary times, many women

Some different paths to contemporary family day care

In parts of Europe—such as Hungary and the former East Germany—state-funded child care centers, staffed by state employees, were commonplace until the late twentieth century. When changes in social and economic circumstances altered national policies, closed down the old networks of centers, and threw many of their employees out of work, family day care emerged to fill the gap with work for care providers and day care for families. It has recently been recognized as part of formal child care services.

In other parts of Europe, family day care has been long established but is now dwindling. In Sweden, for example, nearly half of all children in public child care were in family day care in 1977, but by 1999 this had fallen to only 10 percent.

Outside Europe—notably in Israel—formal family day care services have been established relatively recently not because of a shortage of child care centers but because of concern about the poor quality of care some state-run centers were providing. On the other side of the world, in New Zealand and in Australia, family day care, already an accepted type of child care, has recently been repositioned as part of formally organized early childhood services and is rapidly expanding.

in the English-speaking world have regarded "taking in" other people's children as primarily a way for mothers to earn an income while remaining at home with their own young children: a stopgap until they could return to "proper jobs." But for many family day care providers, that stopgap has increasingly turned into a longer-term commitment, becoming a proper job in its own right. During the 1990s, the National Childminding Association in the United Kingdom and the National Association for Family Child Care in the United States were formed. These organizations moved family day care toward greater professionalism and higher standards, helping many providers onto the first steps of an integrated "early years" career ladder.

Progress has been slow, though, and in many countries family day care is still regarded as a poor relation of nursery or center care, especially as early years education is given increasing importance. Even Sweden, with its long-standing high level of child care and maternal employment and its integrated training for child care workers, treats family day care as a lesser service. Most women in Sweden who open a family day care have chosen to do so rather than seeing it as a compromise between working and caring for their own children, and they are employed by local governments. But nurseries are still seen as having a higher social status, both by the people who run them and by the people who work in them, as indicated by one researcher's discussions about day care with local or national policy makers: "No one says anything about family day care until I ask about it specifically, and then the descriptions and explanations are always offered with a hint of embarrassment."

While all child care is still regarded as difficult to incorporate into the economies of postindustrial societies, family day care seems particularly difficult. Group child care, in centers and nurseries, may offer some economy of scale—though less as the quality of care goes up (see Chapter 2)—with one caregiver's employment enabling the employment of several mothers elsewhere, but there is no economy of scale in the individualized care in a domestic setting, which is family day care's particular virtue. The provider cares for the children of two or three sets of parents while they work at other paid jobs. As long as the provider is self-employed, her earnings are directly dependent on what those parents can afford to pay. And what they can afford depends on the difference between what they earn and what they must pay the provider in order to earn it. Only in exceptional circumstances will the difference be great enough for, say, three families to finance a professional salary for the family day care provider, and many work for less than their country's minimum wage.

MOVING FAMILY DAY CARE INTO A NEW MILLENNIUM

In recent years in some countries, family child care has begun to be seen as a profession. In the past, providers have generally been women with relatively low levels of education and few if any qualifications or women who have spent extended periods out of the labor market while they were having their own children. In the United States and in most of Australia and New Zealand, that is still the case. However, it is increasingly clear that family day care cannot survive unless that changes. The pool of potential providers willing to work for minimal money provided they can do it at home and without much special training is shrinking fast. In the last ten years in Britain, for example, women have gained better access to education and training; many have deferred their own first child until they were established in their chosen jobs, and for those who want to combine earning money with home care for their own children, there are alternative jobs and working patterns available. Everyone in the United Kingdom has the right to request flexible work hours, and a majority are granted it; most women with young children work part-time, and a twenty-four-hour society enables others to work evening or night shifts, leaving their partners in charge of the children at the end of their own workday. Why should women work as family day care providers for less money than they can earn in, say, all-night supermarkets? It is of course absurd to suggest that greater personal satisfaction legitimizes less money.

If family day care is to survive, it has to be professionalized so as to provide better working conditions, including pay, training, qual-

---

Various approaches to funding professional family day care services

In countries of continental Europe and in Israel, family day care providers are usually employed and paid by the local government, as are staff in nursery centers. Other countries maintain the family day care provider's self-employed status but ensure that a third party comes between the provider and the parent, organizing registration and any inspections, placing children, collecting fees, and paying providers. In New Zealand and Australia, for example, family day care providers work within the formal day care service, remain self-employed, and have their work organized by an agency.

All such working arrangements facilitate better conditions and pay than family day care providers achieve when they are operating via direct contracts with individual parents in the private market. However, it is doubtful that real improvements to working conditions, such as leave and health benefits, and to salaries and training standards can be achieved without public funding of the service.

ifications, and support for caregivers, as well as ensuring higher standards of child care. But how can family day care become professional without losing its essential homelike nature? Can it develop a distinctive approach, which is neither "substitute mother" (or babysitter) nor nursery group? How can it be funded so that the provider can afford to do the job and the parent can afford to pay for it? And how can the tensions between dedicated child care and running a small business be resolved?

In the United States and the United Kingdom, family day care funding is still demand-side: parents who want it must find and pay for it (at least initially; some can be partially repaid through subsidies and tax breaks), and family day care providers must act as businesspeople, setting rates, drawing up contracts, sending bills, and sometimes facing nonpayment and the painful possibility of having to terminate a contract to care for a loved child. Ajay Chaudry describes some of the difficulties:

> After these two short spells in kin care, Bethany was switched to what would prove to be her most durable arrangement, one with a family day care provider; this was the one whose ending mother and daughter most regretted. The conflict between Britanny [the mother] and the provider illustrates the unclear guidelines that parents and providers often face when they negotiate care arrangements, which are made doubly hard when the parent and the provider are both low-income and the conflict is over money. In some care arrangements there may be disagreements and misunderstandings over how much to pay for the care, when to pay, and whether to pay for days or periods children miss.

WHY FAMILY DAY CARE REMAINS A VALUABLE OPTION FOR BOTH CHILDREN AND PARENTS

Despite wide variations in different countries and even wider variations in the quality of providers within countries, family day care everywhere has a basic identity and many shared features whose special value deserve wider recognition:

- Because the setting—and therefore the scale of each operation—is domestic, only small numbers of children, perhaps four to six, are cared for at one time, and each child should therefore get a relatively large amount of attention from a consistent adult caregiver.

• The group of children a provider cares for in her home may not only be the size of a large family but also be family-shaped. In most countries, overall numbers, including any of the care provider's own children, are usually controlled by licensing and/or regulation, with fewer babies than older children permitted per caregiver. Apart from these (variable) restrictions, ages and sexes can be mixed as the care provider chooses, and children with special needs may be included.

• Mixed-age groups are a particularly welcome feature of family day care in a world where almost all other provision for children— nurseries, children's centers, preschools, and schools—are organized by rigid age groups. Many children benefit from opportunities to sometimes be the "big one" and sometimes "the baby," and whole families can benefit from siblings being cared for together, perhaps with a toddler in the family care home all day and a kindergarten child joining him after school. When family child care is parents' first choice for their children, it is usually its home-based and familylike features that attract them: "For the very early years I still wanted that one-to-one that a childminder could give . . . a continuity of person. If I couldn't be there I just wanted someone who could. Not *mother* but definitely be the one person to go to; the person they knew would be there in a place that felt like home" (FCCC mother).

• Family day care providers live and work in their communities, unlike the parents of their charges, who may commute. Being cared for close to home helps familiarize children with their neighborhoods and perhaps with their future schools.

• The presence of family day care homes within a community helps to raise awareness of and support for preschools, kindergartens, and public facilities, such as children's libraries, playgrounds, and swimming pools; care providers use the services on offer and inform parents about them and encourage their use.

• Family day care homes can respond relatively easily to a local need for child care as they require neither the investment nor the permissions for a new building or a major conversion project. In particular, they can meet the need for child care in some neighborhoods where center-based care is not possible or sustainable—in rural areas, for example, where the community is widely dispersed.

• Family day care may sustain and stabilize a community's child care places at a time when private nurseries close almost as often as they open and staff turnover within them can be as high as one-third per year. U.K. research has shown that childminding networks, in particular, encourage the retention of childminders in the job.

• Family day care can offer flexible family support services, both formal and informal. In the United Kingdom, for example, many childminders escort or drive children to and from playgroups, schools, clubs, and social activities, and some will take children to dental or medical appointments if necessary.

• With special training and funding, "community childminders" in the United Kingdom care for some children with special needs—physical, emotional, or dietary—that would be difficult and expensive to meet within nurseries/centers. Many registered childminders, parents themselves, can empathize with parents in difficulty and can serve, much as an extended family member might, as someone to talk to or seek advice from on parenting issues.

• Using family day care ensures that siblings can be cared for together and offers continuity of child care and education for babies and children not only up to age five but increasingly right up into the teenage years, which is particularly valuable for families with both preschool and school-age children—and for blended and second families. Many U.K. childminders are spending more time on providing before- and after-school and vacation care than on providing preschool care.

U.K. FAMILY DAY CARE—CHILDMINDING

In England and Wales, there are around 70,000 registered childminders looking after half a million children every week in 319,000 full- and part-time child care places. Thus, family day care accounts for at least half of all child care places and is the largest single source of nonparental care for children under three. The isolation and multitasking of childminders is beginning to diminish as more and more link themselves into networks with a paid coordinator, or as they form connections with children's centers and extended schools. And in the last ten years, the enormous importance of childminding has come to be recognized by government and policy makers.

Cooperating with a British government that has been in power for almost a decade and maintains child care as one of its leading priorities, the National Childminding Association, with 60 percent of all registered childminders as voluntary members, has introduced many measures (such as start-up grants) to make starting as a child-minder easier. Other measures, such as the model for childminding networks called Children Come First and certificates in childmind-ing practice from the Council for Awards for Children's Care and Education, have raised childminding's quality, status, and profes-sional profile.

Today's childminders are usually registered to look after up to three children under five and three children age five to eight, or the part-time equivalents, including their own. Only one child may be less than a year old, unless there is a particular reason, such as twins, for the inspecting body, OFSTED (Office for Standards in Education, Children's Services and Skills), to grant an individual childminder special dispensation. These numbers may be increased for childminders who work with partners or employ assistants, and many also look after older children.

It is impossible, of course, to count the numbers of unregistered childminders, but, while there are probably still a few "paid friends or neighbors" taking in a child or two unofficially, it is unlikely that there are very many, because there is much to be gained from regis-tering as a caregiver and little to lose.

Parents who use childminders and researchers who study them both tend to rate highly the quality of care provided by registered childminders. Furthermore, all registered childminders are sub-jected to exactly the same formal inspections as nurseries and chil-dren's centers, and OFSTED's most recent report shows that the quality of care provided by all childminders and the early years edu-cation of three- and four-year-olds provided by eligible network childminders compares very well with what is provided in child care centers.

However, despite all the improvement, and the acknowledgment of quality by the parents who use childminders and the authorities who inspect their work, childminding still has an image problem, both among parents looking for their first nonfamilial caregiver and among media:

Being in someone else's home you just don't know what goes on all day.
I wanted her in a nursery where I could be sure she'd be with other
children and get lots of stimulation.   —FCCC mother

What a Family Can Expect in U.K. Childminding

Family day care is very personal care, depending almost entirely on
the personality and resources of the childminder. It's important, of
course, that the childminder and the child, as well as the other children she is caring for, get along, but the FCCC study showed that it
is also critical to the success of childminding that the parents and
care provider like each other.

Many childminders still work alone in an ordinary family home.
Outdoor play space is regarded as important, and many registered
caregivers' homes are houses with gardens, but some are apart-
ments. Some childminders adapt and enlarge their homes, and a few
work with a partner or an assistant. The care provision may then be
similar to that described for the United States discussed below.

Childminders vary in how much of their home they allow their
daily charges to use. Some give all the children the same run of the
house enjoyed by their own. Others think it important for the family children to have access to parts of the house—such as their own
bedrooms—not available to the other children except by specific
invitation. Many allocate one downstairs room as a playroom and
perhaps one upstairs room as a quiet space for children to nap.
There is always a bathroom for the children's use and careful safety
precautions regarding the kitchen and arrangements for meals.

A baby or toddler in such a setting will often be cared for much as
the childminder's own children are, or used to be, cared for. His day
"at home" will be a mixture, familiar to every stay-at-home parent,
of playing alone, with the childminder and with any other children
present, and following the caregiver around "helping out" with
household jobs. His day may be regularly punctuated by trips to the
local school to collect older children, perhaps stopping off at a park
or playground on the way home, and his week will usually be punctuated by high spots such as going to the local baby and toddler
group or perhaps to a swimming pool or library. Unlike most stay-
at-home parents, though, a childminder is trained to keep the con-

tinual learning of even the youngest child in mind, to be aware of and to record his progress in different areas of development, and to plan for and offer many different opportunities for play.

Childminders vary in how completely they are willing to take over a child's care during his hours with them and in how flexibly they meet the family's needs. One may require the parents to provide a baby's formula and diapers, for example, while another will expect to buy these items and then be repaid; and yet another may include them in the fees they charge. Most childminders are prepared to welcome children early in the morning and are tolerant of occasional late pickups. A few will even offer late or overnight care to parents on shift work. Almost all will take children to doctor's appointments when necessary, and some will cope with routine appointments for immunizations or dental checkups. All childminders caring for preschool children will drop them off and pick them up from nursery school or from classes, as well as transport school-age children.

Given the range of services childminders may offer to parents and the quality of care they offer to children, the increase in their relative earnings seems unreasonably slow. Most childminders still make less than the national minimum wage, even though, ironically, care by a childminder is no longer an inexpensive option for parents. In many parts of Britain, it costs as much, or very nearly as much, to place a child with a registered childminder as in a nursery; the average cost in England at the beginning of 2007 was around £140 ($225) per week for a child under two years. A childminder who operates at full capacity can make a reasonable income, but because the per-child cost to parents is high, unfilled places and unpaid bills are commonplace.

U.S. FAMILY DAY CARE

In the United States, approximately a million family day care providers care for about 4 million children. This is the most common form of child care used by employed mothers for children under six years. However, U.S. family day care is still viewed somewhat skeptically by the early childhood education community; it is seen as "not professional" because it is not designed and run by university-trained early childhood educators. Indeed, few family day care providers see themselves, or are seen by others, as early years educators. It is also regarded as a relatively low-quality option by parents. American parents who have a choice are probably less likely than British parents to opt for family day care.

Since the United States has no national policy framework for early childhood education services, individual state requirements for the licensing of family child care homes vary considerably, and American family day care as a whole is less regulated than in the United Kingdom, other European countries, Australia, or New Zealand. Some states exempt family child care homes with a small number of children from any form of licensing, and many homes that theoretically require a license operate without one. Recent estimates indicate that 90 percent of American family day care is unregulated. When licensing is required and enforced, it is often limited to ensuring very basic hygiene and safety standards. Some states demand as little as four hours of annual training. Even in states that enforce licensing, the staff-child ratios called for in the 1960s by the Federal Interagency Day Care Requirements (FSDCR) are seldom adhered to. Generally, one licensed provider is allowed to care for between five and ten children, sometimes excluding the caregiver's own.

Recognizing that many states' standards are too low, the National Association for Family Child Care is working to produce a voluntary accreditation scheme to match the one already in place for center-based care. The hope is that by setting higher standards than are demanded by state regulations, as well as more consistent standards from state to state, such a voluntary scheme can attract more state subsidies and perhaps higher fees from parents, thus driving standards up. Some of the highest-quality family day care in the country is provided for Department of Defense families by Military Family Child Care. The nine thousand licensed and regulated providers are encouraged to achieve NAFCC accreditation and offer flexible care to service personnel.

What a Family Can Expect in Licensed U.S. Family Day Care

What a family can expect in American family day care depends not only on the care provider who runs it but also on its locale. Across the nation, family child care homes range from the most informal, where a few neighborhood children are casually cared for—the word often used and sometimes sadly appropriate is "watched"—to the highly professional registered, licensed home that may seem little different from a minicenter and may even be part of a network of child care homes affiliated with a center or within a school or university. Most American child care homes are on the informal, unprofessional, and inexpensive end of that spectrum, but the few on the other end may be excellent.

Unlike U.K. childminders, American family day care providers do not always work out of their own homes or alone. Some places are more like a nursery school, with two or three adults taking care of a group of children. At its best, such an arrangement may be "family day care plus," providing some of the good features of home care without the snags. But, of course, in different hands, it may be "center care minus," providing the worst features of group care without its redeeming features.

Efforts to raise the standards of American family day care are hampered by its relative cheapness. Charges made by all care providers in different parts of the country vary so widely that it is difficult to make valid comparisons between one type and another. However, the U.S. Department of Labor quotes the national average for a toddler at around $611 per month, rising to around $1,000 in many cities and to $1,500 for infant care; and the current Cost of Child Day Care Information (http://www.costhelper.com/cost/child/child-day-care.html) indicates that in any given locality "home care places" generally are a little more than half the cost of places in chain centers. Family child care is the least expensive form of child care except for care by a relative (which is often free) and is expected to be so. Places that need to charge more because they are offering "family day care plus" are therefore disadvantaged.

American parents shoulder the main costs of family day care. Financial help is available for low-income families as in the United Kingdom, though principally by direct subsidy rather than through the tax system. Ajay Chaudry found that at least three-quarters of poor mothers using family day care in New York were subsidized, although those receiving subsidies from city government agencies had to make copayments. For some low-income families (earning less than 85 percent of the median state wage), help is available through the federal Child Care and Development Fund. Families who are eligible for a subsidy can use any provider who meets the basic health and safety requirements, including a family day care provider, but many states have long waiting lists for this program. The effect of minimal regulation and limited public funding is to make the raising of standards extraordinarily difficult.

11. Child Care Centers or Nurseries

Day care centers or nurseries providing group care for children under school age in professionally run institutions are the hub and the aspiration of formal child care everywhere. For most parents who are looking for formal child care, especially for a child past babyhood, a nursery has both practical and emotional advantages over family day care in the caregiver's home or care by a nanny or babysitter in their own home.

> I think we all have more confidence in big establishments for some reason. . . . It's inherently there in most people that if it's a big establishment it's vetted by social services and they are going to have strict guidelines, and you just feel more safe than you do with childminders.
> —FCCC mother

Children are a center's business, so many parents assume that their child will be well cared for there by people who know about safety and hygiene, nutrition and health, education and play—in other words, people who know about *kids*. Many parents assume that all center staff are "professionals." They would be amazed to discover that in many centers only the individuals in charge have professional—or indeed any—qualifications.

> At the daycare they are sort of qualified people and they're pushing her on and sort of teaching her things. —FCCC mother

Because a child care center is a business, its arrangements make it more reliable than any individual can be: always open for its stated hours and days, never closed because a provider is sick with the flu or pregnant, and probably able to cope with even the most

Terrible Two. Having several adults sharing children's care also reassures those parents who are worried about leaving their child with a caregiver who works alone, either because they fear their child might be neglected or mistreated or because they fear their child will be left without care if the caregiver or her own child should be ill or she finds a particular child too difficult to manage. And a well-equipped and well-designed facility is also attractive to many parents:

> I love everything being just the right size for her, like tiny sinks and toilets so she'll soon be able to wash her own hands and she won't need to use a potty or climb on a stool.   —FCCC mother

Most important to parents, though, may be the perception of institutional group day care as advantageous to children themselves rather than being entirely to suit parents' convenience. Parents think that being at nursery is "educational," even for very young babies, and prepares children both socially and cognitively for successful school entry. Instead of feeling vaguely guilty about the hours their child spends in nonparental care, parents can congratulate themselves on the arrangements they have made:

> He'd had me all to himself for almost six months; he needed to learn that he isn't the only pebble on the beach.   —FCCC mother

A preference for group care is certainly encouraged by the approval (and often funding) of policy makers and their advisers, and by a public perception that "early education" cannot begin too early and mostly happens in "classrooms." Whether or not a center offers a specific early years education program, the popular image of such group day care centers in the English-speaking world is that of a nursery school. In the United Kingdom, this has been emphasized by the introduction of free part-time nursery education for all three- and four-year-olds (with imminent extension to underprivileged two-year-olds) that can be delivered in any formal day care setting, and by a curriculum-like program from birth to school age, called the Early Years Foundation Stage, which became legally compulsory in all care settings in 2008. In the United States, the terms "teacher" and "classroom" are used even when it is babies who are being cared for and individuals with no educational qualifications who are providing the care.

> If I had the choice I would probably have gone back to work later. But my partner said to me, "You need to see other people, and not just Jason." . . . And also the fact that Jason needed to see other people as well.   —FCCC mother

In the English-speaking world, fewer than 10 percent of babies under a year old are in center care, but many more parents would opt for a center place if they could find and afford one. Around 80 percent of American and more than 90 percent of British three- and four-year-olds are in formal groups, but that does not mean that only 10–20 percent are in any other type of care. Many of the groups these preschool children attend are nursery school or pre-K classes, primarily early education rather than child care, and usually part-time—often half days and school terms only. A family day care or a nanny may provide care the rest of the time. And even if preschool is full day, there may be formal or informal wraparound care, often by a grandmother, to match the child's school hours to the parents' work hours.

WHY POLICY MAKERS GENERALLY SUPPORT GROUP CARE

Most policy makers and their professional advisers, as well as governments and their treasury departments, promote institutional group care over individual or family day care, not only because of its educational benefits but also because of economies of scale. It is seen as a major economic advantage to have one nursery worker caring for, say, five infants or ten preschool children instead of a family day care provider looking after only two or three children in addition to her own. Furthermore, in countries in which child care is mainly in the private sector, it is big business, operated by highly profitable companies and chains. The U.K. private nursery sector, for example, was worth 3.2 billion pounds in 2006. With 20 percent growth in the year from April 2004 to April 2005, it was the second-highest investment area in the country.

Business means employment. As well as playing a part in getting mothers into paid work, child care centers employ workers who are fully integrated in the tax-paying labor force in a way that many individual caregivers are not. Even family day care providers, technically entrepreneurs running small businesses, seldom make what in any other business would be designated a living wage. Finally, it is much easier—and less expensive—for a local authority to exercise quality-control measures, such as registration and inspection, within fewer large institutional groups than across many small and scattered ones.

Leaving aside the question of educational advantages to children themselves, some of these perceived advantages of formal group care are less clear-cut than they may appear, as earlier chapters have shown. Economy of scale is a risky concept, especially where babies and young toddlers are concerned. As we shall see, a high ratio of adults to children is crucial to the quality of group care, and the younger the children are, the higher that ratio needs to be. It is the basic conundrum of child care that the greater economy of scale it offers, the poorer its care is likely to be for the children. The commonplace institutional practice of grouping children by age exacerbates this because like a parent, a family day care provider may be able to meet the needs of several children at the same time—a baby, a toddler, a couple of preschool children, and two more who are at grade school most of the day, for example—but even two, let alone three, babies together are too many. Ask any parent of twins or triplets.

> I need to sort something with them. . . . She used to drop off to sleep quite happily, but now I've noticed she cries and gets quite panicky, and I think that's because they just leave her at nursery. . . . Mind you, they've got thirteen babies.   —FCCC mother

Child care is labor intensive: staff wages are said to account for 40 percent of the costs of nurseries in the United Kingdom, meaning that day care centers are always expensive to run, and the more and better staff they employ, the more they cost someone. If child care institutions appear economical (and politically acceptable) to policy makers in the United States and Britain, it is because most of their funding comes from parents acting as customers (demand-side

---

European funding of group child care

Finland finances universal child care from birth in the same way as it does education. In other continental European countries, public funding makes a large contribution. In Holland, government policy dictates that child care costs are split equally among parents, employers, and the state. In Denmark, federal law forbids local authorities charging parents more than 33 percent of the costs of a child care placement. And in Sweden, by law no parent may be asked to pay more than 3 percent of their income for day care for a first child (less for subsequent children).

---

funding) with and without a range of subsidies and tax benefits rather than from politically sensitive public funds (supply-side funding) with parents as beneficiaries.

Good care not only depends on adult-child ratios but also on the qualities of those adults. Currently, many parents incorrectly assume that group care equals professional care. While the individuals—managers or teachers—in charge of most centers have early years qualifications of one kind or another, including kindergarten teaching and degrees in early childhood studies, in the United States and to a lesser extent in the United Kingdom, required qualifications and pay for child care assistants are both shockingly low. In some American states, child care is one of the few job options open to young people without high school diplomas and, therefore, is likely to attract a disproportionate number. In the United Kingdom, although the government is making a major investment in training, an individual can still apply to work in a nursery under supervision soon after reaching the minimum school-leaving age of sixteen, even if she is one of the minority who leave without any qualifications at all. On-the-job training and arrangements for time off so that a young caregiver can attend college will be available, but the process of acquiring relevant qualifications by that route is so slow that many will not stay long enough to benefit.

As for ease of quality control: while inspection may be less expensive when child care is concentrated into centers, it is neither impossible nor ineffective in family day care. Furthermore, while licensing tends to be the "stick" used to ensure a basic standard of health and safety, policy "carrots" to encourage improvements in quality work well in both group and individual settings, as experience on both sides of the Atlantic is showing.

In the United Kingdom, all registered child care settings are inspected by the same authority that inspects schools (OFSTED). Posting its findings on its Web site and allowing care providers to use good inspection grades to attract parents have been important motivations for improvements in quality. In the United States, the National Association for the Education of Young Children (NAEYC) has been operating a voluntary accreditation system for center-based child care for seventeen years, and parents in about half of the states pay a higher rate for accredited programs than for those that meet only basic licensing standards.

Although standards vary from state to state, time to time, and chain to chain, some large-scale, high-quality research reports suggest that American group care is mostly of low quality. One study, from the mid-1990s, reported only one in seven centers capable of promoting healthy development and learning, and only one-third "characteristically offering positive caregiving." Ten years later, data from the National Child Care Information Center for the United States as a whole do not suggest that there has been substantial national improvement. Centers in other English-speaking countries tend to be somewhat better.

The quality of British centers is only now being reported, but although recent work suggests that they are not of as high quality as other types of British child care, their transformation into children's centers in every community (see Chapter 12) is certainly improving them. All still compare unfavorably with the best continental Europe has to offer, however. Scandinavian child care centers are widely admired, and Italy, especially the city of Reggio Emilia, has pioneered some of the best in the world.

WHAT A FAMILY CAN EXPECT OF CENTER OR NURSERY CARE

Definitions of child care quality usually rely on quantifiable indicators such as staff-child ratios and group sizes, and parents seeking child care naturally tend to be impressed by bright spacious settings, child-sized bathrooms, and many toys. However, experience from

> *"We went [on a study tour of Reggio Emilia] with the aim of finding an approach we could adapt for Dolphin Nurseries. What we found was far richer. At the risk of sounding weird, this experience was 'soul food.' "*
>
> Martin Pace, CEO, Dolphin Nurseries, England

centers of excellence in other countries suggests that a child-centered approach to child development and early education is what matters most. The Reggio approach, for example, is informed by an image of the child not as an empty vessel into which the right ingredients must be poured but as a being with extraordinary abilities as well as potential. What takes place in the thirty or so centers that cater to children under the age of six in Reggio Emilia could not be printed in a curriculum but is taught, hands-on, to hundreds of visiting professionals from around the world. Great emphasis is placed on encouraging curiosity and innovation, with both children and teachers engaged in a constant process of discovery; children are not seen as a passive recipients of education or care but as active participants; staff are confident and articulate, and parents are encouraged to get involved. The outcomes are not necessarily measurable but are widely regarded as the strongest possible foundation for life.

CONCERNS ABOUT GROUP CARE FOR BABIES AND YOUNG TODDLERS

An educational tradition underpins preschool centers but has little real relevance to infants. Indeed, the postwar nursery school tradition did not include babies and toddlers, focusing instead on children from ages three to five in the United Kingdom, from three to six in North America, Australia, and much of Europe. Younger and younger children have been included not only because more mothers go out to work while children are very young—although that is often assumed to be the reason—but also because formal schooling is starting progressively earlier.

Nursery schools and playgroups that used to cater to three-to-fives now lose children to school or to pre-K when they are four or even three years old, and that means that they have many places to fill and the only children available to fill them are toddlers and infants.

> *"With preschool, [starting age] is an important consideration. Of course, day care is another matter—many parents choose day care as child care for their children from infancy onward, and age doesn't need to be a factor in this decision. When it comes to preschool, however, we believe that parents should send a child only when that child is able to take full advantage of a school experience. The right age varies from child to child. Some two-year-olds are able to express themselves verbally . . . and are comfortable with unfamiliar adults. . . . For most children, three is the natural age of readiness."*
>
> Nancy Schulman and Ellen Birnbaum, *Practical Wisdom for Parents*

Babies are not waiting for preschool groups to join, though. What is demonstrably good for most children from their third year onward is not necessarily appropriate for children in their second and may even be harmful to some in the first year. Each of the main areas of concern about group day care for children under, say, two years has some validity for some children. None is absolutely proven for all.

Separation from mother

Although attachment theory suggests that lack of predictable maternal availability increases the risk of insecure attachment, daily separations from the mother from early infancy rarely damage the relationship between them. The NICHD study, specifically designed to examine this issue, found, as we have seen, that the most important predictor of a secure attachment between mother and baby was the mother's sensitivity and responsiveness to him. In comparison, day care was irrelevant.

Concerns about possible effects of early child care on attachment cannot be completely dismissed, however, because some indirect effects did emerge, suggesting that there was an increased risk of a baby being insecurely attached to his mother if she was relatively insensitive to him and his child care was of poor quality.

Sharing adult attention

Group care usually gives babies and young toddlers less opportunity for one-on-one attention from caring adults than might be offered at home. That "might be" is important; not all mothers, fathers, grandparents, or nannies are highly responsive to children in their care. However, since every aspect of early development—social-emotional, cognitive, and communicative—depends on input from sensitive adult caregivers, anything that reduces child-adult interaction is undesirable, and some research findings do suggest that as a result of little attention being available, infants in center care tend to be more passive and less eager to interact with adults.

Such "bad news" findings cannot be taken at face value, though. While being in group care clearly does reduce both a child's opportunities to interact with caring adults and the amount of time those interactions can take, it increases her opportunities to interact and play with other children. In a good center, such contact might help her to develop social and communication skills, as it is known to do for preschool children. In a poor center, though, or perhaps for an infant of a different temperament, the peer group may be an unwelcome and unhelpful source of tension and challenge, as has been suggested by recent studies tracking the relationship between group care and very young children's levels of the hormone cortisol, which is released in response to stress.

Studies have shown that children's cortisol levels were far higher when they spent the day in (good-quality) center care than during weekend days at home, and they were differently patterned. The children most affected were those who were least confident in playing with other children. The findings are clear-cut, but their significance is not. Although high cortisol levels are known to have ill effects on brain development, there is still much to be learned about the long-term effects of different levels.

Behavior problems related to early group care

The concern that has hit most media headlines and continues to exercise researchers is that early group care provokes adjustment difficulties and behavioral problems later on, especially more aggression toward other children and less cooperation with adults. Not all studies have reported such a relationship, but most of those that have looked for it have found it. The effects are small—far too small to justify published headlines such as "Daycare Breeds Thugs"—but they do seem to be real, both in the United States and in the United Kingdom.

> *"If parents or researchers or policy makers were searching for the single best structural indicator to suggest that young children are receiving warm, sensitive, stimulating attention from their caregivers, it would be [low] child:adult ratio."* Alison Clarke-Stewart, NICHD researcher

IDENTIFYING HIGH-QUALITY CARE FOR UNDER-TWOS

Child care is a fact of modern life, so while it is important to identify problems or risks associated with different types and quantities, identifying the features of high-quality care is equally important and arguably more helpful. The NICHD study followed more than one thousand children and reported on "which observable characteristics of the care arrangement predict higher quality care." What researchers termed "high quality, positive caregiving," assessed by internationally recognized observations, meant care that was "sensitive, warm, and responsive" to each child.

Of the characteristics that contributed to "high-quality, positive caregiving" for babies (six months) to toddlers (twenty-four months), a high ratio of adults to infants was overwhelmingly the most important. Small group sizes often went with this. This probably explains why the highest quality of nonmaternal care was found at home, where babies and toddlers were cared for by (most of) an adult—nannies, fathers, grandparents. The next highest quality care was found in family day care/childminding, where even if the overall caregiver-to-child ratio was not very high, mixed-age groups meant that each child received a comparatively large amount of personalized attention. The least high quality care was found in nurseries or day care centers.

Apart from high adult-child ratios, the main contributors to quality of care for the youngest children, noted by the NICHD team, were:

- Safer, better organized, and more stimulating settings (the "physical/learning environment"), not only because these were good in themselves but also, perhaps, because such settings allowed caregivers to spend less time preventing the babies from doing things and more time helping them find more to do.

- More planning of activities and organization of toys and equipment.

- Caregivers' more liberal views and beliefs about child rearing and discipline also made a contribution to high-quality care.

- Caregivers' education, including specialized early years training, made a surprisingly small contribution to quality of care at these ages.

- Caregivers' experience of child care was not associated with quality at these ages.

These American findings from NICHD were substantially similar to the findings from the English FCCC study: "Observed child-carer ratios in the nurseries were significantly related to most of the measures of observed quality of care at 10 months and almost all at 18 months. The higher the number of 10 month infants sharing one carer, the less positive and the more punitive and detached was her relationship with them. In addition, at 18 months, when carers had more toddlers to care for, the quality of their interaction with them was significantly lower and they were significantly less emotionally responsive to them."

Features of high-quality care, measured by the Observational Record of the Caregiving Environment (ORCE)

- Sensitivity to child's nondistress signals (i.e., positive as well as negative and signals more subtle than outright crying)
- Stimulation of every aspect of child's development
- Positive regard toward child—expecting to like them and usually enjoying being with them
- Fostering child's exploration
- (Not) detached from the child
- (Not) "flat" and unresponsive
- (Not) intrusive or interfering

"Key Working"

Within groups, apart from the possibility of using mixed-age "family grouping," the best possible use of the available staff can be made by utilizing what is often known as "key working": "The keyperson approach is a way of working in nurseries in which the whole focus and organisation is to enable and support close attachments between individual children and individual nursery staff. The keyperson approach is an involvement, an individual and reciprocal commitment between a member of staff and a family. It is an approach that has clear benefits for children and parents, the keyperson and the nursery."

This approach gives a particular adult (and usually another backup person) special ongoing responsibility for several children. The key worker does not just observe the children, do their paperwork, and liaise with their parents; she is committed to providing consistent care and emotional support to each child throughout the day, the week, the month. The role requires her to be "tuned in" to each child and able to establish a personal history with him or her.

When a key-working system is operating as it should, it is almost always the key person who changes a child's diaper, wipes her nose, feeds her, settles her to sleep, and is there when she wakes. The key person changes diapers in the context of a relationship with the child, and may use private songs and jokes; if just anyone does it, or the "chore" of diaper-changing is "fairly shared" among several workers, children may be processed across the changing table like cans of beans across a supermarket checkout. For the approach to work as well as it can, key persons must have the sensitivity, openness, and capacity to enjoy young children's company and manage their demands. Key working also demands organizational flair from a manager who can arrange staff rotations and breaks around the

> *"It's hard for a child being in a nursery. It's 'we, we, we,' all the time, not you. . . . It's really difficult for a child suddenly to stop being 'I.' "*
> D. Selleck and S. Griffin, "Quality for the Under Threes," 1996

emotional needs of the children, and simultaneously trust staff with the autonomy to adapt the day's plans to a child's needs and reshape routines as they think best.

HIGH-QUALITY GROUP CARE FOR OLDER TODDLERS AND PRESCHOOL CHILDREN

The qualities that the NICHD study showed to be predictive of positive caregiving for this age group were interestingly different from those that predicted positive care for infants. For this age group, the number of adults available to the children was not as overwhelmingly important to the quality of care, but who those adults were was far more important. While adult-child ratios still mattered, so now did adult characteristics, such as caregivers' education, beliefs, and attitudes toward child rearing. Even care providers' previous experience now had a bearing.

- Although adult-child ratios were still significant, the quality of adult attention offered to the children had become more significant than its quantity.

- Although overall quality of care was still lower in centers than in family day care or informal care, the difference was much less at this age; centers were coming closer to the quality of other types of provision.

- The physical learning environment made a far greater contribution to positive caregiving.

- A new element was added to positive caregiving at this age—fostering the child's exploration.

- Adults with liberal or child-centered attitudes and beliefs were more likely to foster exploration.

There is more extensive and consistent research evidence concerning preschool care, usually aimed at children from almost three years old and having more or less explicit educational aims, than for any other age group or type. It leaves little room for doubt that educationally oriented preschool experience fosters educationally

> *"The long-term educational benefits stem not from what children are specifically taught but from effects on children's attitudes to learning, their self-esteem and their task orientation."*
>
> Professor Sir Michael Rutter, professor of developmental psychopathology, Department of Social, Genetic and Developmental Psychiatry Research Centre, King's College, London

relevant outcomes, including "school readiness," however it is defined. Indeed, findings from a range of research studies from both sides of the Atlantic suggest that the opportunity for preschool experience should be as much a universal entitlement as a place in school, hence the United Kingdom's recent provision of fifteen hours per week of preschool for all three- and four-year-olds, free of charge.

The Effective Provision of Pre-School Education (EPPE) project is the first major European longitudinal study of a national sample of young children's development (intellectual and social/behavioral) between the ages of three and seven. To investigate the effects of preschool education, the EPPE team collected a wide range of information on more than three thousand children, their parents, their home environments, and the 141 preschool settings they attended. These included day nurseries (public and private), integrated centers, playgroups, nursery schools, and nursery classes. A sample of children who had no or minimal preschool experience was included in the study when they entered school for comparison with the preschool group. Key findings for children from three or four years of age up to school entry are summarized below.

Impact of attending a preschool center:

- Any preschool experience, compared to none, enhanced children's development.

- Full-time attendance had no benefit over part-time.

- Disadvantaged children can particularly benefit from good quality preschool experiences, especially if they attend centers that have a mixture of children from different social backgrounds.

The quality and practices in preschool centers:

- The better the quality of preschool centers, the better the children's intellectual/cognitive and social/behavioral development.

- Good quality was found in all types of early years settings but was higher overall in centers that paid equal attention to "care" and "education" and in nursery schools and classes or pre-Ks.

- Children make better all-around progress in centers viewing educational and social development as complementary and equal in importance.

- For this age group, settings that have staff with higher qualifications, especially those with a good proportion of trained teachers, show higher quality and their children make more progress.

- Effective pedagogy includes modes of interaction traditionally associated with the term "teaching," the provision of instructive learning environments, and "sustained shared thinking" to extend children's learning.

The quality of the learning environment of the home (where parents are engaged in activities with children) promoted intellectual and social development in all children and the quality of that home learning environment was more important than parents' social class, with which it is only moderately associated. What parents do is more important than who they are.

While these findings relate experience in educational settings to educationally relevant outcomes, this does not imply a direct relationship between academic teaching in the preschool period and academic abilities thereafter. Today's thinking on the links between child care in infancy and later school performance emphasizes the importance of the "social context" in which a child lives and learns. School readiness owes more to social skills like cooperating, negotiating, and collaborating with other children than to early academics. So managing feelings, emotions, and a richer mixture of relationships than is available in many modern families is a vital part of early years "education."

Unsocial Hours and Overnight Care

It is not easy for nurseries or centers to offer flexible care to parents who work unsocial or irregular hours, especially to those who may have to work overnight. Apart from essential service personnel, such as doctors, nurses, police, and ambulance and fire officers, it is those earning the most—executives—and those earning the least—cleaners, security guards, supermarket staff—who tend to work the most unsocial hours, and it is the unpredictable shift patterns to which many low-paid workers are subject that make managing child care most difficult. High-earning parents needing maximum or short-notice flexibility may employ a live-in nanny, sometimes also sending a three- or four-year-old to part-time preschool. For working parents with low incomes, finding any affordable, suitable child care is enough of a struggle; irregular hours may render it impossible.

As we have seen, family day care providers may be able and willing to be more flexible than nurseries. Certainly some U.K. childminders pride themselves on being there for families in difficulties and able to care for children unexpectedly with no more upset than they would feel if they stayed overnight with a relative: "She's got a cot and a toothbrush and a teddy upstairs. They're usually for naps, but they're fine for a night, too, if the need arises."

However, anyone working unsocial or irregular hours without backup family support finds it extremely difficult to arrange good child care, especially if she is on her own or her partner also works unsocial hours. More and more nurseries and day care centers, anxious to have a competitive edge in all aspects of child care, are beginning to explore extended hours and overnight care. Former President Clinton, in a 1997 speech expressing his admiration for the day care provided to the children of U.S. Air Force personnel, singled out overnight care for special approval. Doubtless he had equality of opportunity for women on his mind, as well as national security, but the effect of his speech was that he appeared to share the assumption that children's needs for care should not interfere in any way with adult working patterns.

A 2000 report by the U.K. Daycare Trust found that in almost two-thirds of working families, one or both parents were employed outside the traditional working hours of nine to five, and these numbers are still growing. Forty-one percent of single parents and 28 percent of unemployed mothers in couples said they could not take available jobs because of their unsuitable hours. One-quarter of all employees said they sometimes work at night.

A few (currently very few) nurseries are trying to fill the gap, offering overnight care to children as young as six weeks. The parents work in computing, retail, customs, and police work, and occasionally their shifts clash. "All have professions and want to develop careers. They also want quality care for their children and feel they can do both this way," said one nursery's manager. Another nursery manager is planning for a week-on/week-off pattern of overnight occupancy, as she said that this is the pattern for most women working night shifts. Another nursery takes some children occasionally, some regularly—"say two nights every fortnight." The manager said, "It's not ideal, but that's the way things are going."

Most of these few nurseries say that their nighttime provision is for night workers or for parents taking courses. But while one insisted, "It's not a holiday drop-in, or for when parents want a night out with friends," another will provide holiday care for up to two weeks for babies from three months old.

WHAT ABOUT THE CHILDREN?

Asked about the effect overnight care has or might have on a baby or young child, some nursery managers said that the need for such care exists and that they are helping to solve it: "In an ideal world, children would be in bed at home with their parents, but this problem is here and now. Children are being looked after by different people every night, being left alone or looked after by older siblings. I'm not introducing the problem, and I'm not responsible for it. This is something that is going on. The problem exists and we are offering the solution."

Others appreciate the parents' problem but not this solution:

- Children, especially babies, need to be cared for by people they know well and in the ways they are accustomed to. A child at a nursery overnight probably won't be with his special adult; he'll be with different, night-shift staff.

- For older babies and toddlers, being able to take for granted that they will be picked up by their parents at the end of every day is crucial to feeling safe and happy at a nursery.

- If parents don't ask for daytime as well as nighttime child care after a night shift, they may take a child home and be too tired to care for him or her. A child who spends the night at the center should stay at least until the afternoon of the next day so that the parent can get some sleep before picking her up.

For parents who need to work nights, perhaps especially those who need to do so only sometimes, employing a live-in or daily in-home caregiver is probably the best option. It is expensive, but there are ways in which those extra costs could be offset, such as with the U.K.'s Working Families' Tax Credit.

Family day care providers, especially U.K. childminders, already offer a great deal of flexible early morning, evening, and weekend child care; many more could also offer overnight care, which would at least provide one-to-one interaction with a caregiver who is usually seen more as an auntie than as a nurse or a teacher. But if parents really want regular overnight nursery care for their children, it ought to be possible to organize that care so that it is not overnight *as well as* but instead of any day care; and not an ad hoc extra, staffed by strangers, but as high-quality as the best of daytime care.

Instead of leaving it to innovative nursery businesses to meet this "need" for overnight care, perhaps governments and local authorities should be:

- Managing employers' demands for parents to work unsocial hours so that if two parents' shifts clash they are entitled to tell employers, "I can't work that shift because my partner is on call, too."

- Putting the responsibility for extra child care costs onto employers who insist on involuntary overtime and unsocial working hours.

- Encouraging on-site workplace nurseries where overnight and unsocial-hours work is inevitable, such as in hospitals, so that overnight care can allow for parents' goodnight kisses and ready availability for bad dreams or illness.

12. Integrated Care and Education: Children's Centers and Extended Schools

The "formal child care sector," consisting of family day care and group care in child care centers or nurseries, is changing. In the past ten years, many governments, looking to develop policies addressing social problems due to poverty and disadvantage, have focused on the integration of care and education and of infancy and childhood. The trend toward "integrated services" reflects real changes in social attitudes and in knowledge. While care and education used to be considered separate endeavors, one the responsibility of families, the other of schools, it is now recognized that "lifelong learning" begins at (if not before) birth and that schools are only one particular part of, and setting for, education. Clearly, then, all child care is and must be "educational," and all education must be caring. Treating the care and education of infants, toddlers, preschool, and school-age children as separate services is increasingly seen as absurd.

Instead of nurseries or day care centers staffed by child care staff,

---

"[There is] a welcome trend towards increased cooperation between early childhood education and care and the school system, both in terms of policy and practice . . . [and] a greater policy focus on building bridges across administrative departments, staff training, regulations and curricula. . . . [E]arly childhood—from birth to 8—[is being recognised] as an important phase for developing important dispositions and attitudes towards learning."

Organisation for Economic Cooperation Development, 2001

preschools and schools staffed by teachers, and after-school and holiday schemes staffed by play workers, the modern ideal is for services for children, their families, and caregivers to be brought together in what in the United Kingdom (and in this chapter) are called children's centers, staffed by members of an integrated "early years profession."

A Vision for Services

Children's centers, by whatever name, are more the goal than the reality of many contemporary children's services, but they are already making a profound difference to some families and communities on both sides of the Atlantic. In Sweden, Denmark, and Finland, they are the rule rather than the exception; in the United Kingdom there are already many Sure Start children's centers up and running and many more to come, while in the United States, children's centers are being modeled both in national research and development and in state initiatives.

In the English-speaking world, the vision and the actuality of children's centers thus far have been directed primarily at the most impoverished children, families, and communities. The best-known program is Head Start and Early Head Start in the United States, aimed at improving the lives and chances of individual poor children and their families. The United Kingdom's Sure Start came later and was similar in many respects; importantly, though, it was targeted not at individual poor families but at impoverished communities. If a British family lived in a Sure Start area, it could access the services whatever its income level, so using those services car-

---

Early Head Start

"Grantees . . . are charged with tailoring their program services to meet the needs of low-income pregnant women and families with infants and toddlers in their communities. . . . Grantees are required to provide child development services, build family and community partnerships, and support staff to provide high-quality services for children and families."

ried no stigma and helped to meld communities rather than further dividing them. Both Head Start and Sure Start have been largely successful in terms of their outcomes for children and families, and enormously influential in the development of services. However, as originally set up, Head Start lacked the funding and Sure Start lacked the geographical reach to fulfill their potential.

Now, though, Sure Start children's centers are being rapidly rolled out. By 2010, there will be 3,500, and unlike the original Sure Start projects, which were confined to the United Kingdom's most deprived areas, the new centers are spreading throughout the country, some of them building on the original projects, some incorporating nurseries and other early years settings.

In the United States, Head Start and Early Head Start still serve only the least privileged families and are actually available to only a minority of those who qualify, but other state initiatives have wider briefs. Smart Start, for example, North Carolina's enormously successful program, founded in 1993 and funded by public-private partnership, can be used for the benefit of families that are not low income and adapted flexibly to the needs of different communities. Its mandate states: "Smart Start funds may be used for a wide range of services and are not necessarily limited to low income families. The primary goal is to create systemic change that can improve the quality, affordability and supply of child development services for all young children in the community."

Following the Smart Start example, some similar initiatives that encourage and support community planning and service integration have been established, such as the 350 Family Resource and Youth Services Centers in Kentucky, and Project Success, which is now established in almost two hundred communities in Illinois. Most current initiatives, however, are small demonstration projects. The few statewide programs similar to Smart Start provide valuable encouragement for interservice collaboration but no additional funding. In 2001, when the No Child Left Behind Act was signed into American law and the Good Start, Grow Smart initiative was begun a year later to support it, there were hopes of increased federal funding, but the new federal-state partnership carried no new money, although it has stimulated valuable new research.

*Good Start, Grow Smart—the Bush administration's early childhood
initiative: partnering with states to improve early learning*

"Efforts to improve early childhood learning will not work
unless they involve States and school districts, which shoulder
the primary responsibility for providing public education. Since
States and districts are directly responsible for student learning
and achievement in school, preparing children to learn before
they start school is in their best interest. This is particularly true
now that the No Child Left Behind law requires standards and
accountability for every school in America. Many States and districts have already taken concrete steps in recognition that, in
order for students to succeed once they reach school, they must
come prepared to learn.

"The Administration's plan calls on all States to take steps that
will help prepare children before they enter school to be ready
to learn. For example, States should help coordinate the public
schools with the early childhood programs that serve the children they later educate.

"This can be accomplished in part by making available to
early childhood programs information on what will be expected
of children once they reach school and what skills children will
need to learn before school in order to meet State standards in
school."

INTEGRATED CHILDREN'S CENTERS FOR ALL

If integration of services for children is to be meaningful, the body
of children they serve has to be integrated, too, so that all children,
whatever their special needs, and all families, whatever their cultural or economic differences, are included.

Making such services universally available rather than targeting
those in greatest need means spending a great deal of "extra"
money, which is economically challenging and politically difficult.
It is professionally difficult, too, because it renders a "one size fits
all" model of services impossible. Different centers will face and
must address a wide range of needs and levels of need. As a relatively
small and simple example, imagine the extra costs that must be met
by a center operating in a multiethnic community in which every
spoken or printed word that goes out to families must be made

available in three languages. Centers that face a wider range of needs than others will clearly require extra funding. Nevertheless, the temptation to spend only on disadvantaged families and their centers has to be resisted. It is crucial that children's centers be as available in wealthy areas as in disadvantaged ones, in part because affluent areas are often marked by pockets of deprivation. Sure Start's targeting of families in the poorest districts left out many of the poorest families because they lived outside its boundaries. Furthermore, higher incomes do not mean lower levels of need: mental health problems—such as postpartum depression—social isolation, and marital discord are equally likely among high-earning families, and so are child abuse and neglect. Higher incomes do mean, however, that families can pay toward services that in other centers must be free; this is the solution adopted in many countries in continental Europe and being pursued in the United Kingdom.

INTEGRATED STAFFING

Integrated services require integrated training of staff, and that means deciding under what umbrella services for children should shelter. The integrated workforce that is being actively promoted by the U.K. and New Zealand governments, and by many North American experts, must bring together occupational groups that are currently widely diverse. Childminders (family day care workers/ day care mothers), nursery/child care center teachers and assistants, preschool and school teachers as well as their assistants, and out-of-school child care staff (play workers) must share a career structure and work together on an equal footing. That is not easy, as Canada's experience shows.

In the past Canadian teachers have rejected any nonteaching contact with children. Many school boards tried to pressure teachers to supervise nonclass time; teacher unions have been balking at this requirement, and the issue came to a head in Ontario in 2005. A new collective agreement outlined by the Ontario Principals' Council stated that a one-hundred-minute-per-week maximum would be set on time a teacher must supervise children outside of class, but while some boards hire educational assistants and lunchroom monitors to provide the extra supervision, other boards would prefer to force

Department of Public Welfare, Commonwealth of Pennsylvania integrated children's services plan guidelines, May 15, 2008

"Describe the activities of the cross-system planning team that was created as part of the County's integrated children's team and how you plan to continue the work in the coming year. The Plan should be developed through a partnership of county behavioral health, mental retardation, child welfare, juvenile probation, early intervention, child care, education, drug and alcohol agencies, and families and children receiving services from the agencies covered by the plan. . . . Include a list of the individuals that participate on the cross-systems team and their organizational affiliation. List meetings held with the cross-systems team.

"The role of family and youth in integrating services is also critical to success of service delivery. Counties should clearly articulate what steps it will take to ensure families/youth are involved in all steps of system development for integrating services and an update on your progress for engaging families and youth in the ICSP process. . . .

"Counties should indicate how they are engaging their local educational system as part of this planning process and any future steps they may be taking to coordinate services with the educational system."

teachers to supervise in addition to their other duties. Such disputes are widespread.

To make integration possible, all staff need to have equal access to shared educational, training, and salary opportunities. In the United Kingdom and in North America, where a large majority of the individuals who work with children (other than teachers) have low levels of education and little if any professional training, teachers are understandably protective of their much higher status, so this is a very challenging long-term aim and an exceedingly complex one, as the plan guidelines for Pennsylvania, in the box above, clearly show.

Integration is not impossible, however. It has already been undertaken successfully in several European countries and is currently under way in New Zealand. In Sweden, the education and training of all those working with children has been brought together under an education banner. There are no longer different courses and qualifications for people caring for babies and toddlers, working with preschool children, teaching school-age children in the classroom, or working with them outside school hours. There is a single educational framework and a single qualification as a teacher for all early years workers (see Chapter 17). The banner of an integrated service does not have to be educational, though. In Denmark and Finland, children's services are integrated not under education but under welfare in a special profession called "pedagogy."

Pedagogy is the most popular degree course in Denmark. It lasts three and a half years and includes the theory of pedagogy, psychology, social and health studies, communication, and creative studies. There is also a strong emphasis on the importance of outdoor life for children.

Some 15 percent of pedagogy students are male, and 5 percent are from ethnic minorities. The average age for starting the course is twenty-seven. This reflects the fact that pedagogy is often a second career entered after gaining experience in another profession or after real-life experience as a parent. The profession's high status is reflected in basic pay of around £25,000 (nearly $40,000) per year.

The need to increase the training of the early years workforce is well recognized in the United Kingdom, and its Children's Workforce Strategy, but the U.K. government has not committed itself to an overall workforce qualification target. The current aim is to have at least one graduate worker in each child care setting and as many of them as possible (as quickly as possible) qualified with the new Early Years Professional Status (EYPS). This is in contrast to New Zealand, where by the year 2012 the entire child care workforce will be made up of trained teachers.

CHILDREN'S CENTERS AND THE UNITED KINGDOM'S VISION

Integration is the watchword of the United Kingdom's child care policy and planning—integration of all children no matter how special their needs; integration of all families irrespective of cultural, religious, or economic differences; integration of services, whether supplied or funded by the private sector, by voluntary organizations, or by the state via local authorities; and integration between care and education and their staff specialties.

The vision of today's government—like mine fifteen years ago—is of a children's center in every community, one for approximately every eight hundred households. Areas of multiple deprivation—those targeted by the original Sure Start program—have been given priority, but all local authorities are now committed to opening centers for children from birth through age eleven (and soon through adolescence) and their families, providing a comprehensive and joined-up approach to services in health, education, welfare, and leisure. The ambition is for integrated children's centers—bright and accessible places where children and young people can take part in a wide range of activities and every family member can obtain information, advice, and support—to be a focus for all families in the local community with children from birth to sixteen years and a "one-stop shop" for accessing services. They will be community centers *for* children, familiar *to* children and involving children in decision making, as well as being welcoming, interactive, and evolving. Each will offer a range of coordinated children's and youth services, including day care nursery, childminder network, after-school

---

Child places fifteen years ago

"[The] most basic function [of a local child place is] to serve as a drop-in center or informal club for . . . anyone caring for a baby—father or grandparent, nanny or au pair, daycare mother or babysitter. Such a center serves both adults and children. It takes the isolation and boredom out of being home-based with a baby and . . . facilitates . . . gradual separation and eventually stress-free daycare. . . .

"Daycare groups, flexibly constituted to serve parents . . . working any combination of hours, would be in the same setting, so every child's introduction to managing regularly without a parent or permanent caretaker of her own could be gradual and individually planned and paced . . . , building their confidence and independence towards readiness for the (already familiar) pre-school education group, with full-time care for those who needed it."   Penelope Leach, *Children First* (1994)

clubs, play activities, study support, and youth activities. Ideally children's centers are also to be health bases, with health visitors (community nurses), children's dentists and clinics, and additional support for children with special needs. One hopes they will be centers for consultation and participation with parents and children, for training child care staff, and for educating parents and others. Finally, in whatever ways best suit local communities, children's centers will offer crucial and visible support to children, linking into wider initiatives to promote health and well-being, reduce crime, tackle social exclusion and poverty, help parents to obtain employment and training, encourage educational achievement, and build communities.

Even in policy makers' wildest dreams, not every center will provide all that, everywhere, and not everything that is provided will be free for everyone. Provision and payment will both reflect local circumstances. However, while the type of building may differ, depending on the facilities that exist locally, and the services offered will vary according to local need, the range of services in any local center will have a common core:

- Centers will take a primary and strategic role in providing child care places for children up to the age of fourteen for all parents who want them and are working or looking for work.

- School-age child care will include both wraparound care when schools are in session and full-day care when they are not.

- Centers will offer play (and sports) facilities for all children, parents, and caregivers of children.

- They will serve as resource bases—drop-in centers with information about all local services, including employment advice, and all aspects of child care, including child development, health, specialist needs, school, and local support services.

Fifteen years after the blue-sky thinking in the box on page 177, it still seems appropriate to describe children's centers in the future tense, because, while a handful of centers fulfilling that enormous goal are up and running, the vision of centers for all children in all communities in the United Kingdom doing all that is still very distant and therefore vulnerable to political and economic change. There are not yet enough centers, even with 3,500 Sure Start children's centers now operating. Although that number sounds vast, each serves about eight hundred families, providing a very small proportion of the available child care places. Most centers are serving primarily under-fours and their families, and not all are yet offering a wide range of services. Some child care settings that are now called children's centers were previously nurseries and are offering only a few additional services, some of which, such as "advice for parents," are easy to claim but difficult to assess. As one disappointed FCCC mother put it, "It's called a children's centre but it seems like a nursery to me." Other settings are extending their services but only in obvious and easy directions: adult and toddler groups, for instance, offered by playgroups. Centers are not completely integrated, either; in some areas there are still different funding streams or initiatives for different age groups, and separate qualifications are still required for preschool, school, and after-school staff and for education, health, and family support.

But if the United Kingdom still has a long way to go, it has gone a great deal further than the rest of the English-speaking world, and the future for integrated children's centers is bright. There are children's centers in the United Kingdom that are now doing everything in that vision—not many, but some. One center, in Harlow, Essex, opened in 2001. It offers a drop-in group for parents or caregivers with toddlers, early learning and play opportunities for under-fives, family support services, two kinds of parenting courses, and a drop-in nursery. There is a day care nursery next door. The center has six Sure Start workers and fourteen nursery nurses, and it contributes to posts in the local midwifery and health visiting teams. The center runs day trips and holiday treats involving as many parents with their children as possible. It also has occupational therapists and educational psychologists visiting and making informal contact with parents. Currently housed in a former primary school, it is slated to move into a new building, which is almost completed and will include a soft playroom, a multipurpose play space, and a café. Perhaps it is not quite a one-stop shop for parents (you cannot get your children immunized there or their teeth inspected), but it is certainly a community hub.

If that vision became everyday reality for all children and families, the United Kingdom would have undergone a far-reaching social revolution. Making it real would mean building at least ten thousand centers and doubling current government spending on services for children and families from £3.5 billion to £7 billion a year. Once again, that sum sounds massive, but it is far from impossible to achieve. It would still bring funding for children and families in England up to only 0.7 percent of GDP compared with the 2 percent spent in Denmark or the 2.5 percent in Sweden.

Integrated children's centers are not yet commonplace—let alone universally available—anywhere outside the Nordic states, but they are operating very successfully here and there: in Ontario, for example, especially in Toronto. Such centers loom very large in the immediate future of child care in the United Kingdom and in the longer term in the United States. Clearly, though, funding is the crux. Such rich provision costs a lot of money. It is not only a question of whether a government chooses to prioritize children's services, and this aspect of children's services, at the expense of other services or the taxpayer, but also whether attempts to economize in providing centers reduces the quality of the provision. Local authorities can stretch their funding (as they do with American Smart Start centers) by placing centers in existing facilities such as nurseries or schools and sometimes by incorporating services for which they already have to pay—such as lunch programs—into the centers. Furthermore, in both the United States and the United Kingdom, child care is already fee-based, so it is seen as reasonable to charge for it in centers; and where centers are built in more affluent areas, charges may also be made for some activities, such as parenting classes. The balance between what can be provided to parents at no cost and what they must pay for is key to the sustainability of centers, but it is also key to their quality. In the United Kingdom, sadly, it seems likely that children's centers outside areas of disadvantage will provide fewer services and charge much more for them.

EXTENDED SCHOOLS

In its 2001 review of early childhood education and care services in twelve countries, the OECD referred to the development of closer relations between early years services and schools, looking to a strong partnership of equals. Conditions in the Nordic states favor this new relationship of equality, partly because their early years sectors are well established and children stay in them until the age of six, when school begins, and partly because "free-time" teachers tend to be more highly regarded than equivalent play workers in the United Kingdom or youth workers in North America. However, the OECD report recognized a real risk that, even in Sweden or Denmark, integrating other services with schools, bringing all under the umbrella of education, might lead not to the intended equality but to domination of early childhood service. Schools are long-established and very powerful public institutions with a strong professional workforce, liable to colonize other services that come too close.

In the United Kingdom, such an imbalance is even more likely because the early years sector is weakened by the fact that it loses almost all children to school at the age of four. Furthermore, the issue is not only about the relationship between early years services and schools but also the relationships between schools and all other services for children, young people, and families. If extended schools become the hubs of their communities, it may be difficult to avoid the future relationship between the school and other services being colonial in nature rather than all concerned being open to change and eager to form strong and equal partnerships in a new meeting place.

Extended schools are the logical next chapter in the United Kingdom's integrated child care story; they will combine services for under-fives with school-age child care, and leisure time with the school day and term. In North America, though, where integrated children's centers are still in the discussion stage, extended schools may be the first and most central chapter in that story. Certainly, "school-linked, integrated services" is an Internet search term that brings up research and progress reports from across the United States (see www.ericdigests.org). The most visionary of these comes from the Schools Partnership Training Institute (SPTI) in San Francisco: "A joint project of the Jewish Family and Children's Services of San Francisco, the Peninsula, and Sonoma and Marin counties," it was established in 1992 "to provide educators and human service providers with the knowledge and skills necessary to work collaboratively."

The rationale of extending schools' traditional opening hours and functions is twofold: first, using school premises only forty-five weeks of the year and seven hours per day is extraordinarily wasteful. Those resources can and should be used outside what have been known for generations as "school hours." Second, using schools almost exclusively for formal national-curriculum education is wasteful in another way: since there are schools in every community and everyone pays for them whether or not they have children or grandchildren, the facilities can and should be used to meet the entire community's needs.

Many European parents take it for granted that schools will provide not only wraparound child care to fill the gap between their working hours away from home and children's hours in compulsory education but also carefully planned leisure-time activities. An example from Sweden is described on page 56.

EXTENDED SCHOOLS IN THE UNITED KINGDOM

Alongside its rapid development of Sure Start children's centers, the British government has an ambitious ongoing program intended to transform all schools into extended schools by the year 2010. Fifty percent of parents of children under the age of eleven should have been able to access baseline services, including school-age child care, by the year 2008.

It is not yet possible to describe a typical extended school in the United Kingdom because they are still thinly spread around the country, and, since they are resourced to meet local needs, each is different. The baseline is similar to what is already taken for granted in Nordic countries: all schools must guarantee affordable child care for children from five to eleven years old from 8 a.m. to 6 p.m., five days per week and forty-eight weeks of the year. Schools can offer the service themselves or arrange it in a neighboring school or at another site (including a childminder/family caregiver's home), provided they guarantee safe transport for the children.

"Full-service" extended schools (of which there are currently around 250) offer a wide, though flexible, range of additional ser-

An extended school in a deprived English community

The school "meets each challenge as it arises": "As many as 40 local families a year are struck off doctors' lists due to aggressive behaviour linked to poor communication skills. The school highlighted the issues in a drama produced on site and involving parents and much discussion. It was decided to locate a General Practitioner surgery within the school itself. The Health trust providing the surgery owns the space and pays for a proportion of the school's heat and lighting. Parents make appointments as they drop children off.

"The school led a bid for Sure Start funding, putting the cash into a limited company and setting up a daycare facility for children from the age of three months. The nursery is now a Children's Centre and runs the school's wrap-around care until 6 p.m. It also hosts sessions for the parents run by Job and Benefits advisors.

"The school also has a community learning centre which runs a number of Homework clubs open till 6 p.m., run by three members of staff at the school, two local neighbourhood centres and the local library. The clubs are open to local children irrespective of which school they attend.

"The school also provides two after-school and holiday clubs for children under seven and between seven and eleven, open all year. Finally, there's a breakfast club from 8:15 a.m. each day."

vices to their communities. Any service, from health to adult education, can be added and paid for out of government start-up funds, provided it offers direct benefit to the children, families, staff, and local community. There is some priority for services to counteract social and health problems that get in the way of children's school achievement. Services such as child care may be provided on school premises or the school may contract with existing local providers. Schools can and indeed must charge for services (child care in an extended school costs the same as it would elsewhere, and parents are entitled to the same range of financial assistance), but sustainable funding once government start-up money has been used up is the subject of much debate.

TOWARD EXTENDED SCHOOLS IN NORTH AMERICA

North America has neither federal nor state programs for transforming all its schools into extended schools, although there are many examples of similar work at the district or individual experimental level, such as the New Jersey school-based youth services program and the New York City Beacons. It seems clear that if rapid progress toward integrated children's centers is to be made in North America, it will start in schools, increasing their reach into early years and community services rather than the other way around, as is the case in the United Kingdom.

There is considerable pressure to extend the traditional role of schools in the United States, but most of it arises less from a desire to make better use of schools' resources or to provide resource hubs for communities than out of concern for issues that arise from what the literature has termed "Home-Alone America." "Latchkey children" (defined by the Census Bureau as those aged five to fourteen who "care for self" outside school hours) are seen as a growing and increasingly serious problem. They numbered 4.5 million at the time of the 1994 census, and the best available estimates put their current numbers somewhere between 5 million and 10 million. Most of the argument and exhortation seems to be aimed at reversing the trend toward regarding children as self-motivated and self-sufficient and repopulating "parent-free" homes. It seems likely, though, that extended or community schools will gradually be recognized as an easier-to-achieve solution.

KidZinc, the School Age Care Society of Alberta, is leading a campaign to encourage the Canadian government to value after-school care equally with preschool care. KidZinc runs playrooms in local schools from 7 a.m. to 6 p.m. for children up to sixth grade at a cost of around $275 per month and summer vacation care for $600 per month (plus transportation costs). Many parents receive subsidies for these costs, depending on income, and fees for such care can be used toward the child care expense deduction, which can cover up to $7,000 of costs, depending on parental income. KidZinc urges parents to sign a letter it has written, asking the government to provide higher wages for after-school care workers so that there will be better retention of staff. It may be a long time before such letters ask government to pay after-school workers the same salaries as they pay teachers, but it is a start.

Part Three

QUALITY OF CARE

Introduction: Quality of Care from Various Viewpoints

Everybody who is involved with child care wants to know how good or bad it is. If governments and policy makers are going to promote and fund any child care, they want it to be good care. Practitioners want to be part of settings that do good work and to improve those that do not. Parents want the best possible care for their children, and children want that, too. But although everyone who wants any child care wants it to be of high quality, there's no one simple set of measurements that will do for them all. Different people measure child care quality differently, largely depending on their reasons for seeking the information—what they want it for and the use they plan to make of it.

13. Quality of Care from Research Viewpoints

IDENTIFYING HIGH-QUALITY CHILD CARE

The accepted scientific way of judging the quality of child care is in terms of its results: the outcomes for children, how things turned out for them in the medium or long term. Researchers all over the world have repeatedly shown that children who have good-quality caregiving tend to show better cognitive development (measured perhaps by a "baby IQ"), more advanced speech and understanding of language, and more advanced social skills than children in mediocre care, and that the reverse is true for children in poor-quality care, especially among children who are underprivileged in other ways.

So what does the high-quality care that produces these desirable outcomes consist of? It might be thought that if the results of good care are so generally recognized, its features would be obvious. Unfortunately, this is not the case. It's relatively easy to describe the features of quality care, but defining and operationalizing them so that they can be measured, and then identifying their presence or absence in particular settings or circumstances, is even more complex than assessing the results.

"There is an extraordinary international consensus among child care researchers and practitioners about what quality child care is: it is warm, supportive interactions with adults in a safe, healthy and stimulating environment, where early education and trusting relationships combine to support individual children's physical, emotional, social and intellectual development." Sandra Scarr, NICHD researcher

MEASURING CHILD CARE QUALITY

While only those concerned with designing and conducting child care research need to understand exactly how it is done, anybody who wants to evaluate reports of such research should be aware of some of the research issues.

There are two different but interlinked aspects of child care that contribute to its quality. Rather dauntingly, they are termed "process" and "structure." "Process" refers to the nature of children's experience in child care: their interactions with adults and with other children, their learning experiences, the richness and variety of stimulation that is available to them, and the responsiveness of the setting to them. Structural aspects of the care environment are those that are relatively fixed and often open to regulation: buildings and classrooms, group sizes, adult-child ratios, health and safety measurcs, training of staff, and management structure.

Researchers use different methods and measures of child care quality depending on the purpose of the study—and the resources available to it. One of the most difficult choices to be made in designing such research is between collecting information about structure (which may be done from administrative records or interviews with managers) and observing what goes on—process—in child care settings, or striking a balance between the two. Information that is collected by observation is undoubtedly more accurate and more informative, but collecting it is also much more expensive and time-consuming. Unfortunately, although structural features of a day care setting certainly have a bearing on the process within it, they cannot be relied upon to predict it. This was very clearly demonstrated by a study of 120 American centers in which the interaction of structure and process was studied. Out of six structural (and regulatable) characteristics, only one—the highest wage paid—was significantly correlated with observed process quality, higher wages being significantly likely to go with higher-quality care. And even that correlation did not fully explain the difference between one center and another so that wage rates could be used on their own as a surrogate measure of quality. Even the ratio of adults to children—a structural (and regulatable) variable known to be extremely important to children's experiences of care—cannot be used as a measure of quality without also using observations. A large study in the United States did indeed find that process quality rose as the adult-child ratio increased. But these were not official ratios reported by administrators but observed ratios, noted every fifteen minutes over several hours of observation in each child care setting. Official ratios cannot be relied upon to predict process quality because they may not be routinely met in practice. And just as there may be a difference between administrative descriptions and actual caregiver behavior, so there may be differences between what caregivers themselves say they do and what they actually do.

In a study of the "climate"—the atmosphere and relationship between children and adults—in Swedish day care centers, observers identified three different "group climates." The first (termed "future focused") was highly cooperative and facilitative with the children; the second ("present-focused") was more authoritarian and controlling, and the third was mixed. The staff were then given a questionnaire from which their attitudes toward their work were defined as "relaxed," "strained," or "mixed." When the two sources of information were put together, caregivers' responses to the questionnaire were found to bear no relation whatsoever to their observed behavior. Any attempt to pick out the most relaxed groups, for example, on the basis of what the staff had said, would have been highly misleading.

Of course, relationships between structural qualities of child care and its effects on children's outcomes can be identified, but studies show that when structural features contribute to good outcomes, they usually do so indirectly by producing positive changes in some aspect of process quality. For example, if excellent architecture and equipment in a center is shown to be related to excellent child outcomes, it will probably be because that well-designed and enjoyable environment encourages enthusiasm among the staff and may contribute to keeping sickness absence low and staff stability high. Structural features seem to provide (or prevent) the necessary conditions for process quality, such as positive staff-child interaction. As such, they facilitate but do not guarantee high-quality experiences for the child.

The example in the following box, taken from the largest U.S. study to focus on child care staff, illustrates some interconnec-

---

Some interconnections between child care structure and process

- When staff have had more formal education, more early childhood training at college level, and earn higher wages and benefits, they tend to provide more "appropriate and sensitive caregiving."

- When children attend centers with stable staffing (i.e., with lower staff turnover), they are more competent in social and language development.

- Higher-quality centers pay staff higher wages, provide a better adult work environment, and have a more highly educated and trained staff with lower turnover.

---

tions between structural and easily regulated variables concerning staff characteristics, and process effects concerning adult-child relationships.

Most studies of child care quality attempt to measure something of every aspect of child care settings—the environment; the materials and ways they are used; the staff, their backgrounds, training, and the manner in which they behave; and the children and their backgrounds and behaviors. However, more specialized research techniques are especially suited to investigating particular questions. Academic and research-oriented methods, principally from the United States, are used primarily to test ideas about the relevance of different aspects of care quality for various child outcomes. The measures themselves are complex and detailed, but when the findings are put into statistical models, results from these measures are often simplified, sometimes being reduced to single scores. These may be adequate for demonstrating a relationship between, say, high-, medium-, and low-quality child care and children's scores on a vocabulary test, but they are not very useful for explaining such relationships. When the quality of child care is being measured for the purposes of regulation and licensing, or to help improve child care programs or training, different methods may be needed instead or as well. When estimates of quality are needed for national statistics, or day care inspections and registration are legal requirements, they usually highlight structural aspects, as these are easier to observe and to control, and the resulting global estimates of the quality of care provided in each setting may be adequate for that purpose. However, if the focus of investigation is on explanations—why some children progress more than others over time, for example—process variables, especially interactions between staff and children, such as the provision of appropriate learning opportunities and caregivers' responsiveness to children, may be more important, and measures that focus on the behavior and quality of individual caregivers and therefore on individual children's unique experiences will be needed. It cannot be assumed that a nursery of generally good quality is necessarily giving a particular child good-quality care: he may be profoundly influenced by spending time with one or two insensitive caregivers, whose shortcomings would be lost within an overall rating. Measures focusing on individual caregivers may be particularly useful in planning or evaluating staff training.

QUALITY OF CAREGIVERS

Children's relationships with the people who take care of them are an important—probably the most important—aspect of the overall quality of child care. Research studies have identified a range of caregiver qualities that make good relationships with young children more likely, including sensitivity, empathy, and attunement. Being cared for by adults whose work is informed by these qualities and attitudes can help babies and young children to feel confident in themselves and encourage them to communicate and talk, think and have ideas, discover and learn.

It is not enough for a caregiver simply to have these qualities, however. Children cannot benefit from her unless she is with them. A caregiver who not only has these characteristics but also is readily and consistently available to individual children has recently been shown to be a key feature of high-quality care. Warm personal relationships between care providers and children are featured in the United Kingdom's Key Elements of Effective Practice and are part of the ten key principles that made up the influential guidance package in Britain called *Birth to Three Matters*. These findings also link closely with the concept of the key person in group child care (see pp. 163–64), a way of working that became compulsory in the United Kingdom in 2008.

Caregiver availability, including the amount of time a particular caregiver spends with particular children, is often described as part of a wider variable called "caregiver stability." This also includes the number of changes of primary caregiver (or key person) and the number of different child care arrangements or settings children experience, as well as the overall rate of staff turnover. Children who experience greater caregiver stability have more secure relationships with their caregivers and show higher degrees of social competence.

Caregiver stability partly depends on, and can certainly be facilitated by, structural aspects of child care that affect quality and can and perhaps should be regulated. Adult-child ratios, group sizes, children's age at entry and number of hours spent in the facility, and caregivers' qualifications have all been found to be predictive of sensitive, positive caregiving and of children's early socioemotional development. Along with lower staff turnover rates, these are associated with children's increased social competence and adjustment and positive caregiver-child relationships. A comparison between the quality of different types of child care in the FCCC study, as measured by research observers rather than by outcomes for children, showed an unambiguous relationship between the number of toddlers each caregiver was responsible for and the quality of the care given: the more charges, the lower the quality of care the children received. In the NICHD study, children's outcomes were predicted more powerfully by the quantity of child care children experienced than by its quality. More time in nonmaternal care across the first four and a half years of life predicted more problem behavior, particularly antisocial and aggressive behavior at four to five years of age. These effects were moderated by high-quality child care and by maternal sensitivity, but quantity of child care had a clear independent effect, and quality of care had no separate main effect. In a major Australian study, however, the advantages of high-quality care counterbalanced the disadvantages of high quantity, and in an American study of Early Head Start, children who spent more time in high-quality child care did better than children who spent less time, perhaps because these children were from underprivileged families.

VALUES, ETHOS, AND CULTURE

As if the relationships between structure and process in child care were not complicated enough, there is yet another powerful set of influences on quality that underlie both: the values, ethos, and culture of child care and early years settings, which strongly influence children's personal, social, and emotional development. Settings that are inclusive of all children, whatever their disabilities or special needs, and value systems that embrace all children, irrespective of ethnic background or creed, and are equally committed to the well-being of all, have been highlighted as particularly likely to provide high-quality care. Inclusiveness may be important not only because it reflects a socially desirable and child-friendly ethos but also because the quality of any child care group partly depends on the characteristics of the children who attend it; any form of selection (or "targeting") will restrict their range and balance. In postwar Britain, for example, when the only children admitted to publicly financed nurseries were those who were considered to be "at risk," the resulting clustering of vulnerable children led to high levels of aggression and behavior problems. It is likely that in such circumstances children learn problematic behavior patterns from playing together and watching one another. Young children who attend selective centers or preschools may learn "desirable" behaviors by similar mechanisms, but at a cost to the pool of children from which they are drawn and to their own social and emotional development.

Leadership and management have important impacts on the values, ethos, and culture of child care settings, through the ways in which relevant national and professional standards are interpreted and implemented and the extent to which a whole-setting approach is taken toward personal social and emotional development. An outstanding result of the initial evaluation of Britain's Social and Emotional Aspects of Learning (SEAL) materials was that these worked well where, and only where, there was a cocoordinated and coherent whole-school approach.

Current studies of child care quality do not tell us everything we need to know about early years care and education. Child care quality certainly matters, but it is by no means the dominant influence on children's development; the quality of home care and relationships with parents matters far more. And although outcome studies are essential to "evidence-based" research, developmental outcomes of child care are not the only possible criteria of its quality. There is growing interest in studying child care quality in relation to children's current experiences of it and their immediate well-being. In the United Kingdom, for example, there is a new interest in developing a theoretical framework (and consequent methods of assessing quality) that can be directly incorporated into good practice, inform day care providers, and establish ways to improve services. This conceptualization incorporates a "children's rights" approach, suggesting that young children have a right to the best-quality child care that can be provided irrespective of whether there are measurable differences in long-term outcomes. Such an approach is seen as working both ways: a child care setting in which children are not fully engaged and happy is not good child care, however excellent the outcomes for children in terms of their "readiness for school" may be when they leave. But a child care setting in which children are cheerfully engrossed is good child care no matter how the children's cognitive test scores compare with others when they emerge from it.

The best-known theoretical framework for child care and early years education is probably that which has come to be known as the Reggio approach. The small Italian town of Reggio Emilia is the hub of a network of world-renowned centers for children from birth to six years, based on the philosophy and the actual pedagogical guidance of the late Loris Malaguzzi. The Reggio approach is about children's rights and children's potential, as one of its many visitors, Martin Pace of Dolphin Nurseries, describes:

> Reggio practitioners are united in their view of the child as a competent human being and as a new source of hope. In Reggio preschool educationalists start with a bigger question than most. They ask, "What is this life all about?" and they see children as joint investigators in the process of inventing new answers. . . . Imagine an educational approach where children are the main protagonists in their own growth and where meanings are created not supplied.

Developing a theoretical framework is one important element in raising the quality of child care; improving the qualifications (and motivation) of the workforce is the other. In the United Kingdom, the government's recent Ten Year Strategy for Childcare accepts that "key explanatory factors" for better-quality child care are "staff with higher qualifications . . . trained teachers working alongside less qualified staff . . . [and] staff with a good understanding of child development and learning."

Surprisingly, despite these sentiments, the U.K. government has not committed to a workforce qualification target beyond undertaking to have at least one graduate worker in each child care setting and two such workers in child care settings in areas of special need. Clearly, the impact each highly qualified individual could have depends upon the size of the facility: one person might raise the overall quality of care given by six caregivers but would be unlikely to make a very great difference in a large children's center employing thirty. In contrast, New Zealand's child care workforce will be entirely made up of trained teachers by 2012, while most northern European countries already have a relatively highly skilled and trained early years workforce.

In Sweden, 60 percent of the workforce is already educated to the university-degree level, and most of the rest are in training, while Danish pedagogues must train for three years. Such workforces offer dramatically higher-quality child care than is generally available in the United Kingdom or the United States, but this is the fruit of

---

Skilling-up the workforce in New Zealand

Child care in New Zealand is undergoing a period of sustained change. Previously fragmented early years services are being brought together by a single Early Childhood Education agency, organized under a coherent framework of early learning, funded to enable access for all, and regulated to ensure standards of care are high. An important part of this is raising the standard of the workforce. An ambitious target has been set to have the entire workforce staffed by trained teachers by 2012.

The government in New Zealand has recognized that this is an expensive ambition, in terms of the cost of training existing staff and of temporary replacements. To ensure that staff are able to improve their skills, the government provides grants to meet some of these costs.

almost half a century of development. With their experience to serve as a model, however, improvement need not take so long. There is evidence that with concerted state interest and involvement, major changes in child care can be made relatively quickly. The Smart Start program in North Carolina has set up "Local Partnerships" to deliver child care and has made a large investment in it. The results have included a dramatic increase in the number of college-educated child care workers from less than 20 percent to more than 80 percent in a decade, and a concomitant increase in the number of children whose child care is classified as high-quality from 20 percent to 70 percent.

INTERPRETING RESEARCH FINDINGS

Comparing the results of one study with another and deciding how far research findings can be generalized from one group, place, or country to another is fraught with difficulties. Standards, settings, and staffing vary from country to country, state to state, and community to community, so even a study as large and groundbreaking as the NICHD study of early child care in the United States cannot

---

Smart Start: Raising the Status of Child Care

In 1992, child care advocates told North Carolina's general assembly that virtually anyone was allowed to take care of children in their state. In just over a decade, Smart Start grants have dramatically increased the skills of child care workers and the quality of child care itself.

Local partnerships between business and nonprofit organizations work to improve existing facilities, make child care more accessible to low-income families, and provide access to health and family support. The North Carolina Partnership for Children (NCPC) board of directors includes representatives from local social services—health, mental health, and child care services. Local businesses, faith communities, and parents are also represented.

More than 55,000 extra child care places have been created in North Carolina since 1993, benefiting 160,000 families. Children from "Local Partnership" care had higher school-readiness skills and fewer behavioral problems than children in other forms of care. These differences were still apparent at age eight.

necessarily be applied elsewhere. We have seen, for example, that in many European countries, early years care is a popular course of study at university, while in the United States many workers take jobs in child care out of necessity rather than choice and have neither qualifications nor ambitions.

Given the importance of the ethos and values of child care, consideration always needs to be given to the values inherent in a study of it. Ethnocentricity is always a possibility, especially if research findings are likely to contribute to value judgments about care characteristics. With the bulk of child care research having come out of the United States, many European and Australian investigators (and some Americans, too) see the need to develop measures that reflect a cross-cultural orientation to child care and do not necessarily reflect North American practices or ideals.

However, child care networks are, by definition, so deeply embedded in the socioeconomic and political value systems of their country or culture that it is often difficult for colleagues from different backgrounds to understand one another's viewpoints. The approach to child care of researchers from the Nordic countries Sweden, Denmark, Norway, Finland, and Iceland, for example, is quite different, even opposite in some respects, to that which is taken for granted in North America or Australia. For example, whereas American child care training seeks to minimize the differences between children's experiences at home and in child care, the Nordic conceptualization, known as "dual socialization," states that radical differences between the two reflect reality. Scandinavian children no longer grow up and live only or even mainly among people who share their experiences and backgrounds, nor in one consistent environment, but constantly shift between different "social arenas," one public and one private. One Danish researcher stated in 1994: "[In child care research] the crucial interaction between the family and day care is grossly overlooked. What is needed instead is a broad holistic approach to the understanding of children growing up in family and day care. . . . Instead of regarding day care as a substitute for home care, as held by traditional beliefs, with the mind set on whether this substitution in general harms children, day care can be seen as one of a number of possible care settings that contribute to children's total experience."

Dual socialization

"The Nordic countries, notwithstanding some variations between them, have all realized a Scandinavian welfare state model. This comprises public child care services provided to a large proportion of the young children in these states. To a large extent both the mothers and the fathers of young children in the Nordic countries are gainfully employed outside the home, as well as involved in the daily care of their child, and the child spends part of its everyday life in a public day-care institution as a member of a group of children of more or less the same age, supervised by professional child minders.

"Part of modern childhood thus is that from early childhood on children regularly commute between at least two different social settings, viz. the family and the day-care institution. These settings combine to form modern childhood, that thus is constituted by the interaction between two fundamentally different worlds. This interaction between the different worlds of childhood we label the process dual socialization."

D. Sommer and O. Langsted, "Modern Childhood:
Crises and Disintegration, or a New Quality of Life"

Even the very hallmarks of high-quality care or high-quality staff cannot be assumed to be the same everywhere. In North America and in the United Kingdom, for example, poor center care is largely ascribed to the youth, inexperience, poor education, and lack of qualifications of many caregivers and to the related facts that pay and job satisfaction are both low and staff turnover is high. Yet in a study conducted in Haifa, Israeli day care centers were found to be of very low quality, although the mean age of the caregivers was forty-three, they had an average of eleven years of experience, and their pay and job satisfaction were high. The reason was that at that time and in that society those "stable" caregiver characteristics were not desirable and good for children as they would have been in the English-speaking world. In fact, they were the opposite, describing women who were of such low socioeconomic status in Israeli society that they had very limited alternative employment opportunities. As the study's author put it, "a high stability of unskilled caregivers within an unfavourite and hectic ecological context of routine day care activities may even perpetuate the low quality consequences."

14. Quality of Care from Parents' Viewpoints

Parents' ideas about what makes for high-quality child care are often very similar to those of researchers, but their judgments of the quality of any child care arrangement or setting they actually use are often very different. The parent is telling it as she or he sees it, while the researcher is trying to make an objective assessment. So while a researcher may conclude, "This is a high-quality child care center; it just happens not to be doing well for child X," the mother of child X will start from her own child's experience: "This is not a good center. My son hates it, and I'm going to have to move him. I don't know why it's been rated so highly." Parents' judgments are value judgments; the judgment made by the parent of another child, by a child care inspector, a teacher, or (if we ever asked children) by a child might each be very different.

Parents judge child care settings from their own points of view as well as their children's. Many of the practical reasons for choosing one setting or caregiver rather than another are also reasons for appreciating it—or not. Does the child care fill the parents' needs for flexibility of days, hours, and pickup times? Is it comfortably affordable, or does it, at least, provide what feels like good value for the money? Does it actually deliver what its brochure promised, or are there unexpected and unwelcome differences in organization or everyday staffing? Has the child care lived up to any verbal assurances that were given on an early visit, perhaps about the children's access to outside space, the frequency of outings, or the provision of healthy food? Negative answers to such questions are likely to reduce the parents' perception of the quality of the care.

As we have seen, parents' judgments may also be affected by the extent to which the child care matches their own culturally based beliefs about early child rearing. The extent to which parents from diverse cultural backgrounds use formal child care services may depend in part on the availability of child care that reflects their values.

Reasons for parents' level of satisfaction with child care and why they consider it high-quality have not been studied as extensively as their reasons for choosing one type of care or one particular caregiver. Most early child care research assumed that parents would be satisfied if their child care was "affordable" (in somebody's judgment) and reasonably reliable. That was clearly an oversimplistic view, but even today we do not know as much as we should, partly because high demand for scarce child care in many countries makes it difficult for parents who have obtained places to be openly critical of them or to vote with their feet by moving children out of care they regard as poor. At the same time, high fees and waiting lists mean that some private providers see no particular advantage in canvassing parents' opinions. Almost half a century ago, however, a study was designed specifically to ascertain the characteristics and attitudes mothers of preschool children wanted in what were then referred to as "mother substitutes." The results of this study became the basis for the Parent Satisfaction with Child Care Scale, versions of which have been used in most subsequent major studies of satisfaction with child care.

Despite these useful research tools, parental satisfaction is still not always easy to establish or to understand. According to some American research, once a child is enrolled in a facility, parents are predisposed to be enthusiastic about the child's care and caregivers, often rating a particular child care home or center more highly than independent observers do. In the United Kingdom, parents sometimes support child care settings that professionals judge inadequate. Some inspectors have found that on the rare occasions when a child care facility has failed its inspection and is to be closed down, parents protest and circulate petitions to keep it open. There are several possible reasons for such protests. Often, of course, parents are provoked by the prospect of the disruption to their work schedules, and perhaps to their income, that losing a child care place will cause. Sometimes there may be a genuine difference of opinion between the parents and the inspectors regarding the quality of care that is being offered. And recent research also suggests that mothers' judgments sometimes reflect their own relationship with the caregiver rather than the caregiver's relationship with her children, so parental satisfaction is likely to be especially high when parental involvement is encouraged and the care provider is friendly. However, alongside such reasons there also can be an element of wishful thinking in parents' favorable assessments. Once they have committed their child to a child care setting, many parents find it difficult—even painful—to be critical of it, because that would mean admitting to themselves that every day they are leaving their child in a place they know is not good.

> Yes I do think it's good actually. Maybe not perfect, but . . . Yes I do. Well I'd have to really, wouldn't I? Paying all that money and leaving my baby there. If I thought it was *bad* I'd have to leave.
>
> —FCCC mother

Parents' Views of Child Care in Theory and in Practice

Whatever specific reasons parents may have for thinking highly of the child care they use "in practice," the degree to which it is consistent with the kind of child care they wanted or approved of "in principle" is not likely to be one of them, any more than it is likely to have affected their choice of that child care in the first place.

Characteristics of satisfactory child care often mentioned by parents

- The care setting's convenience, dependability, reasonable price, nutritious food
- Competence of staff, appropriate discipline, ability to teach children new things
- Care that provides children with love and understanding
- Care that provides parents with worry-free substitute child care
- Care that is viewed positively by the child
- Care that is viewed positively by husband/partner

Indeed, interpreting research findings concerning both parents' choices and their opinions of child care is complicated by the fact that they don't always say what they mean. The characteristics of child care that parents endorse as important to them from a research worker's list (such as those given in the box on p. 203) are often completely different from the features they describe as important in their child's actual care situation. In one very large sample of American parents, for example, almost every one (99 percent) selected health and safety as the most important from a list of features of child care. However, when those parents described what was important to them about the real-life care facilities their children were in, fewer than 9 percent mentioned health and safety.

If what parents actually want is not the same as what they say they want, it is difficult for policy makers to have meaningful public or parental consultations on child care. A recent U.S. study found that the opinions of low-income African American parents about what made for high-quality child care were very similar to those of child care professionals. Both groups stressed the importance of caregivers' qualifications, experience, training, and warm, stimulating behavior with the children, and the parents said that they would be willing to pay premium rates for such characteristics. However, these parents did not translate their own guidelines into practice when choosing a place for their child. Many of their children were in low-quality child care with too few and ill-trained staff. Of course, parents who need child care do not have free choice: care that meets theoretical criteria of high quality may not be available or affordable in real life. But the parents in this study who had expressed such high ideals were not dissatisfied with care that fell far short of them. It seems that parents' ideas about "ideal" or high-quality child care sometimes get lost in a gap between abstract thinking and practical arrangements.

Ideas about desirable child care may get lost in time, too. Parents often tell researchers that they would prefer a different type of child care to the one they are actually using. In two large-scale American studies of mothers using a range of care types, roughly one-quarter were not using the type they said they most preferred. In a study of parents who had chosen family day care settings, 62 percent said they would have preferred a different care type, 39 percent would have preferred nursery or school care, and 19 percent would have preferred to care for the child themselves. But many of these opinions are based on hindsight. Parents who put a child in, say, family day care a year ago now feel that a nursery would have been better. But would they have opted for nursery rather than family day care at the time? "Retrospective studies" cannot give us an answer. In fact, research that asks parents today to describe what they did yesterday and why they did it cannot tell us anything certain about the present or future relationship between parents' attitudes, beliefs, and behaviors.

While one mother may choose a particular child care for her child partly because it is the type that she has always believed to be the best, circumstances may lead another mother to select child care that is different, even opposite to any she had previously considered. That mother is then likely to revise her earlier beliefs in order to resolve an uncomfortable conflict. One such mother interviewed during the FCCC study put it this way: "I always wanted professional care so we chose a nursery way back when and hoped he'd start there when I went back to work, but now I think we're quite glad the place isn't coming up until much later. It feels much better while he's so little, that he's at home with my mum."

"Ideal Care" in Relation to Satisfaction with Actual Care: Follow-up in the FCCC Study

The FCCC study, being prospective rather than retrospective, allowed for some exploration of these issues. The child care of more than one thousand English mothers was studied from the time their children were three months old until they started school. When the babies were three months old, the mothers were asked what they would consider the ideal child care for the future. At that time, the mothers were on maternity leave and had no immediate need for child care nor any practical experience of it for the current baby. As described earlier, when the babies were close to a year old, fewer than half of these mothers were using a type of child care that matched their ideal; furthermore, the mothers who were using the type they had thought would be best were no more likely to be highly satisfied with it than mothers whose actual child care bore no relation to those ideals.

Qualities of caregivers valued by mothers in the FCCC study

The personal characteristics of caregivers, and their "warm" and "responsive" relationships with the children they care for that are such an important part of child care quality from the research viewpoint, were of great importance to FCCC mothers, as they had been to earlier American mothers. When caregivers were more detached from the children, as observed and reported by the researchers, mothers were less satisfied with their child care. When these mothers were asked to rank qualities of child care in order of their desirability, the quality most frequently included among the top three was providing a "loving and caring environment" (77 percent), ahead even of "providing a safe environment" (68 percent) and "providing worry-free child care" (41 percent).

Many mothers also emphasized the importance of trust; indeed, as we have seen, the issue of trust overrode all others for many mothers: "I think trust was the big thing. There was no question whether I trust them [grandparents] or not. I do."

Trust was not simply a matter of being certain the caregiver would consistently take good care of the child or that she would do so in accordance with the parents' culture and beliefs but also that she would act according to their wishes in small matters as well as in large ones.

> I did say he could have banana, but I said "mashed" and she decided to give it to him in little bits to eat in his fingers. That wasn't for her to decide. It's up to me when my child first has, like, finger foods. I need to be able to trust her to do as I say.   —FCCC mother

Even outside the specific issue of trust, the kind of adult relationship mothers themselves had with the caregiver was important to many of them. Indeed, a variable labeled "ease of communication with the caregiver" emerged as a key to the FCCC mothers' overall satisfaction with their child care. Interestingly, there was no relationship between the quality of care observed by the researchers and mothers' confidence in communicating with the caregiver. Concerns about their children feeling comfortable with the caregiver were separate from their own need to feel comfortable with her. In detailed discussions with some of these mothers, it became clear that a sense of adult acceptance and shared values, perhaps potential friendship, with anyone who cared for their child made an important contribution to some mothers' satisfaction with the child care as a whole.

FCCC mothers' satisfaction with different types of care

These mothers had babies less than a year old who were in nonmaternal care for at least twelve hours and an average of thirty hours per week. Overall, the mothers who were most satisfied were the few whose babies were being cared for by the father (or mother's partner). The mothers who were least satisfied were those using nurseries or centers. Between those extremes, levels of satisfaction were similar for mothers using childminders (family day care), grandparents, and nannies. An earlier study using a single-item measure of child care satisfaction found similarly that American parents using care at home by a relative or nanny were significantly more satisfied than those using either center or family day care.

The features of child care settings that were most frequently mentioned as important may help to explain those differences in satisfaction. The principal area of concern was the ratio of adults to children and the total number of children in the group. Care by father or by a grandparent or nanny at home would obviously come close to a ratio of one to one, with family day care providing a higher adult-child ratio and a smaller group size than center care. Equally, since their own relationship with the caregiver was so important to these mothers, the fact that they were likely to have less in common with young, usually childless nursery/center staff and to have less regular opportunity to chat with them may have predisposed some to be more enthusiastic about other types of care.

Mothers' main reason for concern over staff-child ratios, however, was the amount of adult attention their children were getting. It was not entirely a case of "the more the better," as is suggested in many research assessments. FCCC mothers tended to feel strongly about whether the most desirable care setting was a nursery group, a domestic-scale group as in childminding, or even one-on-one care with a relative or nanny. Different mothers felt equally strongly in favor of each type of arrangement, and among those who felt very strongly that only a group could offer high-quality care were some mothers who specifically did not want their babies to have a lot of attention from an individual caregiver who might "share," encroach on, or even dilute their own relationship with the baby:

> If she is going to get one-to-one attention, I want it to be from myself or Matthew, rather than a childminder.

Other mothers who preferred group care felt unable to trust an individual who worked alone and was not a relative:

> How do you know what goes on once the door closes?

However, most of those who had chosen group care talked about wanting a child care setting that provided learning and social experiences:

> I liked the environment. They've got nice equipment and it seems caring and busy.

They not only felt that a group could provide those experiences but also that lack of stimulation (perhaps with too much television viewing) would have been very likely if the child was with an individual caregiver:

> Being in someone else's home—or even your own—you just don't know what goes on or whether the TV is on all day. I wanted her in a nursery where I could be sure she'd be with other children and get lots of stimulation.

A very similar proportion of these mothers of almost-one-year-olds felt equally strongly against group child care. They felt that what mattered most was that their baby's caregiver should take a mothering or nurturing role, and most felt that this was more likely in childminding or at-home care than in a nursery:

> For the very early years I still wanted that one-to-one that a childminder could give as opposed to a nursery. A continuity of person. If I wasn't there I just wanted someone who could be, not Mum, but defi-

nitely the one person to go to . . . the person they knew would be there.

Most of these judgments were clearly related to the child's age. Like mothers in earlier studies on both sides of the Atlantic, some mothers felt that domestic-scale "homelike" care by an individual was appropriate while the child was very young but that group care in a nursery might become the best choice later on.

Work-home balance among the FCCC mothers

For a lot of women who are the mothers of babies or young toddlers, better child care is less nonmaternal child care. Although almost all the FCCC mothers expressed themselves contemporaneously as satisfied with the choices they had made, more than half of this group of mothers were ambivalent or anxious about their overall situation and lifestyle.

There was remarkable consistency in the general tenor of what

---

FCCC mothers of babies in child care aged six to eight months talking about their work-home balance

"There are pros and cons. . . . I think originally we just thought that we would have a child and I would go back to work full-time and we would just almost carry on as we were . . . and financially we'd be better off. I don't think we appreciated how tiring it would be and I don't think I appreciated how much I would feel I would miss out if I did as well."

"I've always enjoyed teaching and being in the classroom, so I didn't expect to feel that I could spend all day at home. I didn't think I was the sort of person that could do that. But since Mark was 4 months old I realized that yes, I could. And that's surprised me."

"I thought I'd sort of do a few months and see how I coped but now I've done three months of it, I think, I sort of know the [child care] hours are too long and I'm looking to review the whole situation for the rest of the year."

"In an ideal world I would take another 6 months off . . . well I'd love to take a couple of years off [laughs] but I can't. Nobody is forcing me; it was just the pressure and the investment in my career that was forcing me to go back really. I really would rather not have gone back to work."

these women said. Those who felt their work-home balance was not ideal felt that correcting it would mean fewer hours at work and more hours at home with the baby. Some of the mothers who were working full-time said that they would have preferred not to; several mothers who were working three days a week said that they wished they could work two days instead. None said that they would prefer to work more. This group of women had very positive attitudes toward paid work in general and their own jobs and workplaces in particular, so what was being expressed was not "antiemployment" or "pro stay-at-home mothering" but real ambivalence.

VIEWS ON WORK-HOME BALANCE AND CHILD CARE QUALITY EXPRESSED IN OTHER STUDIES

FCCC findings concerning mothers' feelings about their work-home balance are more detailed than most but are not unique to England or to mothers with infants. They are echoed in other studies on both sides of the Atlantic. A major pre-election poll of all provinces in Canada in 2006, for example, found that more than 80 percent of Canadians thought the most satisfactory type of child care was having a parent at home, and if that was not an option, care by a relative was the second best. Those opinions were consistent with responses to monetary questions: asked whether the option of up to a three-year paid parental leave would be satisfactory for Canada, 70 percent said it would; asked how they would like the government to spend $5 billion per year on the care of children, most suggested a tax deduction for all parents, regardless of household income, rural or urban position, or parents' age. The polling firm concluded that most Canadians do not support a national child care system and that both those with and those without children would prefer direct support to parents so that they can freely choose their own balance between work and home.

Importance of mothers' own relationships with care providers

"Ease of communication with the caregiver" makes an important contribution to mothers' satisfaction with child care, according to major studies in the United States and in Australia as well as in the United Kingdom. Furthermore, the American NICHD study showed that when mothers and caregivers acted in a freely communicating partnership in the care of three-year-olds, the quality of the children's interaction with each of them was improved; so was the care children actually received and their mothers' perception of it.

Communication and trust

The Australian Institute of Family Studies' report *Child Care in Cultural Context* showed how important communication with the caregiver was to the overall satisfaction of Australian parents and especially to those for whom English was not the first language. This study, which included mothers and children from Somali and Vietnamese as well as Anglo-Australian backgrounds, also emphasizes the importance to some parents of child care that reflects not only the culture and values of the parent—including caregivers' ability to talk to mothers in their first language and to serve children with food familiar to them from home—but also shared attitudes toward aspects of child rearing, such as whether "obedience" and associated good manners and compliance are more or less valued than "independence" and associated personal responsibility and curiosity. A paper aptly called "Who Says What Is Quality?" describes the efforts made to establish consensus between parents and caregivers in order to build a meaningful accreditation scheme for American family child care.

Parents' preferences for group or domestic-scale child care

In the United States and in much of continental Europe, as we have seen, high-quality child care is assumed to be group care in nurseries or child care centers. Family day care is often regarded as second best, while nonmaternal care by relatives is often disregarded. As a result, there are few recent studies comparing mothers' views of different types of care other than the FCCC research in England. A very different piece of research carried out in the United Kingdom, however, produced very similar findings. This was a survey of two thousand mothers of children under five carried out by Discovery Home and Health Channel. The feelings of the mothers who took part in the study echoed those of the FCCC mothers about different types of care. More than a third of mothers who were using nurseries said they were dissatisfied with the treatment their child was receiving, and a fifth said they had moved their child for this reason. The mothers who reported being most satisfied with their child care were those using nannies (5 percent), but, like some of the FCCC mothers, they worried about the nanny getting too close to the child and usurping part of their role. Care at home by the father—used by 4 percent—was the solution most said they would have preferred. Libby Rowley, presenter of the program, which commissioned the survey, said that what working mothers really wanted was "a wife" to care for their children at home while they were at work.

15. Quality of Care from Children's Viewpoints

Do children share their parents' views of what constitutes good child care? It is almost impossible to tell because, unlike their parents, the youngest children cannot be asked how satisfied they are with which aspects of child care, and even the older children who could and perhaps should be asked rarely are. It is still important to look at child care quality from children's points of view, though, not least because it helps to shift our perspective from child care as a necessity or convenience for parents, employers, and economies to child care as a service for children.

The idea of consultations with children is currently fashionable in English-speaking countries. Interactive Web sites seek young people's views; many "reality TV" programs encourage their participation; and some service providers are proud to present a child-friendly image. In the United Kingdom, an amendment to the 2006 Childcare Act, for example, made a praiseworthy gesture toward consultation with children, passing regulations requiring local councils not only to have plans for children and young people's services but also to consult with them on drawing up such plans: "In discharging their duties under this section, an English local authority must have regard to such information about the views of young children as is available to the local authority and appears to them to be relevant to the discharge of those duties."

While current attempts to ascertain or to act on children's views are welcome, most are halfhearted, and few are likely to be very effective. The duty imposed on local authorities in the United Kingdom is to pay attention to information about the views of young children "as is available." It places no duty upon them to collect such views. Arranging and carrying out consultations with children under school age is difficult, so most "children's forums" consist of older children and adolescents, whose views of issues such as child care may be very interesting but are unlikely to reflect the feelings of toddlers or preschoolers. An Australian study is a case in point. This was an honorable attempt to collect information from children, but only from older children. Furthermore, the commissioners did not talk to the young people about individual care providers or settings or about what they considered made for high-quality child care; instead, they focused on children's attitudes to their parents' work that made child care necessary. They concluded:

> Formal child care not only helps parents to compensate for the shrinking extended family and community networks but can be socially beneficial for children. However, if it is to benefit children child care needs to be of high quality. . . . [I]ts quality is an issue of concern.
>
> Children and young people tell the Commission that their families and the relationships they have with their families are the most important thing in their lives.
>
> Most children value their parents' paid work, understand it as necessary and find it beneficial to their own security, however only those from the poorest households would have preferred more money rather than more of the parents' time.

The report does make clear that children want parents to have time to take part in their activities and interests, including school sports and projects:

> Everyone is so busy trying to make money and trying to get on top of things that they have no time for their kids.   —boy, age eleven

> I'm in a single parent family with just my Mum. And she works a lot. Sometimes she just hasn't got time to talk. So you've got to find someone else. It's not her fault, she probably really wants to help but she's so busy trying to be three people in one.   —girl, age fifteen

A 2007 study from the U.K.'s Jobcentre Plus called *Working Parents Do Their Kids Proud* produced rather similar results, although the words used to report them seem more positive than the statistics: "New research from Jobcentre Plus shows kids like their parents working." In the study, 46 percent of children said they liked their mum or dad going to work (so presumably 54 percent did not); 33 percent said it made them feel proud (so 66 percent did not say this); 37 percent agreed that their working parents still made time for them (but 63 percent did not agree).

Without direct reports of children's levels of satisfaction with different types of care and caregivers, it is tempting to assume that children who have good outcomes must have had high-quality child care experiences (and therefore that children with poorer outcomes must have had worse care). It is a temptation to be resisted, though, because it means assuming that outcomes the adult world approves of are also the ones that matter to children themselves. While that is usually the case, it is not necessarily so. The English-speaking adult world tends to prioritize "educational" outcomes, often rather narrowly defined in terms of "readiness for school" and especially readiness for academic learning. We do not know what preschool children think of this, but there are disagreements among professionals and among parents about the relative importance of aspects of child care that are designed to lead to the best possible cognitive outcomes as soon as possible and those that are designed to maximize creativity or motor development or confident sociability, with cognitive performance following on. Some children, perhaps especially boys, might be better off with more active play and less time sitting at a table, more time outdoors and less classroom time.

Despite accumulating knowledge of different "learning styles" and their relationships to gender and temperament, extraordinarily little is done to fit child care to the child. In the United Kingdom, for example, where much has been done to improve the availability and quality of child care and early education during the ten years of New Labour government, policy has moved toward ever more tightly defined and all-embracing "frameworks," each replacing the last. The most recent is the Early Years Foundation Stage, a comprehensive statutory (as of September 2008) framework of standards for the care, development, and learning of all children from birth to age five and their assessment. Published in 2007, the framework includes targets for literacy and numeracy by the age of five, which many people regard as aspirational rather than realistic and therefore likely to give many five-year-olds (and their parents) feelings of failure.

Even when there is general adult agreement about desirable out-comes for children and the best ways of achieving them, an outcome approach to child care quality disregards children's current happi-ness in their particular child care setting. Indeed, the possibility of defining and measuring children's happiness and the extent to which children being happy should be considered an attribute of high quality child care are important issues that are still open. In a com-parison of the daily lives of American children attending a high-quality child care center with those attending a low-quality center, one researcher pointed out that the effects of poor quality are imme-diate for the children involved. For children in poor-quality care, "and for their parents, who may perceive the effects of mediocre care without understanding their origins—the conflicts and trade-offs that compromise quality are irrelevant. What counts is that their experiences have been miserable, at the same time that their more fortunate peers in centres of good quality have had wonderful times—making new friends, coming to know and love other adults who are good to them, learning many different kinds of things each day, coming home radiant and eager to return the next day."

Even today, though, considering the quality of care from chil-dren's viewpoints tends to be more a matter of commenting on what is thought to be good for children in the long run than what they might enjoy in the short term. The mother who answered a ques-

---

Talking to parents

How would you know that a child care setting was really good for your child?

If she wasn't anxious about going; no tears at breakfast or on the way; no more than a tearful moment when I left her. And then really knowing her teacher—going to her when we arrived, telling me things about her, wanting to tell her things that had happened at home. And being all enthusiastic about other kids and the activities. When I picked her up, not being angry at me for being away from her, or desperate to get away, but wanting me to see what she'd been doing or maybe wait while she fin-ished something.

tion about child care that was "good for her child" entirely from the child's point of view (see box p. 216) was one of very few.

As that mother clearly realized, the two or three years during which it is least possible for children to tell about their happiness or unhappiness in words is also the period during which they tell us most in their behavior. A child who is too young to report on his feelings is also too young to cover them up. An older child may try to be brave, be anxious not to worry parents, hope to live up to parental expectations or to measure up to the peer group, but a very young child who is miserable, anxious, lonely, or scared will cry a lot, cling when he has anyone to cling to, and withdraw when there's no one. Usually this means that a young child who seems fine prob-ably *is* fine, but adults should take notice of the child who doesn't seem fine, because even if the care setting she is in seems wonderful to her parents, it probably is not, at that time, right for her. Unfor-tunately, many people are so unaccustomed to looking at daily life from children's points of view that both florid unhappiness and lack of joy may be dismissed as "natural" or "just a stage" or ignored as unimportant.

We cannot expect small children to know what's good for them long-term or to understand that they're going to enjoy tomorrow when today's strangeness has worn off, so it is often up to parents to help them find out. But helping a child find ways of coping with a situation is not at all the same as ignoring the unhappiness or anxi-ety he is feeling. Starting in child care is now known to be stressful for many small children, and for some, acute or chronic stress—manifested in levels of the hormone cortisol in their saliva—may actually be damaging to aspects of brain development.

However, provided that they do take notice of children's apparent feelings and consider children's points of view along with their own whenever possible, parents cannot usually do better than to assume that what they think will be good for their children will indeed be so. Most children, most of the time, are better off—happier and more confident of themselves and their love relationships—when they are doing what parents expect and they therefore feel approved of. Children's feelings about adults who are important to them and the adults' feelings about them are crucial to children's immediate happiness and long-term success at all ages. As earlier chapters have made clear, much evidence from research studies carried out both at home and in child care strongly suggests that it is personal relationships that have the most, and most positive, impact on children's development, especially in the first three years. Good outcomes take many forms, but they are all related to high-quality care. Whether that care takes place at home or in a child care setting, its quality depends on the quality of the relationships between children and adults.

FIRST RELATIONSHIPS

Apart from growth, the most dramatic development of the first year of life is the establishment of attachments between children and adult caregivers, usually mothers and fathers but sometimes also others. For infants, relationships with caring adults do not just dictate the quality of care; they *are* the quality of care. This is why questions about whether (or for how long) children in general are better off in the sole care of their parents or would benefit from nonparental child care are unanswerable. Particular answers depend on the quality of the individual's relationships.

Secure "primary" attachments correlate with better development because children who have warm, predictable relationships with the adults who care for them are better able to use those adults to help them explore their environment and learn about themselves in the world. This is true for babies and toddlers at home and in child care settings.

When people talk about "attachment," they are usually referring to babies and children being attached to a grown-up, and usually that grown-up is the mother. However, taking children's viewpoint highlights the fact that adult caregivers (parents or others) who are more securely attached to *them* fulfill the vital function of "safe base" more satisfactorily than insecurely attached or more distant caregivers.

Primary attachments, usually to parents, are, well, primary. But when an infant or toddler is away from his mother or father, a secondary attachment to whoever is taking care of him is critical to his happiness today and his development tomorrow. Babies and toddlers don't need to be able to tell us that in words; it is clear to see in their behavior. The security of that secondary attachment and most of the aspects of good-quality care that go with it crucially depend on the amount of access the child and his caregiver have to each other. Much has been written about employed mothers who are inaccessible to their babies during the working day, much less about the inaccessibility of caregivers who may be on the premises but overwhelmed by the number of children for whom they are responsible.

Stability of Care

Babies and toddlers show richer patterns of social interaction when they are securely attached to their caregivers, and they are usually more strongly and securely attached to well-known and regular care providers than to those who are occasional or less familiar, so stability of care is clearly an important aspect of quality from children's viewpoints. We can go further, though. Since young children's relationships with stable adult caregivers are better, all their relationships and many aspects of their development may suffer when adults are not stable. Changes of caregiver are sometimes associated with increased aggression and less cooperative play. Furthermore, the loss of a caregiver who knows the children well enough to be sensitive to each individual child may undermine many aspects of their overall development, particularly speech. Young children who are learning to understand other people's words and gestures and to build up a repertoire of ways of communicating with them often use idiosyncratic gestures and made-up "own words." Parents and caregivers who have known a child well over a long period will know what he is trying to convey—know that a "ban-ban" is a ball, for example—and will therefore be able to respond quickly and appropriately. A new caregiver may be unable to understand what the child is saying and may not even recognize "own words" as budding speech. From the caregiver's point of view, her inability to respond sensitively to what the child is trying to communicate is due to his absence of language; from the child's point of view, the sudden failure of his dawning communication system is incomprehensible and may be both alarming and frustrating to him. In a longitudinal study of children from birth to six years conducted in London, children with more instability in their child care arrangements and more changes of care provider in the first three years showed poorer language development than those with fewer changes. These differences were still evident at the age of six.

Even without being able to ask children about their feelings, we know that every time a familiar caregiver leaves, children suffer some degree of loss. If this happens over and over again, some children will stop trying to establish sustained loving relationships with care providers, and the complex communication and understanding necessary for maximizing developmental potential will be greatly reduced. Staff turnover in child care centers in the United States has been documented at 37 percent per year and soon may reach 40 percent. The situation in the United Kingdom is similar. If more than a third of the staff leaves each year, it is most unlikely that the children in centers of average size will have the same caregiver for a whole year, and some children will have several changes of key person in the same period. Although this is generally recognized as unfortunate, it is often described from the adults' viewpoint as a management problem. For children, it may be an overwhelming quality problem. Frequent staff changes may mean that a center that seems to researchers and to parents to provide "good-quality care" is experienced by children as the opposite. Where staff retention is a problem, stable staffing for the youngest children should certainly be the priority, because they cannot have good-quality care without it. Stability of care matters for older children, too, though as anyone who has followed the fortunes of a classroom through a succession of substitute teachers knows, what matters from children's points of view is not just having enough adults but having the *right* individuals. The ratio of adults to children is crucial, but so is the closely related issue of continuity and stability.

BEING WITH OTHER CHILDREN

Regular opportunities to play with other children and get to know and feel part of a stable group are key benefits of the expansion of preschool provision both from parents' and from children's viewpoints. Without it, many of today's children would spend very little time with other children and get to know very few of them well enough for real friendship—or rivalry, or enmity. In dwindling and mobile families, many children have no siblings or cousins who are close in age and proximity, and they have little opportunity to play with peers in their home neighborhoods because of increased concerns for the safety of children playing outside unsupervised. Parks and their ubiquitous playgrounds, and now-popular soft playrooms and other indoor play facilities, are valuable, but they are not adequate alternatives, even in families that have time and resources to take children often. Playing where other children play is better than always being the only child, but the kind of peer relationships that teach three-year-olds basic lessons about the meaning and purpose of taking turns, or why it is better to solve problems by speaking than hitting or crying, and that foster the most socialized and complex play and the most sophisticated role-playing and problem solving are the real friendships that can form only in stable, predictable groups of children. Stable groups of children are, of course, more likely to be found in higher-quality centers and family day care. In the United Kingdom, it is not unusual for childminders to care for the children of two or three families from infancy to secondary school.

From an adult viewpoint, it matters if young children have contact with other children because greater experience of peer interaction in the first three years of life dramatically improves children's social skills; from a child's viewpoint, it matters because playing with other children is (usually) fun. Even in high-quality child care, though, being part of a group is not something all young children find equally easy. Some take much longer than others to begin to participate and to form ongoing friendships with other children.

Indeed, some of the research on stress in child care has suggested that the toddlers who are most stressed when in their groups are often those children who find it most difficult to socialize and play with other children. From children's points of view, then, there needs to be high-quality care available in smaller-than-usual groups, with shorter-than-usual hours and extra attention paid to settling children in.

EDUCATIONAL OPPORTUNITIES

Learning opportunities are the most vaunted benefit of preschool child care but difficult to approach from children's perspectives. "Preschool education" has traditionally been aimed at children from about three years old, and its educational aims have more or less explicitly included "preacademics." The findings of study after study make it clear that educationally oriented preschool experience fosters educationally relevant outcomes. For example, British children who attended nursery education in the 1980s did better in primary school than children of matched ages and backgrounds who attended playgroup. And the Effective Provision of Pre-School Education project, reporting in 2004, found that professionally staffed and run preschools produced better outcomes for children than any other type of child care, not because there was a direct relationship between academic teaching in the preschool period and academic accomplishments thereafter, but because three- and four-year-olds acquired a lasting predisposition to learn.

Children do not start learning about learning only when someone starts teaching them at age two or three, however. From birth, children are continuously learning about the environment and people around them, and about themselves in relation to it; furthermore, since the formation of rich interconnections within the brain is most rapid in the first year (and then the second), the learning opportunities of even the earliest child care—including care by a parent at home—are at least equally important, and some would argue more so. Sometimes learning opportunities are explicitly planned for and provided; sometimes they are inherent in the child care setting and the daily activities that go on there. If an infant is at home with an adult—perhaps a parent, perhaps a nanny—who is constantly and creatively bearing him in mind, he can pick up all the concepts and skills he can use from playing with and around adults and watching and sharing their everyday activities and conversation. Nevertheless, some planning of activities and provision for a range of kinds of play is recognized as a feature of higher-quality nonparental child care—and one that is sometimes missing from informal care settings, such as grandparents' homes. Planning—and the thoughtful interest in children's development that it implies—helps to make sure that all the children present are offered a wide and balanced range of activities: some already familiar, some new; some easy for the child to manage, some more challenging. And it also helps to ensure some balance between different types of activities, with energetic outdoor play interspersed with quieter play indoors, and effortful concentrated building or painting combined with more relaxing water play or stories. Equally important, planning lends predictable shape to the children's day and helps to minimize aimless wandering about doing nothing much in particular, or equally aimless TV viewing.

The benefits of planning activities and particularly learning opportunities are difficult to assess from children's points of view, though. Too much preplanning can limit the free, unstructured play (which is often mistaken for "doing nothing much in particular") within which children experience unique combinations of joy and learning. Not all wandering is aimless; peaceful thinking or mulling-over time is valuable, and so is the spontaneity that can be lost in too much and too rigid planning. The learning that takes place because a child's attention happens to be caught can be especially valuable:

> It was story time and I was reading to them. Paris came up in the story and one of the children said "What's Paris?" and we started talking about cities and ended up finding pictures of different cities in the baby encyclopedia. . . . It was a really good session.
> —childminder, personal communication, 2007

So while adult-laid plans and routines are important from the children's points of view, it may be at least equally important that their own interests and activities usually take precedence, especially over adult convenience. Movement from a rule-driven, clock-driven routine to a child-oriented responsive routine will engage children more in their daily experience, and engaging children themselves in planning decisions fosters cognitive development and communication skills.

Staff should ask themselves, and should encourage parents to ask them, whether routines are actually fostering children's development.

> I hate that they *make* him sit at the table and do fiddly things. He's at a stage when he wants to rush about; ride the vehicles; climb; yes, push and shove the other little boys as if they were puppies. . . . They have to make them make the damn father's day cards and stuff because like all good preschools they're thinking "school readiness." But I really hate for him to have to.   —New York mother

PARTICULAR BENEFITS OF HIGH-QUALITY EARLY YEARS CARE AND EDUCATION TO CHILDREN FROM LESS PRIVILEGED FAMILIES

As earlier chapters have shown, many research studies report that children who come from relatively deprived backgrounds are espe-

---

Penny-wise, pound-foolish policy choices: Wasting money and lives

Do investments in quality child care and early childhood education bust budgets or save money? Extensive analysis of the results available from the ongoing, publicly funded Chicago Child-Parent Centers demonstrate overwhelmingly that these are wise investments.

Economists, looking at this, other research, and their own analyses, concluded that spending on early childhood programs is among the best investments government can make in education. As Nobel Prize–winning economist James Heckman at the University of Chicago put it, "Skills [including social skills] acquired early on make later learning easier."

Chicago's Child-Parent Center federal- and state-funded program has been providing quality early childhood education and parent training to almost 100,000 at-risk kids since 1967. A study tracked almost 1,000 children who attended the centers in 1985–86. Compared to very similar children who attended all-day kindergartens but not the CPC preschool centers, by age twenty these children had 26 percent greater high school graduation rates, were held back in school 35 percent less often, and were less than half as likely to have been arrested two or more times as juveniles. The program saves the government, the public, and the participants combined almost five dollars for every dollar invested.

cially likely to show far-reaching and long-lasting benefits in their overall development from good-quality child care and education. In fact, in light of the comments on some well-known early years programs, summarized on page 226, it is astonishing that every state and country does not make early childhood education a universal entitlement as they do the education of five- to sixteen-year-olds.

Outcomes for vast nationwide programs targeted toward underprivileged families such as Early Head Start (as well as Head Start itself) in the United States and Sure Start in the United Kingdom are also notably positive and lasting. While these state-of-the-art preschool programs have been shown unequivocally to benefit children in otherwise deprived circumstances and might also benefit more privileged children, caution is needed in using these findings to argue for the benefits of child care in general. Comparing such programs with "ordinary" child care is like comparing apples not just with oranges but with potatoes. Early Head Start, for example, is not full-time child care, 8 a.m. to 5 p.m. without a parent or personal care provider, but half-day nursery school with parents often present and involved in the classrooms and, crucially, with home visits to provide parent education and support.

The best-known and internationally most admired of all U.S. preschool programs, the Perry Preschool Project (PPP), was recently put under a spotlight during a debate in Canada about

---

The Perry project (1962) was neither day care nor preschool. It had five components:

1. Parents participated in regular meetings with teachers.

2. Teachers did 1½-hour weekly home visits.

3. Children spent 2½ hours per day in classroom setting.

4. The child-teacher ratio was five or six to one. (For comparison, British Columbia preschool regulations allow fifteen children per staff; day care ratio is eight to one.)

5. Purpose-trained teachers provided a specially designed intensive, exploratory play and problem-solving program.

Helen Ward, Kids First Parents Association of Canada

Building their futures: How Early Head Start programs are enhancing the lives of infants and toddlers in low-income families

An evaluation of three thousand families in seventeen Early Head Start (EHS) programs across the United States found that two-year-old children in the program performed significantly better in cognitive, language, and social-emotional development than children who were not in the program. Parents in EHS showed more positive parenting behavior, reported less physical punishment of their children, and were more likely to promote learning, language, and literacy at home by reading more to their children and engaging in more structured play activity than parents not in the program.

In June 2002, a follow-up report on the same children at age three showed continued improvement both compared to the previous year and to the control group.

Early Head Start findings in three-year-olds:

- Better cognitive, language, and social-emotional development

- Higher scores on standardized tests of infant and toddler development

- Larger vocabularies and the ability to speak in more complex sentences

- More positive parenting behavior and less physical punishment

- Promotion of learning, language, and literacy through increased reading at home

whether the state should fund children who are in formal child care and, if so, whether it should also fund children who are cared for informally or at home. Helen Ward, president of the Kids First Parents Association of Canada, an organization that campaigns for state resources to be allocated to give more support to parents who choose to care for children at home (and therefore less support to enable formal child care), has made a detailed study of the PPP and considers that it is entirely inappropriate to use the results of that project to support the merits of child care.

The excellent results of the PPP are not being called into question. Children who took part in the project were less likely to be

*Florida State University Center for Prevention
and Early Intervention Policy*

Poor-quality care can negatively affect children's development, especially for very young children. Tragically, care for infants and toddlers consistently rates worse than care for preschoolers. Poor-quality centers with large group sizes and poor ratios of caregivers to children have been correlated with harmful levels of the stress hormone cortisol in children. Centers with inadequate ratios of caregivers to children are challenged to provide even basic custodial care, much less cognitive stimulation or emotional nurturance. Often babies in these centers languish in infant seats or mechanical devices like swings, with propped bottles rather than receiving nurturing human touch, smiles, and eye contact. High staff turnover and frequent changing of a baby's environment may negatively impact attachment. Poor-quality care has consistently been linked to increased behavior problems, as well as delays in school readiness, social-emotional development, and cognitive and language skills.

labeled mentally retarded, were more likely to finish high school, and, as young adults, had fewer arrests by the police than a control group of children without such help. However, these were not what Ward calls "average kids" in typical child care but "58 African American kids aged 3–4, not 0–2 as in infant/toddler daycare . . . selected partly because they had below average IQ's and assessed low 'socioeconomic status.' They lived in a very high crime area. Their mothers were not at paid jobs. They were single and on welfare—and most had been teens when the children were born." Applying the data from the highly resourced experience of a small group of at-risk preschoolers to all children, including under-twos, and their short half days with parents involved with highly trained teachers to eight hours a day in child care is questionable.

If most child care fails to measure up to state-of-the-art remedial programs, some child care is of truly poor quality. There are other less studied and far less often quoted research projects whose findings suggest that poor-quality child care is at least as bad for children as high-quality care is good—and in many places there is more of it.

WHO IS CHILD CARE FOR?

Outside the Nordic states, where democracy is a powerful and largely realized ideal that includes children among those whose views should be heard and respected, child care policies are more informed by what it means to be a parent than by what it means to be a child. When services "for children" are provided at all, they are mostly provided to address the problems and needs of parents rather than children. And sometimes, of course, meeting recognized parental needs contradicts ignored childish ones. By clicking on www.emergencycare.co.uk, British parents can access a database of care providers who will supply emergency child care not only for parents who know in advance that they will need cover for their child care provider's vacation but also for mothers whose nannies phone in sick three hours before they need to be at work. Given the undisputed link between high quality of care and close relationships between children and caregivers, care by someone they have never met before (and whom their mothers have never met before either), whether in their own home or in a house that is new to them, and with other children they have never met before, may be the best the parent can provide that day, but it is not good child care from children's point of view.

Where children are regarded as principally private family business, no outside person or public body has a duty to provide services just because children could benefit from them, let alone just because they'd enjoy them. Public duty comes into question only when children have a "real need" (definitions vary, of course) and all else—including hapless mothers—fails to meet it.

If this view of responsibility for child well-being ever reflected reality, it does not now. Very few contemporary families, good or bad, rich or poor, intact, broken, or melded, can provide everything children need—and parents themselves know it. Children need input from their communities, and from their points of view, it should be a universal right, with every support, enrichment, and opportunity that is offered to any child available to all. Take the summer school vacation. Because it is assumed that parents will cope one way or another and it's nobody else's business how they do it, camp costs overwhelmed many North American parents, as usual, and local authorities in the United Kingdom felt compelled to provide only a few short play schemes for particularly hard-pressed families. But suppose it was assumed that school vacations should actually *be* holidays for schoolchildren, and that interesting, fun things to do and people to do them with should be there for all, whatever arrangements their families were able and willing to make. Think of the bliss for children and parents—and, yes, think of the costs . . .

It is not only the actual expenditure that makes such universal provisions for children (and their enjoyment and education) unthinkable, though. There is also a moral issue about entitlement. The greater the range of people entitled to a service, the more public alarm there is about the dire possibility of hard-pressed taxpayers' money going to people who "don't really need it." When the United Kingdom's universal (though taxed-as-income) child benefit was discussed in 1996, shortly before New Labour came to power, the most heartfelt (though ultimately unsuccessful) argument in support of introducing means testing (or "targeting," as it is now more often termed) was that as long as Child Benefit was for everybody, even Princess Diana would be entitled to claim it, just like her domestic help. Although the arguments for targeting poor families as a way of making the best use of limited resources are powerful, such compensatory provision often stigmatizes the targeted group, offends the excluded middle, and does nothing to contribute to community cohesion or convey respect for children. The United Kingdom's free school lunch program, for example, makes an important contribution to the nutrition of children from underprivileged homes, but finding discreet ways for entitled children to take their meal without paying for it, and deciding how many of the choices available to children who pay should be available as part of the free meal, takes almost as much effort as providing it. Services all families use, such as those ubiquitous playgrounds, locally subsidized swimming pools, and now endangered children's libraries, are in sharp contrast.

16. Choosing Child Care

Whatever people do or don't do concerning children's care, upbringing, and education, there will always be questions. Research is crucial to helping everyone ask the right questions and to guiding policy makers and politicians toward getting the large-scale answers right. Parents and families, though, tend to need small-scale and immediate answers to very personal questions—not "What kind of child care should public money be invested in?" but "Which day care should I pay to look after my child starting next week?" Research cannot answer that kind of question directly, and media reports that suggest it can and does are often misleading.

What Parents Are Up Against

How can parents find high-quality child care? Unfortunately, there isn't an answer that applies to everyone. Without a battery of observations and assessments and a team of researchers to make them, parents have to use research findings indirectly and well mixed with their own, because high-quality child care is either a statistical entity or it's a value judgment. We can talk about high-quality care in general or about a brilliant childminder or nursery in particular, but turning either (or both) into definitions of brilliant (or just good) child care settings for the benefit of people in search of care is a different matter. As we've seen, it's crucial to know whose point of view we are judging from. Parents may give a center top marks for being open long hours and friendly about late pickups and slightly feverish children, but that's no guarantee that it gets top marks from the licensing authority; maybe its educational provision is below average. Children may love the center, too, but if they do, it may be for the ride-on train in the garden or one particular teacher. Meanwhile, staff might be disillusioned with the center because it doesn't pay them for providing those extra services for parents, and the community might not be happy with it because of issues that have nothing to do with children, such as disputes over parking or a problem with the planning authority.

How can parents select the best available child care? The short answer is "by observing it." If there's sometimes a gap between the child care parents want in theory and accept in practice, there's also often a gap between what care providers think about their jobs and what they actually do. Staff attitudes toward their work, whether collected in face-to-face interviews or through questionnaires, bear little relationship to how they actually behave. If you want to know how a particular caregiver does her job, you have to go and watch her doing it, which is not as obvious in real life as it appears on the page. Some of the FCCC mothers who started back to work in the first year of their babies' lives settled on family day care homes (childminders) that they had visited only after the children had gone home for the day, accepting that it was difficult for the care provider to talk while she was working. Many started their babies in center or family day care without following the settling-in guidelines most of them would have endorsed:

> I did take her and stay all the time, once, but of course she sat on my lap so neither of us really got a feel for it. Then when she started they told me, "Look, she's bound to cry when you leave her whether that's now or in an hour. So get it over . . . ," so I told her good-bye like they say you should, and I left. I hadn't meant to do it so quick but it made sense.
> —FCCC mother

An Australian mother asked her two-year-old what he'd done during the first day she had left him at child care.

Did you play in the garden?
No.

Did you have a story?
[No answer]

Did you do painting?
I done crying.

Talking to parents about child care choices

Help! I've read this whole book, but I'm still confused! Can you sum up the pros and cons of possible types of care from the ideal of a live-in nanny downward?

A care provider who lives in may seem to offer parents the ultimate freedom to come and go, but don't forget that your home will also be the live-in nanny's home. She will have every right to be there when you don't want her as well as when you do.

A trained nanny who is competent to take "full charge" of your baby or toddler may undertake nothing but child care so that you end your working day cooking her evening meal and spend your weekends doing household chores.

A mother's helper/housekeeper will probably do anything you would do if you were at home but may find the job just as lonely, boring, and underpaid as you did (and after all, it's your child!).

Au pairs can be marvelous and may neatly fill particular needs (such as bridging the gap between the end of school and your return home), but most are no better around the house or more child-centered than you were at that age; don't speak the fluent English you want your child to hear and learn; and seldom stay longer than nine months. That's a lot of losses for your child.

Daily care providers are sometimes easier to get along with because neither of you has to share private lives or draw lines between time "on duty" and time "as family." A daily nanny or mother's helper who has children may experience some of your own difficulties in balancing work and home, though.

Sharing a daily nanny with another family is a way of achieving affordable high-quality child care that is increasingly popular in the United Kingdom. If she is to care for both households together (rather than sharing the week between them), make sure the adults of both families are compatible and that the children are manageable together.

A daily mother's helper or housekeeper may be happy with part-time work to match your hours away, especially if she is working her way through college. Make sure she has enough interest and energy left over for your child.

Nonfamily carers in their own homes (childminders; family day care providers). This kind of day care exists in every country but is different in each. In some American states, many providers are not registered or inspected, so their care is regarded as a risky second-best to a child care center. In the United Kingdom there are registration and inspection procedures, strict controls on the permitted numbers and ages of children, and increasingly (but not yet very) widespread provisions for training (including training for work with children with various special needs). In many other European countries, the training of family day care providers is of the high standard required of all other early years workers, and they are employed by state or local authorities rather than providing services directly to parents. Many family day care providers offer more personalized and flexible child care than most centers, including enabling siblings to be cared for together.

Family caregivers in your home or their own. Grandparents provide a large proportion of nonparental child care in most countries. If another relative or a friend offers to care for your child informally and with little if any payment, think before you cheer. She is unlikely to be, or to need to be, registered, licensed, or inspected, so you have only your personal relationship on which to base the assumption that your baby will be safe and happy with her. Furthermore, favors this big are sometimes offered with more enthusiasm than forethought and quickly go sour.

Group care (child care centers; nurseries). National and local policies concerning the provision of day care places vary widely. In some countries, day care centers or nurseries run by public or charitable bodies devoted to children's welfare provide places for almost all who want them and set national standards of excellence; in others, they are oversubscribed or confined to groups with particularly pressing needs.

Forward-looking employers sometimes provide workplace child care as a perk to staff. Sometimes it is on the working premises, more often in less-expensive accommodations in the area. As well as some financial subsidy, these have big advantages: you need be away from your child only during your actual working hours; you can visit during breaks; and you are on the spot in case of illness or crisis. But there are also large possible snags, including rush-hour travel; your child's isolation from your home community; the fact that if you are off sick, she probably has to stay at home, too, and that if you change jobs, she loses the child care.

Numbers of chain and individual private day care centers are increasing to meet booming demand. Although quality (and costs) varies tremendously, standards of good practice (especially educational content for all ages) are being agreed on, which is a necessary, if not sufficient, step toward meeting them. Demand for places is usually highest of all for babies and toddlers, but not all nurseries will accept under-twos because both the regulations and realities of their care demand extra resources.

When an individual parent watches what goes on in a particular room of a child care setting, she'll judge the quality from the point of view of herself and her child—and that's fine. But if that same parent listens to somebody else's judgment, she needs to know where that person is coming from. If her source is another parent, she needs to be sure the two of them have a shared agenda. A mother who has recently dropped out of her profession to care for her children full-time, for example, may be understandably hyper-critical of all nonmaternal child care—and perhaps of mothers who plan to use it. The father whose four-year-old has just been excluded for disruptive behavior may find it easier to see the nursery as "too rigid" than his little boy as "too wild." If the source of your infor-mation about a nursery is a professional—a kindergarten teacher, for example—her perspective may have to do with outcomes: the better the children perform upon entering school, the higher qual-ity it must be. So when she praises a particular center, she may be talking more about what it will do for your child in the long term (and possibly in terms of entry to a desirable school) than about what it will be like for him (and therefore for you) right now. The fact that someone is giving you an "expert opinion" tells you noth-ing except that this person's opinion is based on some information and experience. Another "expert" might judge the same day care differently. Of course, if they both single out a center's emphasis on preacademics instead of "just playing," the chances are that their agreed information is valid—the center does emphasize reading and writing and number activities. The fact that one approves this emphasis and the other does not leaves you free to form your own judgment.

Other people's judgments about family day care/childminding are even more difficult to assess because, as discussed in an earlier chapter, mothers tend to like the caregivers whom they feel they can communicate with: people they get along with as one adult to another. The fact that your friend really likes the woman who runs a particular day care doesn't mean that you will, much less that she'll be exactly the right care provider for your child. As for nannies, babysitters, and au pairs, although a "reference" from a friend (and perhaps her children) feels enormously reassuring, it should never replace checking real references from previous employers. These are especially important when you're considering employing someone who does not have to be registered for work with children or have her work inspected. Don't rely on references written "To whom it may concern." Employers who write these are sometimes eager to get rid of the employee and/or anxious not to upset her. You are likely to get more information from a private phone call.

The FCCC study explored more than a thousand English mothers' information and beliefs about types of nonmaternal child care and where their information came from. Mothers cited a wide range of sources as useful, including printed materials (books, pamphlets, and magazine articles) as well as direct communication with health professionals. Family and friends were the most influential, though grandmothers were widely seen as being on the wrong side of a generation gap: "She listens but she just doesn't know what it's like being a mother today." That did not prevent mothers from accepting actual child care from grandmothers, though; in fact, many were more willing to accept care from grandmothers, other relatives, and even family friends, because they were "family" or "known," and therefore deemed trustworthy, than from a family day care provider or childminder because she was "a stranger," albeit someone whose home would have been inspected for safety and who would herself have had a background check.

While parents' personal knowledge and individual judgment are the keys to choosing good child care, the processes of using them may be daunting, even impossible, for some. When advice from the American advocacy group Project Child Care was shown to a group of single mothers, it evoked comments such as "They need to get real" and "In my dreams."

Nevertheless, some general guidelines that a parent might find useful when searching for the best available care for a particular child can be garnered from the research detailed in earlier chapters and are summarized here.

GENERAL GUIDELINES TO FINDING HIGH-QUALITY CHILD CARE FOR A BABY OR TODDLER

As earlier chapters have shown, the quality of child care matters more to children than its type or even, usually, than how old they

---

Some tips for parents from Project Child Care
(Manatee County, Florida)

1. Plan well in advance searching for your child's day care needs. Some facilities have limited openings or waiting lists.

2. Check out at least three day care centers or child care homes before choosing one for your child.

3. Visit each center or home and talk to teachers/staff at least twice—one announced visit and one unannounced visit.

4. Ask for the qualifications and length of employment of teachers/staff.

5. Review health and safety inspection reports at the state Department of Health and Rehabilitative Services child day care licensing and regulations office.

6. Talk to other parents who use the services you are considering.

7. Buy the best care you can afford.

8. Once you find day care, get involved. Get to know the teachers.

---

are when they begin or how many hours per week they spend there. Quality has many components that have already been discussed, but the ones that seem to underpin all the rest, especially for the youngest children, are a high ratio of adult caregivers to children and consistent care by the same adults. This is illustrated by the NICHD study's findings concerning the components of what they call "positive caregiving."

For this age group, caregivers' education, including specialized early years training, made only a small contribution, and caregivers' experience of child care made no difference at all.

Findings from the American NICHD study are echoed by some findings from the English FCCC study. For example, at both ten and eighteen months, the observed quality of home-based care (by the father, a grandparent, a nanny in the child's home, or by a child-minder in hers) was higher than the quality of care observed in care groups (nurseries or child care centers). In care groups, the adult-

*"Positive caregiving" from six months to two years,
summarized from the NICHD study*

For these age groups, high ratios of adults to infants (which were often accompanied by small group sizes) were overwhelmingly the most important contributors to "positive caregiving." Differences in these ratios accounted for much of the variation in the amount of positive caregiving found in different types of child care.

The most positive caregiving was found at home, where babies and toddlers were cared for on a one-to-one or nearly one-to-one basis by fathers, nannies, or grandparents. The next most positive caregiving was found in childminding/family day care, where groups were very small and often of mixed ages, so instead of competing directly for their attention, babies and toddlers were sharing their care providers with older children whose needs were different from their own. The least positive caregiving was found in nurseries or day care centers.

Other factors that went with more positive caregiving were:

- Safer, better organized, and more stimulating settings (the "physical/learning environment"). Along with their intrinsic benefits to the children, such settings also allowed caregivers to be less restrictive with the babies and to have more fun with them.

- More planning of activities and organization of toys and equipment.

- Caregivers' liberal beliefs about child rearing and discipline.

child ratio was clearly associated with the observed behavior of the staff. The more children each member of staff had to take care of, the less positive and more punitive she was with the babies and toddlers, and the more detached from them, too. In addition, at eighteen months the quality of the overall interactions between care providers and children was lower, and caregivers were less emotionally responsive when each had to care for more children.

IDEALS IN INFANT AND TODDLER CARE

One way of using these guidelines is to ask yourself how closely the setting you're considering matches most of these:

- **Ratios:** The higher the number of adults relative to the number of children they care for, the better. International professional opinion suggests that, ideally, one caregiver should be responsible for no more than three babies, and a ratio of one to two is better for under-ones, especially when they are being greeted at the beginning of the day and at mealtimes. However, these ratios will be more aspiration than reality in most nurseries and child care centers, and they are not even aspired to in many American states or in Australia, where recent compulsory accreditation requires ratios of one to four or one to five.

- **Group sizes:** Small groups are better for very small children. In a large nursery or center, babies should be in rooms containing no more than six children (and two adults). Beginning at one year, young toddlers may be in groups of nine children (with three adults). From around eighteen to thirty-six months, the usual recommendation is an adult-child ratio of one to four and a group size of up to twelve children (still with three adults).

- **Family group ratios:** When a center (or a childminder/family day care provider, or a shared nanny) cares for children of different ages in "family" groupings, there should be no more than two children under two years or one child under one year in a group, unless there are special family reasons, such as twins or very closely spaced siblings.

- **Care environments:** The physical conditions in which children are cared for are obviously important but are subject to such widely varying social norms and state regulations that only the most general recommendations can be made. In domestic settings or in any care that is not inspected, care providers may not always be up-to-date on safety issues, so checks on safe habits (such as putting babies down to sleep on their backs and washing hands after using the toilet) and on childproofing (not forgetting safety and hygiene precautions concerning any pets) are important.

- **Outside space:** Although charming decor and tiny toilets may mean more to you than to your child, it does matter to children how clean and warm and well lit the center or playroom is, how much daylight and sunshine come in (a windowless room or an entirely north-facing environment can be extremely depressing for staff as well as for children), and whether very small children can see the outside world through the windows.

    It is difficult to imagine high-quality child care with no outdoor play space, especially if the child care space is a single room. Even if it is spacious and well equipped, one room is a very limited environment for any child, especially one who is there all day, every day. Look for outside play space that is used freely, or at least daily, and inquire about the availability and frequency of trips outside the premises.

Consider the amount of unencumbered space available to each group. Try to look ahead. If your child is a currently immobile baby, can she sit on the floor without fear of being knocked over by those who crawl and walk? If she is a toddler, can she push wheeled toys and learn to run without terrorizing others or being reproved?

- **Organization of care:** Look for intimate and consistent individual care. From the moment he arrives, your child should be the special (though not necessarily the exclusive) charge of one particular adult. In a nursery or center where there are several caregivers, he should be allocated to a "key person" (though she may be given a different title) who, within the limits of her working hours, shift patterns, breaks, vacations, and sick leave, will be primarily responsible for his hands-on care, especially the highly personal daily routines of greeting, diaper changing, feeding, and settling for naps.

  Since a key person cannot be available to a child every minute of every day, her care should be supported by one or more deputies (sometimes known as "key-person buddies") who are well-known to the child. When two small groups share a room, two key workers can stand in for each other, since they will already be familiar to the children. However, that means one of the key workers will be temporarily in charge of twice the usual number of children, so each key worker will need to have an assistant. If your child is in a group setting full-time, his key person's shift will probably not be as long as his day. If someone else takes over his care for the last couple of hours (when he will be tired), it should be one of the well-known deputies on a split shift rather than a scarcely known stand-in.

  In some countries, centers are encouraged to organize themselves so that key workers "move up" with their children from baby room to toddler room and perhaps from toddler room to preschool. Bear in mind that although two or more years with the same principal caregiver may provide welcome stability, it may not. If the child and particular caregiver are not well matched (or become less well matched as he gets older), the stability may not be welcome but burdensome. And if the plan is for each caregiver to stay with the same group of children for two or more years, there is an even higher than usual chance of her leaving them before they are due to leave her.

- **Consistent care/staff turnover:** Once a child has become attached to a care provider in any setting, his security depends on her staying in the job. You cannot, of course, hold any individual to caring for your child for a particular length of time, but you might want to explore the intentions of a relative or the career plans of a nanny and to consider carefully whether a commitment of only a few months is enough to make the arrangement the one you want to choose. In group care, standards of good practice suggest that everything possible should be done to reduce turnover of staff. You might want to ask how extensive turnover has been in the past year and what is being done to lower it or keep it low. A center that is giving due importance to this question should be addressing it not only in obvious ways, such as working toward better salaries, holidays, or easier hours, but also by exploring plans for listening to and supporting staff and for providing for their professional development.

• **Stimulating, developmentally appropriate play:** Look for much more than "babysitting," even if your child is a small baby. Babies learn from the beginning, and the opportunities and stimulation they are offered affect not so much *what* they learn but *how* their capacity and enthusiasm for learning develop. Sometimes home-based care, despite its high-quality relationships, doesn't include many planned day-to-day activities and offers a poor range of play opportunities. If a child is put in front of the TV instead of being given lots of different things to do, being taken out and about, and shown things and told about them, the care will not reach its quality potential. Relatives do not have to be "trained" in order to give babies high-quality care (after all, parents are not), but they do need to be interested in the baby's stage of development and aware of the kinds of experience that will help it along. Most parents pick up an enormous amount of information about infant development from their reading during pregnancy and afterward and, above all, from talking to other parents in prenatal groups and in the local park. Grandparents and other relatives may not have up-to-date information or parent networks to get it from. In center care, a planned "educational" program must be an integral part of high-quality care, even for the youngest babies. The aim is not that babies should be taught "subjects" or even that they should be directly taught skills but that each should be offered and encouraged in a wide range of play activities tailored to his particular developmental stage. When observing a baby room, it is useful to note the range of different "activities" available and how long babies spend in each. A windup swing, for example, may be interesting and enjoyable for five or even ten minutes, but then the occupant will probably enjoy being on the floor to practice sitting or crawling while another baby has a turn in the swing. Left in the rewound swing for half an hour, a baby is being kept safe but not much more.

- **Respectful care:** Wherever babies and toddlers spend their days together or with older children—in a biological or melded family as well as in a day care home, a nursery, or a center—the adults who are caring for them need to be aware of the importance of each child developing a strong sense of him- or herself as a valued individual, and of the need to support, protect, and build every child's self-esteem. There is room for respect in the minutiae of everyday life with small children: listening to them and really trying to understand the communication of babies who are not yet verbal or toddlers whose talk is fast and inaccurate; responding readily not only to distress but also to affection or humor; helping children to manage things for themselves rather than saving time by doing it for them; and, perhaps above all, avoiding not only the punishments that can feel like bullying but also the sarcasm and the teasing that can so easily humiliate. Even a one-year-old has a sense of personal dignity and deserves to be laughed with but never at.

  As much as possible, physical care arrangements should allow for individual differences: Must every child eat the same food and take the same-length nap at group times? Are older toddlers helped toward toilet mastery on an individual basis rather than trained as a group?

  Books and toys and ceremonies should reflect the cultural diversity of the nursery and the community and be positively nonsexist and antiviolent. This is central to the quality and atmosphere of the center, so it is equally important to all parents, irrespective of their own background. Staff should deliberately avoid stereotyping language, value diversity, and model sensitivity to particular disabilities or problems.

- **Care you can share:** Anyone who takes care of your baby or toddler should be not just willing but eager to work closely with you and with anyone you designate as important in your child's life. Fathers should automatically be included in all contacts made with home. Where parents are separated, double invitations should always be sent.

  To get the best for your child out of shared care, though, you have to feel able to work closely with the staff, and some people find that surprisingly difficult. Parents want children to be happy in child care but perhaps not *too* happy. Of course, they are grateful and flattered when a childminder loves their baby or a nursery teacher loves their toddler, but that doesn't stop mothers from worrying privately about how much the baby or toddler loves *her*.

  There is no evidence to suggest that relationships with care providers ever threaten or dilute secure and sensitive relationships with mothers or fathers, and quite a lot to suggest the contrary.

Going back to work after maternity leave, or any time when a mother would really prefer not to leave a child, can be stressful and sad. But nobody who feels ready to go to work or has to should torment herself with the possibility that her child will forget she's his mother because someone else nurtures him. *No chance*.

GENERAL GUIDELINES FOR FINDING HIGH-QUALITY CARE FOR PRESCHOOL CHILDREN

The differences between the aspects of quality that are important for preschool age children as compared with babies and toddlers are again well illustrated by the NICHD study's findings.

When research findings concerning center care for babies and toddlers are considered, there is an inescapable possibility that some children might be better off in individual or family day care. For these preschool children, the reverse is true: by the time children are approaching their third birthday, most of them enjoy and almost all of them benefit from being part of a close-knit group of other children; from close contact with nonfamily adults and trained teachers; and from a wider and more carefully planned range of opportunities, activities, and equipment than most private homes can provide.

Research evidence concerning "preschool" care, usually aimed at children from nearly three years old and having more or less explicit educational aims, is more extensive and consistent than the evidence concerning any other age group or type. Experimental studies consistently show that preschool educational experiences lead to far-reaching and long-lasting benefits to children's overall development and that these are especially marked in children who come from relatively deprived backgrounds. For example, U.K. children who attended nursery education in the 1980s did better in primary school than children who attended playgroup. It seems so clear that experience in high-quality educationally oriented preschool groups fosters educationally relevant outcomes that even if your three-year-old has satisfactory home-based care—with a parent or a nanny, perhaps—she might soon benefit from part-time attendance at preschool. Part-time is quite enough. The Effective Provision of Pre-School Education study, reporting in 2004, showed very clearly that full-time hours provide children with no extra benefit. How-

Positive caregiving from two to four years in the NICHD study

By the time children had reached this age, the factors associated with positive caregiving had changed considerably. Most notably, where positive caregiving for babies and toddlers was overwhelmingly identified by a high adult-child ratio, positive caregiving for this older age group was related far more strongly to care providers' characteristics than to their numbers. *Caregivers' education, beliefs, and attitudes* to child rearing, previously of only marginal importance, are now central to child care quality.

The quality of adult attention offered to the children has become more significant than its quantity: how the caregivers respond rather than how many there are.

Positive caregiving is still lowest in centers, but the difference is much less at this age.

The physical/learning environment makes a greater contribution to positive caregiving.

A new element is added to positive caregiving at this age—fostering the child's *exploration*.

Liberal or child-centered adults are more likely to foster exploration.

ever, the quality of preschool education is crucial: both this study and the Neighbourhood Nurseries Initiative, reporting in 2007, emphasized that high-quality preschool education means attendance at a group run by or at least closely supervised by a trained teacher.

Research studies also emphasize the importance of the following:

- **A high ratio of staff to children so that personal attention is available.** Although a very high ratio of adults to children is less important to this age group than to the youngest, classroom ratios of perhaps one teacher to fifteen children are still too low unless teachers are supported by classroom assistants. When the staff-child ratio is more favorable, children engage in more cognitively complex play with objects; show higher levels of language skills; are more securely attached to their teachers; and show less evidence of aggression, anxiety, and hyperactivity.

- **Carefully selected well-educated and trained staff.** Higher-quality care and education for children in this age bracket tends to be

provided by staff who have higher levels of formal education and
more early childhood training at the college level. If all members of
staff do not meet these criteria, there should be at least one person in
each group or classroom who does.

- **Continuity of staffing and low turnover among staff** who are paid
wages that allow them to be comfortable in their jobs. Children are
more competent in social and language development when they
attend centers with consistent staffing, and lower staff turnover goes
with higher wages and a better adult work environment.

- **A planned curriculum** appropriate to the developmental stage of
each group of children and adapted to each individual member of the
group. Freely chosen and self-directed play is essential, but in addition look for considerably more than "Monday: puzzles; Tuesday:
cutting and pasting, . . . Friday: cooking."

    The value of that planned curriculum depends on how it is deliv-
ered. Try to see some projects in progress. For example, if the children make celebration cards (for Mother's Day, Christmas, or Diwali,
for example), what arrangements are made for children whose personal circumstances or religion make the current project inappropriate? And do children who are working on the project understand the
point of these cards and create them for themselves, or do they simply "finish" (color, glue, decorate) cards prepared by the adults?

    Proper procedures for keeping track of individual children's
progress are important so as to ensure that no child's particular problem with learning—poor hearing or color blindness, for example—
goes unnoticed and so that children's dawning interests are noted and
encouraged.

- **Adult support and encouragement** for children to explore natural
materials, discover "natural laws" such as gravity and volume con-
stancy, and test their own physical agility and strength, for themselves, in their own way and at their own pace. Children should
likewise be encouraged to explore the creative possibilities of many
different materials and many different roles and relationships.

- **A consistent approach to conflict between children,** encouraging
them to reflect on their own and each other's feelings, plan different
ways of resolving the quarrel, and predict the consequences of particular actions. Such an approach has the double benefit of reducing
aggressive or antisocial behavior and fostering cognitive and social
development.

• **Adequate support services** (such as cleaning and cooking) to ensure children's safety, health, and nutrition without reducing the available teaching time. The lower staff-child ratio that is adequate for this age group assumes that additional support staff will be available for domestic care.

• **Partnership with the children's parents and with their community,** so that children's child care and family experiences are integrated.

Talking to parents

My daughter has been with her grandmother until now, but she's coming up to three and I want to start her in a half-day preschool. I am visiting three settings and plan to spend a morning in each. I'm concerned that I may not recognize the indicators of good quality. Are there specifics I should look for?

Planning is important. Ask if written plans for the session you're observing, for the day, the week, and perhaps the term, are available.

Adults' training is important. Ask how many trained teachers there are on the staff. If only the manager or principal is trained, ask how she ensures high standards, consistent policies in handling the children, and continuing professional development of staff.

Ask how many of the "juniors" or "classroom assistants" are in training. A high-quality center will schedule at least some staff meetings/staff support sessions as well as arranging "day release" so that junior staff *can* undertake training.

Adult-child ratios still need to be high enough to ensure that no child can get "lost" or be ignored. Ask what the maximum number of children is in any one group and whether teachers work alone or have assistants.

Ask how the domestic aspects of the school day are managed. Who prepares and cleans up snacks and meals? Who takes children to the bathroom? Who takes care of a child who is unwell?

Continuity of care is still very important. Ask how many staff have left in the last year and how quickly they were replaced. Ask how "cover" is arranged for a teacher who is sick or for one who requests family-friendly (probably part-time) hours.

SOME EASILY OBSERVED INDICATIONS OF HIGHER-QUALITY CARE (THE MORE THE BETTER)

This mental checklist may be useful when visiting a preschool facility:

- Most of the time, children are reasonably cooperative with one another. Although one or two may seem shy, most talk a great deal, and their play is enthusiastic and innovative.

- While new arrivals receive a lot of adult help in managing their relationships with other children, adults intervene very little between settled children, and self-control (or "self-regulation of behavior") seems commonplace. Children clearly know how they are expected to behave, and most of the time most of them do so.

- Problem behavior (such as tantrums, biting, pulling hair, throwing toys) is very rare for most of the children. It would be cause for concern if you saw more than one violent incident in a single morning, but less so if all the incidents were caused by one child (who was clearly having acute problems) than if such behavior was normal for the group.

- When conflicts arise, adults encourage children to reflect on (and talk about) their feelings, plan alternatives, and predict the consequences of particular actions.

- No formal punishments (such as time-outs) are used; any physical restraint is kept to the absolute minimum necessary to prevent children from hurting one another or themselves, and adults do not talk to children in ways that shame or humiliate them.

- Adults listen to the children and respond to them whenever possible. Most of the children seem securely attached to their teachers, smile at them, converse freely with them, and readily comply with their requests.

- A range of activities is available, and since most of these are interesting to almost all the children, it is likely that they are changed frequently.

- Children are encouraged to choose what they want to do and organize themselves to do it. When a particular activity is "oversubscribed" (for instance, more children want to play in the "House

Corner" than it can comfortably accommodate), teachers take the trouble to ensure fair turn-taking.

• Changes of activity and pace are sensitively handled with children given adequate notice.

Contradictions of the above points and the points listed below may raise questions about the quality of the setting. Remember, though, that you may be seeing a good group on a bad day, especially if its regular teacher is not available. Unless you have already decided that this is not the right place for your child, raise any negative points with the manager at the end of your observation period. (Any unwillingness to interact with you, a potential parent, in this way is a warning sign.)

SOME POSSIBLE INDICATIONS OF POORER-QUALITY CARE

• There is not enough staff to cope with the unexpected: a spilled drink brings teaching to a halt while the teacher mops up; an urgent phone call to a sick child's home takes the teacher out of the classroom. Every transition (such as getting ready for lunch or clearing up at going-home time) stops classroom activities, leaving the children with nothing positive to do. Absent staff are sometimes filled in for by adults the children do not know.

• Many children play alone over long periods.

• There is a lot of aimless wandering about; most of the children seem to find the available activities uninteresting or the other children daunting.

• When there are classroom activities provided (such as circle time), not all children join in, and little is done to involve those who are reluctant.

• Children do not look happy. At any one time, many are frowning, some look withdrawn, and at least one or two may be crying.

• There are more quarrels than conversations between children.

• During frequent conflicts between children, staff seem content simply to separate them, doing little to help the children resolve their differences.

- Adults do not look happy either.

- Few are entirely engaged with the children they are teaching but seem to spend a lot of time chatting with one another (e.g., when children are playing outside).

- When adults do talk to children, it is often to scold or exhort, or even to tease.

SCHOOL-AGE CHILD CARE

There is very little research on which to build criteria for choosing school-age child care because in most countries there is even less choice for schoolchildren than for younger ones. In the United Kingdom, North America, and Australia, it is sparse provision that limits the likelihood of choice, but in some countries of continental Europe, there is ample provision but only of one, usually school-based, type. In most countries and communities, it is easier for parents to find provision that meets their need for child care before and after school, matching children's school day to their own conventional working hours, than to find provision to meet their child care needs during school holidays.

As we have seen, any setting or person providing infant, toddler,

---

Talking to children about after-school care, Boston, 2002

(Three six-year-old boys and the eight-year-old sister of one of them)

So you'll be there for three hours? How is it?

One: There's lots to do.

Two: But there's lotsa kids . . . too many kids.

One: Yeah, it's noisy for sure.

Three: It's OK, but I'd rather go home . . .

One: Home? Me too.

Sister: I wish. I used to, you know. When I was little. When *he* was at the day care we went home after school. Can't now.

Wouldn't you be bored in the afternoons if you were home?

Sister: No, ma'am.

and preschool child care may also offer before- and after-school care, and sometimes vacation care, to school-age children. In addition, holiday programs are run by some park and recreation departments, public and private schools, religious institutions, and youth groups (such as Ys, scouts, boys and girls clubs).

No one type of school-day child care program is necessarily better than another. Some children are happier in small groups or homelike settings. In the United Kingdom, for example, after-school care by childminders (family day care providers)—often the same caregivers who had looked after the children before they reached school age and sometimes are still caring for younger siblings—is popular both with parents and with children. Other children thrive in larger, center-based programs. In any type of care, school-age youngsters need a program that lets them enjoy their out-of-school time, relax, play, pursue hobbies and other interests, build relationships with trusted adults who are neither teachers nor family, and socialize with children who are not necessarily classmates.

Parents need to know that their children are in a safe place under the supervision of competent adults. For many parents, convenience and cost are important considerations. Most child care programs that serve school-age children in the United States—as in the United Kingdom—must be regulated. For example, services for schoolchildren in New York State must meet regulations established by the New York State Department of Health:

- Parents have the right to drop in at any time to observe the program or see their children.

- Adult-child ratios limit the number of children each adult cares for, which helps to ensure that children are properly supervised and get the attention they need.

- Child care providers must receive ongoing training in areas such as child development, health, safety, and nutrition.

- The child care facility must be clean and safe, with space enough for active children.

- There must be a written plan for program activities and routines, and the plan must be shared with parents.

- There must be a plan for the identification and prevention of child abuse and maltreatment.

- Every licensed program is inspected at least once before the license is issued or renewed. At least 20 percent of all registered programs are inspected annually.

LOOKING FOR THE BEST AVAILABLE SCHOOL-AGE, SCHOOL-DAY CHILD CARE

Once you have established that the facility you are considering is licensed and has a current certificate to prove it, you will need to consider whether it is manageable for you in terms of cost and perhaps transportation, and whether it is the kind of before- and after-school care your child would prefer—or at least will tolerate. The school-based center already attended by his friends, for example, may be just what your son wants, and he will join with every intention of enjoying what it offers. But the same center, already attended by children with whom she is having problems during the school day, may fill your daughter with dread. If she thinks she is going to hate it, she very likely will.

Every child needs the following from the care program:

- A clean, safe, friendly environment with enough separated spaces (including outdoor space) for some children to be physically active while others play quieter games or perhaps do homework. Hard surfaces make for noisy environments, exhausting after a long school day. On school premises or in a large center, some areas should be carpeted, and "quiet corners" with soft seating and lighting are an advantage.

- Responsible care providers, at least some of whom are qualified play workers and all of whom positively enjoy working with school-age children at leisure rather than as all-day care providers for younger children or as classroom teachers. Play matters; expertise in play leadership makes a difference.

- A variety of activities that complement the school day, present opportunities for achievement at differing levels of skill, and encourage school-age children to make choices and risk trying new things.

- A program philosophy that sees the purpose of school-age child care not just as "watching" children after their parents leave for work and until they get home again but as giving children the opportunity to relax with friends more safely than they could at the mall or on the street, as well as time to pursue individual interests and the guidance of competent adults to develop new skills.

- Nourishing breakfasts before the school day begins; after school, healthy meals and snacks that will appeal to children, many of whom are in a period of rapid growth and some of whom may not have eaten much at midday.

- A philosophy of inclusion of all children, irrespective of their gender, race, religion, or particular challenges.

- Respect for the importance of parents and other family members to children and to the child care program.

VACATION CHILD CARE

Increasingly, settings that offer before- and after-school care are also offering vacation care or "play schemes." This is a welcome trend, but many schemes still take place only during the long summer vacation, and not for the entire time. In many communities, there may be nothing available during Christmas or Easter breaks. Even in summer, whole-day, whole-week care makes heavy demands on staff; it is far more difficult to provide children with a complete substitute for school than to complement it. Only the very best can provide programs that keep children of all ages enthusiastic and involved all day every day. Many registered children attend reluctantly, irregularly, or not at all. Some reluctant children may find it more amusing to misbehave than to cooperate. The dropouts may be hanging around the neighborhood unsupervised.

Children are more likely to be enthusiastic about vacation care that is completely different from their after-school program. Countries such as Norway and Sweden, which take children's leisure-time activities as seriously as their schooling, often lend their summer programs more excitement by establishing them in new environments, a mountain or forest camp, for example. North America has

> *"A wholesome escape from the pressures of school and vices of urban sprawl.*
> *Camp is a wonderful change of pace, environment and context. . . . [A]t*
> *camp young people bond with positive adult role models whose integrity and*
> *leadership-by-example tower over those of celebrities or sports 'heroes.'*
> *High-quality camps are places where young people . . . realize their poten-*
> *tial to do good in the world."*   American Camp Association

a long (since 1861) tradition of summer camps in interesting rural
environments.

There are currently about seven thousand sleepaway camps and
five thousand day camps in the United States, according to the
American Camp Association. Canada and Australia have similar
programs. In the United Kingdom, the camp tradition was slow to
take hold, perhaps because a large minority of well-to-do children
used to be sent to boarding school, so they spent vacations at home.
However, in 2006 thirteen thousand children attended a U.K. ver-
sion of camp, termed "activity holidays," with a range of offered
activities similar to American camps, though with rather less spiri-
tual uplift or moral intent.

Many camps, sleepaway or day, are the holiday child care of
choice for children over about eight years. In fact, the best of them
provide glorious summer holidays. From parents' points of view,
though, they have some major snags that prevent them from being a
real solution to child care needs during vacations: they take place
only during the summer holidays, and they are either very expensive
or very brief (some are both). Children can stay in privately run
American camps for as much as eight weeks, but the costs are very
high indeed. Not-for-profit camps, run by agencies such as the
YMCA, and camps run by cities for disadvantaged families are low-
cost, even free, but in order to offer opportunities to as many families as possible, the time any one child can spend there is usually
very limited. Camps specializing in particular sports or targeting
children with particular health problems, such as obesity, may have
grants available but are still costly and brief.

Part Four

MOVING ON

Introduction: Is Better Child Care a Priority?

As the title of this book suggests, most of the information gathered here is about child care and what it is like today. However, the book's subtitle, "Getting It Right for Everyone," suggests a wider agenda. One would hope this examination of Western child care in the first decade of the second millennium has not only described how it is but also how it might, or even should, be.

Studies of child care from different places, different times, and different researchers repeatedly focus on the same issues and produce similar findings. The picture—or rather the patchwork quilt—that emerges shows us what is widely established and accepted about child care but also shows us what is left out, highlighting by default both what is known but seldom acknowledged and what is not known at the moment but clearly needs to be. Putting the information and the omissions together gives us some indication of how we might move on, but they are signposts rather than highways, manifestos rather than policies, questions as often as answers. Who and what is child care for? Where do we want it to go from here, and what do we want it to be like?

There is complex thinking to be done and difficult decisions to be made by all the adult stakeholders: politicians and policy makers, professional care providers and parents.

BETTER CHILD CARE: EVERYONE'S PRIORITY?

All those who plan, provide, and use child care maintain that they want the best for children, now and in the future. If that is the case, bringing all early years child care and education up to the standard of the best ought to be everyone's immediate priority. Evidence of the importance of the quality of care children receive in their earliest years is woven through every chapter of the book. While there are a few studies of child care whose designs and analyses did not include measurements of quality, there are none that I know of that measured quality and found that it made no difference to children whether their child care was good, mediocre, poor, or terrible. Better child care is better for children and for parents, now and in the future, and eventually better, too, for the communities and societies in which they live. We know that.

We know a lot—though not everything there is to know—about what contributes to high-quality child care for different children in different countries and how to measure it. As we have seen, there is no single measure of child care quality, but there are multiple methods for measuring various aspects of child care environments, some designed and many validated by the NICHD Early Child Care Research Network. These include the overall ratings of "positive caretaking quality" described in Part 3, which include measurements of many aspects of the care provider's relationship with the child and stimulation of his or her development, as well as quantitative measurements of aspects of the child's experience in the care setting, such as amount or frequency of language stimulation, positive talk, positive physical contact, positive interaction with other children, and interaction with stimulating physical materials. These aspects of quality apply to child care anywhere. Furthermore, while carrying out the assessments in any particular child care setting is

"The vast majority of [American] child care is of unacceptably low quality and in the first 3 years of life does not meet even minimal recommended guidelines. Positive caregiving by nonparents in child care settings is rare. In the first 3 years of life, only 12% of the children studied in these 10 [NICHD study] sites received child care that fit the definition of 'highly characteristic' of positive care! When extrapolated to the United States as a whole, only 9% of children are estimated to receive such levels. In contrast, at every age, well over 50% of the children receive care that is either 'very uncharacteristic' or 'somewhat uncharacteristic' of positive care. . . . This is shocking and intolerable; it is also well-concealed from most parents and the general public."

Sharon Ramey, director of the Center for Health and Education,
Georgetown University

demanding of an appropriately trained observer's time and concentration, they are not part of a psychological mystique. Everything that is measured could be observed by informed parents as well as by those charged with inspection or regulation of child care. Measurement of "positive caretaking quality" has made an important contribution to child care research to date and could play an even more important part in improving child care quality in the future.

Higher-quality child care and education goes with better physical, social, emotional, and cognitive development and outcomes for children. And in several countries, those have been shown to be crucially important not only to children's ability to fulfill every aspect of their potential but also to the economies in which they live. There is widespread—and growing—agreement among economists across the political spectrum that investments in early years care and education pay startlingly high dividends. Individuals who have had higher-quality early years experiences do better at school and in the workplace, so overall they make a greater contribution to society than children who have had lower-quality care. The national economic advantages don't stop there, either. In the United States, it has been shown that the children who have had good child care are less likely than others to use welfare programs or get involved with criminal justice systems; so, along with contributing more to society, they cost society less. It is because these wide-ranging and far-reaching effects of good-quality child care are recognized that people not only want the highest-possible quality for their country, state, or service as well as for their individual child but also are reluctant to acknowledge that what they have might be poor.

Studies of low-quality child care are rare, so we know less about its features and outcomes than about those of high-quality care, but we do know that in most countries there is a great deal more of it. Research suggests that outside a handful of northern European states, most countries where studies of child care have been undertaken have fewer than a quarter of children in high- or very high-quality care, and at least a quarter in settings where the care is poor or very poor. Some authorities believe that for the United States, even this is probably an underestimate.

It seems likely that bad child care is at least as bad for children's development and nations' wealth as good child care is good, but we

need to know more than research scientists tell us about its characteristics and measurement. Research seldom studies bad child care
directly. Instead, it usually presents its findings as if good and bad
lie at the top and bottom of the same measurement scale, so child
care that gets a low score on a quality-of-care measure and is therefore "not good" is viewed as bad. "Not good" and "bad" may be the
same and probably often are, but we shouldn't assume that is always
the case. Bad child care may need indicators and measures of its
own. We know, for example, that care in which children lack close
relationships with their care providers cannot be of high quality.
What we do not know, and certainly need to know, is whether being
without those close relationships damages children in the same
ways and to the same degree if it is because well-intentioned caregivers have too many children to take care of or because they favor
some children and discriminate against others. It could be cogently
argued that while a low adult-to-child ratio prevents a child care
setting from being of high quality, discrimination by staff between
one child or group and another makes it bad.

Even in the present state of knowledge and understanding,
though, we do know a great deal about what would need to be done
to raise the quality of all early years child care and education, not
only the worst but also the best and everything in between. We
know how to do it, and there is no doubt that it could be done if it
was made a priority and the necessary resources were allocated. Of
course, that is true of many social programs; not all can be priori-
tized, nor can scarce resources be spent twice, so positive change is
unlikely to be complete or rapid. However, given the level of individual, local, national, and international agreement on the importance of good child care, it is surprising—even reprehensible—that

> "I judge that the basic descriptive findings about the generally low quality
> of care that children experience are minimized in the scientific articles
> about this [NICHD] project. That is, many of the studies emphasize the
> relationship between quality and child 'outcomes' and tend to gloss over the
> basic finding that so many children spend so much time in low to medium
> quality care, and such a small percentage are in consistently high quality
> care."   Sharon Ramey

so little is being done to improve it. Almost everywhere much more is being done to increase the supply and improve the accessibility of child care in its current forms than to raise the quality of children's experiences in such care.

Although the political issues and policies concerning child care are different in every country and state, and professionals and parents are differently situated, the absence of answers to the four interlinked questions noted here seem to act as brakes on action everywhere. If early years child care and education is to move on, these questions need to be addressed:

1. What model of child care are we working toward?

2. How is child care to be funded?

3. How do attitudes toward child care, family responsibility, and parental (especially mother) care mesh?

4. Is nonparental child care bad for children?

17. Politics and Policies, Models and Money

A national "model" of early years child care and education may seem very distant from the local nursery that needs improvement or the poor qualifications of family day care providers—too abstract a concept to be relevant to this pressing everyday issue. But although child care is an everyday issue for individual families, its solutions have to come from the top down. No country is likely to be able to move confidently and competently toward better child care services until or unless all stakeholders—politicians, policy makers, professionals, parents, and children themselves—share an agreed-upon destination.

In the English-speaking countries, child care is primarily about parental work and only secondarily about child well-being. The political driving force behind any public provision or subsidy of child care is getting parents into paid work so as to combat poverty (especially the child poverty that comes from being raised in a workless household) and enrich economies by relieving them of paying out benefits, bringing in money from parents' expenditures and taxation instead. Under the mantra "work is the way out of poverty," workfare imposes punitive monetary sanctions on parents who are not employed, irrespective of the ages and needs of their children. In the United States, it is shamefully the case that whether a mother can stay at home with her new baby depends not on her choice or judgment, or on the best interest of her child but on her wealth. The fact that for some families at particular times the best child care may be parental care is disregarded for any family requiring welfare support. The American emphasis (echoed in the United Kingdom but padded by paid maternity leave and by child benefit) on the importance of making child care accessible to underprivileged families, especially single mothers, as part of workfare arrangements makes it clear that nonparental care is a benefit for the adult world rather than a service to children, something most parents must use whether or not they or their children like it rather than a positive part of children's lives.

It might seem that any democratic government that uses its economic controls to compel parents to use nonparental child care should be expected to do everything possible to make that child care good. Regrettably, this does not always follow. In the United States, despite the existence of large bodies of data demonstrating the need to overhaul the standards of care for young children, there are powerful groups actually lobbying directly against attention—and tax dollars—being spent on child care. Even when they accept that available child care is mostly of poor quality, such lobbyists continue to argue for the status quo on the grounds that high-quality child care is unaffordable and consequently unattainable.

The scientific and academic communities, therefore, produce research findings that are politically sensitive and would certainly be unpopular if they were widely disseminated, and seem somewhat shy about pressing them to their logical conclusion. Some researchers are concerned that talking publicly about the true state of American child care will heap yet more guilt on already anxious parents or put pressure on those who are already poor to forgo a vital second income or devote even more of it to paying for higher-quality child care. Other academics seem paralyzed by the magnitude of the task of reforming and monitoring the nation's standards for care, seeming to hope that somehow things will get better and parents will figure out solutions on their own. Sharon Ramey of Georgetown

"To what extent the scientific community will focus on discovering effective ways to communicate and collaborate with those who shape and implement public policy, as well as those who are engaged in the everyday transactions that affect parents' decisions and children's care, is far from certain. What is certain is that there are major barriers that have forcefully kept our scientific and professional fields from acting in ways that truly place children at the center of the agenda. . . . [There are many] different ways in which reliable information generated can be used versus ignored or denigrated by special interest groups."   Sharon Ramey

University, invited commentator on the work of the NICHD Early Child Care Research Network, describes the situation like this:

> In the professional and political circles I know best, there is a culture of silence and defeatism that has crept in. People and groups are frankly fearful that criticism of existing standards and the quality of publicly funded programs, such as subsidized child care for welfare-to-work families and Head Start and pre-K public school programs, will lead to a total withdrawal of any public support for very low-income families or those with two working parents. . . . [M]any of us suspect that poor-quality care may be increasing, and that many parents remain ignorant about how really bad the child care is that their children are receiving. . . .
>
> We choose to ignore that the United States remains an outlier in its lack of attention to this urgent national crisis; and we fail to place our children truly at the center of our agenda.

Getting parents into the workplace and combating child poverty are the driving forces behind public child care provision in the United Kingdom also. But this adult-centric view has been modified during a decade of Labour government in which positive outcomes, especially cognitive outcomes, have been recognized for children in high-quality care. A series of "frameworks"—first advisory, such as "Every Child Matters," now brought together and made statutory in the Early Years Foundation Stage—convey a clear understanding of how children under school age are to be cared for when they are not with their families and a commitment to making those regulations a reality in all child care settings, including, as we have seen, children's centers in all communities.

This government has both paid attention to other people's research and funded its own. When the government-funded Effective Provision of Pre-School Education (EPPE) project showed clear developmental benefits of preschool experience not only for children from age three upward but also from age two, the government took note. A pilot project was initiated, and as a result of its findings, the fifteen hours per week of free preschool currently available to three- and four-year-olds is being extended to a large number of disadvantaged two-year-olds. However, despite the growing conviction that early child care and education can improve school readiness and life chances, especially in children from less privileged homes, and the provision of governmental models of good practice, U.K. planning is guided only by outcomes, especially cognitive achievements. Although an unprecedented amount of government-level attention has been devoted to it, the United Kingdom still lacks a clear theoretical framework for children's services, and the focus of its child care planning has scarcely changed since the interdepartmental child care review published in 2002 put it like this: "This review has emphasised the importance of childcare to Government objectives of extending employment opportunities and tackling child poverty, as well as other objectives such as boosting productivity and closing the gender pay gap. It has also highlighted significant benefits to children . . . when good quality childcare is delivered alongside early years education, family support and health services."

Where nations have developed theoretical frameworks for children's services in general or for child care in particular, there are substantial differences between them, the philosophies behind them, and their working models of good practice. New Zealand, for example, has adopted much of the education-centered Swedish model for its child care but with a view to realizing its own unique aim of bringing Maori child care and education into the mainstream. Even the theoretical frameworks of those northern European countries whose child care is the best in the world are not as similar as many in the English-speaking world might assume. The literature on this topic is too substantial to include here, but the following issues, whose formulation owes much to the work of others, are the ones that most urgently need resolving before the planning or the practice of child care can move forward.

ISSUE 1. INTEGRATION

Relationships between care and education

The importance of integrating care and education—some would rather say, of acknowledging faults in the web of their intrinsic connectedness—is internationally recognized (see Chapter 12). Physical and emotional care, learning and play (and in some models, such as Denmark's, every aspect of children's upbringing) need to be brought together and equally valued in all early childhood services. Some models of good practice, including Sweden's, extend the concept of integration from bringing together care and education in institutions for infants, toddlers, and preschool children to bringing preschool institutions and primary and secondary schools together, creating what the OECD called a "strong and equal relationship."

Although many countries, especially the United Kingdom with its expanding program of children's centers and extended schools and New Zealand with all children's services now under education, have moved a long way toward integration, it has been achieved only in the Nordic states, most notably in Sweden and Denmark. Elsewhere, there are still important (though not always openly acknowledged) differences in the quality of care available in more and less affluent neighborhoods and the fees charged for them; in families' access to schools, preschools, and child care services; and in the staffing and the funding of each. Child care is still often perceived as distinct from education, while play workers tend to be assigned a still lower status. A care provider in a nursery may be happy to be referred to as a teacher (as she often is in North America), but the reverse seldom holds.

Sweden's and Denmark's models for their children's services may be equally integrated, but they are importantly distinct from each other. In Sweden, all the services come under the education department. All who work with children of any age from one (when most parental leave ends) to nineteen are teachers (or trainee or assistant teachers), and children's education is continuous, the quality of each phase being dependent on the quality of what came before. It is widely accepted by specialist teachers that the work of a secondary school is affected by the work done in the children's center a decade earlier.

In Denmark, those who work in children's services are neither teachers nor care providers but members of a special and highly regarded profession: pedagogy. Pedagogues may work with adults as well as with children, and pedagogy is the most popular degree course in Denmark, attracting many mature students and quite a large minority of men. Lasting three and a half years, it covers psychology, social and health studies, communication and creative studies, and emphasizes the importance to children of outdoor activities. Pedagogues are responsible not for what children learn but for how they learn: for their physical, emotional, and cognitive development, socialization, and relationships with others. Respected both by parents and by teachers, pedagogues are regarded as making a special contribution to children's lives.

Just as New Zealand has adopted for its child care program those parts of the Swedish educational model that are relevant to its particular needs, so other nations could choose either one or any combination of these and other models to fit their particular circumstances. Pedagogy is not only foreign to many non-Europeans but also difficult to define. Nevertheless, unlabeled elements of its approach can be incorporated, as they are in the United Kingdom. An educational model is easier to understand but may not be the best way forward everywhere. Schools are long-established and powerful institutions, and the teaching profession's position is entrenched. Even in Sweden, there are fears that such models may dominate preschool and leisure-time institutions.

Training and working practices

Whatever its model, any integrated service designed to meet all the extrafamilial needs of all children requires an integrated workforce with a common core of skills and knowledge. That core needs to be consistent and transferable, providing a starting point for employment in a day care center as well as in a nursery school and the base from which caring individuals can move on to construct their own career ladders, building specialisms ranging from play leader at the vacation play program or physics teacher in the secondary school to autism specialist in the special education department.

The best existing model is the university-based teacher training put in place by Sweden in 2001 after two decades of preparation. This training is the only route into any kind of professional work with children. It encompasses work with children from one year to six years in "preschools," children from six years through adolescence in schools, and "free-time children services" (school-aged child care and vacation activities/care). All students follow the same course for the first eighteen months, whether they want to work with babies or teenagers. Students then choose an area in which to specialize, and at least two more years of study follow. At the end, all qualify as teachers but with differing profiles depending on the areas in which they have specialized.

Integrated training programs are available in New Zealand and are being developed in some North American states. In Britain, a new graduate qualification as an Early Years Professional (EYP) describes individuals who are trained not only to provide an excellent standard of child care and education themselves but also to supervise, lead, and inspire less well qualified child care workers. However, none of these programs jumps the still enormous gap between preschool and "real" school. British EYPs will be highly qualified, and they will be teachers, but only through the "foundation stage," not into compulsory schooling. Furthermore, none of these programs starts out with Sweden's years of preparation behind them nor with adequate commitments of long-term public funds. While the Nordic states have been able to build new early years professions mainly from among new undergraduates, others now have to start with individuals who are already working in child care, often with little education and minimal training, and find ways of enabling them to accumulate credits toward higher qualifications. That would be difficult in any field but is particularly difficult in this one. Child care is understaffed almost everywhere, and individual staff members are vitally important to the children they work with. Arranging to release individuals to attend courses for professional development is therefore extraordinarily difficult. If a children's center plans for day release of its staff, it must also plan to put in (and pay) replacements so that the staff-child ratio does not suffer. But even if that ratio is protected, the stability of care offered to the children may be threatened. In family day care, acquiring training and qualifications while working in the field is even more difficult. A childminder who works alone (as many in the United Kingdom still do) has no way of replacing herself for day release. If she takes time for training during the workweek, she inevitably lets down the working parents (and their employers) who depend on her. It is to the credit of workers in family day care that so many give up their scarce family and leisure time to attend training in the evenings and on weekends. It is a slow struggle, though. Currently, U.K. plans to have everyone who works with children of any age or in any capacity qualified to university-degree standard and equally regarded seem closer to aspiration than actuality, while in the United States such plans are not even aspirations but utopian.

ISSUE 2. ECONOMICS: CHILD CARE FUNDING

Child care costs money. Better child care costs more money, and the best child care we know how to provide costs the most of all. Funding issues—not only what the costs are but also how and by whom they should be met—are the stiffest brake on progress in children's services. Whether the model of child care that is adopted is a public service, like education, part of the private sector, or a mixture of the two, its viability depends on its economics.

Demand-side funding

Child care in the English-speaking world largely relies on "demand-side funding" rather than the "supply-side funding" of many European countries. Demand-side funding usually means that the service is paid for by those (and only those) who want to use it: by parents directly paying for the child care they use. Supply-side funding is usually understood to mean that child care is paid for by those who supply it—the state or its local authorities and perhaps nonprofit organizations such as churches—and in practice usually means that the service is paid for out of taxation. In North America, however, demand-side and supply-side funding are reinterpreted as "private/for-profit" and "public/not-for-profit." It is often assumed that governments grant money preferentially to nonprofit child care, thus ensuring that nonprofits have higher standards. While this may be true of some grant-giving bodies, there is no evidence of it in national policies. If nonprofits have higher standards, it is usually because they attract new ideas and better staff.

Like private education or hospital care, private child care and early education places inevitably cost more than any but a tiny minority of parents can pay out of their taxed income. All countries that rely on demand-side (or for-profit) funding therefore mediate parental fees through means-tested fee subsidies and tax credits, often of enormous complexity. In the United States, for example, up to $5,000 per year paid by an employer into a Flexible Spending Account for Dependent Care instead of to the employee can be claimed by the employee free of income and other taxes against child care receipts. Fine, if the particular employer offers FSA; if the employee can accurately predict the next year's child care spending during the open enrollment period (if she puts $5,000 in the account and spends only $2,000 because a grandparent took over, she loses the difference); and if her child care provider will provide receipts. In all such schemes, it is extraordinarily difficult to ensure that every family entitled to such easements actually receives them here and now rather than at some future rebate time, and it is impossible to ensure that they pass the money on to their care providers. So such "systems" do not work well either for the users or the providers of child care. Parents struggle to pay, so consideration of the out-of-pocket costs of child care often overwhelms considerations of quality. Care providers struggle to pass inspections and to raise their standards without the secure income necessary for future planning and investment.

Currently, American and British child care is big boom-bust business that parents buy mostly from private "for-profit" providers but also from a patchwork of voluntary and nonprofit organizations. It is clear that this system (or lack of system) cannot consistently deliver high-quality early child care services. In any given country or state, the best of current early years child care and education is invariably found in the public sector or in trailblazer or demonstration projects with special staffing and funding. If demand-side funding cannot consistently deliver today's best care, it clearly cannot deliver the major reevaluation, reform, and reeducation of the workforce that is needed to make that standard general, rather than exceptional, tomorrow.

Fifteen years ago, it looked as though a way forward might be found in corporate responsibility for child care funding. "Workplace child care," in which nurseries were provided close to (though seldom in) workplaces, or places in centers were held by employers for their employees and vouchers given to employees as a "perk" that they could spend in any type of child care, looked promising for a while. In the 1990s, an Australian program gave parents vouchers they could use for either nonprofit or for-profit child care, and a tax benefit in the Netherlands allowed employers to work with either child care sector. Both schemes were said to work well at the time, with the standards in private child care equaling those in the public sector and the supply of new places being increased. However, economic climates have changed, and neither workplace child care nor vouchers seem appropriate in a world of global markets and short-term contracts. Children's child care places are not secure if they are dependent on parental employment, which is now so often insecure and short-term, and child care providers cannot achieve the secure long-term funding on which quality-raising investments depend.

Lack of secure long-term funding not only puts brakes on investment but also reduces the impact and spread of many excellent initiatives, even those in the supply-side or nonprofit sector. Head Start, Early Head Start, and Smart Start are all North American examples of superb services that have been and remain so underfunded that they serve more as demonstration programs and flags for governments to wave than as real services. Some of the programs targeted to underprivileged communities in the United Kingdom during the first years of the New Labour government faced similar risks. Sure Start, for example, was fully funded with start-up grants (which could not be spent for any other purpose) to the relevant local authorities from central government. However, when those Sure Start services were handed over to local authorities—health trusts and education authorities—it was up to each authority to decide what priority to give them. Inevitably, that priority varied, and not every Sure Start program could maintain its high standards and wide reach.

In the United Kingdom, a system of child care tax credits was designed (and redesigned) with the specific intention of softening the impact on families of demand-side, pay-as-you-go child care funding. It was originally thought that such a system could stand in for supply-side funding, but it does so very inadequately. The wheels of the tax system turn so slowly that in some families claimants' circumstances change faster than the system can follow. If someone is laid off, the increase to which he or she is entitled is needed immediately, not months later. Some parents have even been made to repay money given to them earlier and long spent; when eventually their circumstances improved, they were found to have overpaid. From the providers' point of view, whether working alone in family day care or trying to build a chain of nurseries, tax credits (and similar demand-side funding systems) do nothing to help them plan, because they cannot predict how many parents will take the tax credit and how many of those who do take it will pass the money on to a particular child care provider.

Supply-side funding

Many countries, especially in continental Europe, regard universal early child care and education as a social essential like other health and education services. They have come to recognize the difficulties of demand-side funding and take it for granted that child care, early years education, and leisure services should be paid for out of national tax funds, just as education is paid for once children reach compulsory school age. There is often a means-tested parental contribution, but it is always capped and usually at a rate many English-speaking parents find incredible, such as 10–30 percent. Supply-side (public) funding does, of course, come with a high price tag for all taxpayers, not only parents. In Sweden, for example, public expenditure on early years and free-time (after-school and vacation) services is four times as great as in Britain (almost 2 percent of GDP compared to less than 0.5 percent), and this is one part of the reason why Swedish citizens pay higher taxes than U.K. or U.S. citizens. It should be noted, though, that when a newly elected Swedish government promised to lower taxation by reducing spending on parental leave and child care, it was rejected by voters of all parties, nonparents as well as parents. Taxpayers pay more, but they also get a great deal more for their money. Outstanding returns to parents include very low rates of child poverty; generous parental leave that is well paid; and child care and education services with good staff recruitment, retention, and training, universally available as a right and universally affordable. All these benefits are funded by economies that are no more successful than those of the United States or the United Kingdom, so to say that they could not afford a similar system is clearly absurd.

Mixed funding

Governments in the English-speaking world are reluctant to treat optional early years care and education in the same way as compulsory schooling or to accept the tax and political implications of doing so. Such a change of policy would be regarded as especially radical in the United States, where there are no publicly funded universal health or welfare services. Indeed, when Nordic social policies, especially child care, are described to American audiences, scornful or incredulous dismissal is commonplace. Of course, the fact that a system works in one part of the world is no reason to assume that an identical system would be right for another. Complete acceptance and outright rejection are not the only possibilities. Some public funding is essential if all children are to have better child care and eventually the best child care we know how to provide, but public funding can be arranged in many different ways. In New Zealand since 2004, for example, an early childhood service that is education-based like that of Sweden, but with a different scheme of parental fees and income-related subsidy, has been made available to all. It is paid for by a combination of direct funding of each child care place provided with further funding made available setting by setting as staffing and other standards are raised.

Meanwhile, some commentators see the way forward as being a compromise regime that has been called "the social investment state." The British Labour Party's Third Way, proclaimed by the

---

From the social welfare state to the social investment state

"The welfare state at the start of the 21st century appears to be in the midst of a transformation. The original consensus was that, if the market economy was sufficiently productive, it could be taxed to support social expenditures. These social expenditures were assumed to be a diversion of capital from production and a drag on economic growth.

"Today, the assumed competition between social protection and economic growth is being challenged. There is increasing recognition that social spending for some purposes and/or in some forms can contribute to both economic growth and social development. Reflecting this, the best social policy alternatives will move beyond the idea of consumption-as-well-being, toward what Amartya Sen identifies as capabilities. Building people's assets is one policy pathway to both increase capabilities and eliminate the trade-off between economic growth and social development in the process."   Michael Sherraden, *Shelterforce*

Blair government, came close to this model, and analysts detect its emergence in other liberal states such as Canada, as well as much discussion of its principles in the United States.

The overall meaning and detailed arrangements of "the social investment state" are far from being universally agreed upon. However, it is thought countries such as the United States, which currently rely on demand-side (private) funding, will find it more acceptable than outright supply-side (public) funding, because it maintains what might be termed the "moral dimensions" of social provision and stresses responsibilities alongside rights. This model continues to stress the importance of individuals being self-sufficient (no nanny state or welfare dependency) and productive through paid work, while still justifying tax-based funding of some aspects of human capital, especially early years child care and education, as an investment that is necessary to sustain the nation's competitiveness in a global economy.

It seems possible that "social investment" will become the concept that pulls diverse politicoeconomic systems toward the center. As English-speaking nations move to incorporate some aspects of the Nordic welfare states' child care arrangements into their own, there are signs of Sweden moving toward a more liberal, market-based approach with encouragement (and equal subsidies) to private providers. Exactly where the center will be remains to be seen.

18. Families and Child Care

Unease about the relationships between families and child care, and especially between parents and caregivers, complicates discussion about desirable models of child care and policy decisions about how it should be funded. After all, politicians, policy makers, and professionals are all members of families, and many are parents. When they talk about what these relationships are, what they should be, or what parents want them to be, their views are partly personal. Perhaps it is a pity that many of them are privileged citizens. Their own feelings seldom illuminate the range of all families in the country.

The topic "relationships between parents and caregivers" sounds anodyne but is not. While there is a great deal of research into parents' feelings about care providers, as we have seen, very little is known or recorded about caregivers' feelings about parents. In the English-speaking nations, care providers, especially young nursery assistants, are often disapproving of parents for using the child care facility in which they themselves work and very quick to criticize lapses in parenting, such as being late to pick up a child or forgetting to send in something the center requested. Parents, many of them already vulnerable to guilt about using child care, sense such disapproval; children may also.

Behind the day-to-day relationships parents have with care providers lurks a question that is so sensitive it is often left unasked. The question is this: "When children spend adult working hours in child care, who brings them up? Who socializes them?" In the English-speaking world almost every parent would answer, "We do," adding a slightly indignant "of course" in their tone if not their words. Even if a child spends fifty hours each week from infancy onward in a nursery group or with a family day care provider, parents take it for granted (or struggle to believe) that whatever specific developments and skills, friends, or manners their child acquires in child care, her upbringing (seldom defined) remains in their hands. As we have seen in earlier chapters, they are largely right. No matter how much time children spend in any type of child care, relationships with parents matter more to them than those with care providers, and the quality of parenting and home life affects their development even more than does the quality of child care.

When parents really understand and believe in their own unique importance in the lives of their children and the relative unimportance of other caring adults, using child care is likely to be less conflict-ridden, and they are less liable to feel guilty about it. In fact, a general recognition of the primacy of parents might help many to feel less threatened by child care services and be able to take a more positive view of child care and perhaps offer more respect and support to care providers. Unfortunately, when acknowledgment of the primacy of parents is made, the message most generally understood in the English-speaking world is that *only* parents matter, so maybe they ought to be there all the time.

Many mothers and fathers believe that if they had the time, money, and inclination to remain home based, their children wouldn't need anyone or anything else before they started school, and that they would be better off. Since most parents don't remain home based, at least not right through the several years until school age, they have to acknowledge that it is they themselves who need child care and caregivers for their children; but many are uneasy about it, and many, some of whom I've quoted in earlier chapters, especially resent and resist the idea that sharing their child's time with nonparental caregivers means sharing his or her upbringing.

> I have to work; I have to lead some adult life, but I sort of wish that while I'm doing it I could put Jessica on ice or away in a safe cupboard until I come home. I know that sounds awful but she's *my* baby: I really don't want other people telling her things, making her laugh, influencing her. —FCCC mother

A parent who feels this way is certain to be conflicted about balancing home and work and may feel that it is selfish of her to use child care (or so much child care), which she sees as being entirely for her sake and not for her child's. Furthermore, whether they recognize it or not, there is a sense in which such parents may not *want* child care, or a particular care provider, to become too important to their children or central to their development, so they actually do not want child care to be as good for children as we know how to make it.

In much of continental Europe, on the other hand, a child care group is seen as complementing rather than competing with or substituting for home and family life: a child's world that is separate, even private from the family. Indeed, in the Nordic countries, the Netherlands, and Italy, for example, many children's centers serve as the hubs of their communities, just as children serve as the hubs of their families, and most parents would acknowledge without pain that caregivers play a big part in children's upbringing.

THE INTERFACE BETWEEN HOME AND INFANT CHILD CARE

Parents' responses to the question "Who brings up or socializes our children?" have an important bearing on how they view child care and caregivers and how they would like to see them change.

Where child care is perceived as existing primarily for the convenience of parents rather than for children—as is common in the United States, the United Kingdom, and Australia, for example—parents and other stakeholders seek to smooth out differences between what children experience at home and in child care and to minimize the differences being in child care makes to a child's home relationships. Parents and professionals alike talk of the importance of keeping as closely as possible to an infant's or toddler's home routines when she is in child care, especially of the importance of providing each child with a key person so that she can be treated as an individual rather than as a member of the group. Mothers sometimes refer to care providers—especially in family day care or in the home—as "substitute mothers" and want them, perhaps even expect them, to care for the child as they do themselves. Such control over the details of a child's daily life and care is an important reason for employing a nanny, who can be told what to do, or enlisting the care of a grandmother who will rear the child as she reared the mother.

Minimizing the difference between child care and home, care-

giver and parent, certainly reduces the impact on babies and toddlers of a transition from twenty-four-hour-per-day home care to
eight or more hours per day in child care and eases them into their
new lifestyles. A "settling period," in which the infant first spends
time with the mother and the care provider, and then, as they get to
know each other, gradually spends more and more time with the
caregiver alone, is widely recommended. Easing a child into it,
however, does not alter the fact that child care is a new lifestyle for
him. The child care setting is not home; the caregiver is not mother
or father. Parents who cannot fully accept this reality of the child's
separation from them and life without them, and cannot detach
themselves enough to support and encourage his efforts to adapt,
may make it exceedingly difficult for him to do so. And if a child has
trouble adapting to care, his parents are likely to feel critical of it
and the caregiver likely to feel criticized. A vicious circle can
develop in which all the stakeholders are unhappy, and the mother's
feeling that only she can care properly for this child is reinforced.
To avoid this situation, she and the caregiver must talk openly and
often—not to make sure that the caregiver knows the mother's
wishes and follows her instructions but to try to help the mother
come to trust the caregiver to do as she thinks best.

Developing that kind of trust is not always easy, but neither is it
always desirable, of course. As we have seen, not all child care is of
high quality, and where it is not, the judgment of some care
providers may be questionable. In the final analysis, parents are
responsible for trusting and acting on their own judgment about the
quality of care their child is receiving. Moving a child from one
child care setting to another may cost parents time, money, and
work-related stress, but continuing to leave a child with a caregiver
they do not feel able to trust once they and the child have gotten to
know her is hard to justify.

Where child care is expected to be positive for children and is
perceived as their right irrespective of parents' convenience, child
care and home are seen as parallel worlds. Only children inhabit
both these worlds, and they are recognized and respected as the only
people who can be fully integrated into them. Parents accept (or try
to accept) that the children's center is their child's domain, which
they themselves will never fully understand. Children's upbringing

> *"Enrolling children from age one in full-day preschools has become gener-*
> *ally acceptable [in Sweden]. What was once viewed as either a privilege of*
> *the wealthy for a few hours a day or an institution for needy children and*
> *single mothers has become, after 70 years of political vision and policy-*
> *making, an unquestionable right of children and families. Parents now*
> *expect a holistic pedagogy that includes health care, nurturing and educa-*
> *tion for their preschoolers."*
>
> Gunilla Dahlberg and Hillevi Lenz-Taguchi,
> *Preschool and School—Two Different Traditions and*
> *a Vision of a Meeting Place*

is therefore seen as a process of what has been named "dual socialization." The adults of both worlds—parents at home, caregivers at
child care—must all contribute to and work at cooperating with one
another and sharing information about the child.

Instead of aiming to minimize the differences between children's
experiences at home and in child care, dual socialization describes
differences between those two parallel developmental worlds as creative and complementary. It is considered a virtue of child care that
it offers children different experiences, has different expectations of
them, and offers them opportunities to play different roles and be
different people from those they are at home. The child care setting
is a more public venue, and adults' behavior toward children there,
while friendly, is more emotionally neutral and instrumental than in
the home. Relationships in the family, on the other hand, are primarily emotional and based on intimacy and individuality. In the
home, children can express a range of emotions, such as love, frustration, and anger, that are more controlled in the group setting. A
leading exponent of the concept of dual socialization contends that
the role of day care centers in Scandinavian countries can thus be
seen as socializing children into acceptable group behavior and that
learning such behavior while very young may be an advantage in
social development.

Dual socialization is not all positive, though. Although a large
majority of Nordic infants do not start child care until they are at
least a year old, they are then confronted with developmental challenges that some—especially the very young and those who lack

sensitive parental support—find difficult to meet. While he is in child care, the child must interact with several, perhaps many adults and learn to meet their social demands and balance them with the very different demands made by parents at home. His success is thought to depend on parents' being sensitive to the conflicts he faces at child care and calmly responsive to the emotional outbursts that are commonplace when he arrives home. Even within high-quality centers in Nordic countries, children who are having a difficult time at home—perhaps because of the fallout from parental divorce or the arrival of a new sibling—may find child care very stressful, especially if care providers are not privy to or sensitive to what is going on at home. Furthermore, even within a high-quality service with well-trained staff, not every care provider is an excellent match for every child. So while dual socialization sounds like and may be a double benefit, its success in making child care something positive for children is just as dependent on communication between parents and care providers as is the success of a system that seeks to minimize the difference between them.

Where child care is run by trained pedagogues, notably in Denmark, the approach to that question about who brings children up is different again. Children themselves are seen as being the central force in their own upbringing. "Upbringing," in its most general sense, was the subject of the original German concept of pedagogy, and the modern pedagogue addresses the whole child from birth to adulthood (pedagogues work with adults also): her body, mind, and emotions; her past, present, and future; seeing every kind of care and learning and every aspect of upbringing as inseparable parts of his or her daily work with children. Within pedagogy, these are not separate fields that need to be integrated but interconnected facets of life that cannot be envisaged separately.

There are wide differences among these three schools of thought about who raises children and even wider differences among child care models generated in and brought from other parts of the world. The difficulty for politicians and policy makers is that each model and mode of family–child care interface seems self-evidently right to those brought up within its tradition and close to incomprehensible to those outside it. A Danish parent would not wish to bring up children without input from pedagogues, but an American might resent the wide range of pedagogical expertise and feel that it intruded into private areas of her parenting. A British parent might find it impossible to imagine that the child care center was—or should be—her child's own private world and almost as important to him as the home he shares with her, but a Swedish parent might be equally astonished and rejecting of attempts to minimize differences between home and day care, which seem to her both obvious and desirable.

Is Child Care Bad for Children?

This question originated in the United States, where most twentieth-century research in child care was carried out, and children below school age are still regarded as rather exclusively family business. The question is placed here in a chapter slanted toward family concerns because the possibility of negative effects of child care on children, or indeed children's viewpoint on any aspect of child care, is scarcely acknowledged among politicians or policy makers. There is plenty of literature on measuring or raising standards in child care to make it even better for more children but very little on measuring or changing aspects of child care that might be damaging to children.

"Is child care bad for children?" is not a question often heard in languages other than English, but in the English-speaking world, it is constantly reiterated by parents and by the media, so that the question has become part of our problem with child care: a distraction from what we know and need to know.

Since nonparental child care is an integral part of modern life, discussing whether it is bad for children is no more useful than discussing whether we would all be better off without television or the Internet. It's the *wrong question*. Proposing a blanket indictment of child care invites, almost forces, people to line up as pro or anti and distracts from the real issue, which is "How can we make any part of children's lives that they spend in child care good for them?" and sidesteps the many more meaningful questions put forward in earlier chapters: Which children? What effects? What type and quality and quantity of child care? Child care when, where, and by whom? Individuals and organizations, perhaps especially media, who ask

> *"This study [NICHD] unequivocally demonstrates that both the quality and the quantity of nonparental care influence children's development. Stated directly and summatively, poor quality care is harmful. Conversely, high quality care can be somewhat beneficial, particularly for somewhat older children and particularly for children whose own family home environments do not consistently provide high levels of stimulation. Further, children in extended care—for more than 30 hours per week and starting very early in life—do show outcomes that are in a non-optimal direction. This is not uplifting news; it means that no one can credibly claim that we do not know whether child care really matters. Child care makes a difference and given the overall low levels of high-quality child care and the long hours many children spend in nonparental care, the risks are real."*
>
> Sharon Ramey

rhetorically if nonparental child care is bad for children and answer "yes" often seem ignorant of the fact that in the English language the opposite of "bad" is "good." They do not suggest that the answer to bad child care is good child care but assume that it is *no* child care. They regard full-time parent care (usually in the form of care by mothers financed by fathers at work) as the "gold standard" against which all other kinds of child care must be measured. That is patently unhelpful. Many contemporary mothers and fathers choose—and more would like—to be home based with children for a while, but that doesn't indicate a return to that disproportionately influential postwar period of nuclear family living when exclusive mother care until the youngest child went to school was expected. That is over and has been for half a century. It is partly because we haven't entirely abandoned the attitudes of 1959 that we are finding it so difficult to move forward in 2009.

There is much that we still need to know about the effects of child care experiences: we especially need to know more about the balance between "positive" and "negative" effects for different children at different ages. How, for example, do the most vaunted benefits of child care and early years education, such as increased readiness for school and a larger vocabulary, balance against the relative lack of cooperation reported by teachers? How significant are the higher levels of the stress hormone, cortisol, produced by some toddlers in group care? And knowing that family relationships and poverty have far more impact on children's development than any aspect of child care experience, just how significant in the real world, as opposed to statistical tables, are any child care effects? Above all, though, knowing how important the quality of child care is to children, we need to know more about improving both child care and children's experiences of it.

Given the way global capitalism impacts families, we have to have nonparental child care. Outside academia, no policies that might change that are even being discussed. Much is being done to increase the numbers of child care places, but in the English-speaking world, much less is being done to improve the quality of those places or to make them truly a service for children. It seems that we are not sure which services we want children to have or what we are willing to pay for them, financially or politically. Thinking through the brakes on progress discussed above may help us to get moving, but knowing which way to go depends on developing a clear sense of purpose.

19. Some Signposts to the Way Forward for Politicians, Policy Makers, and Professionals

STARTING SCHOOL

The age at which children start school has a major bearing on the size and the influence of the early years sector. In North America and in the United Kingdom, the age at which children start school has crept further and further down. The United Kingdom, which already had the youngest compulsory school-starting age in Europe, the school term after a child's fifth birthday, now offers school reception classes for four-year-olds and free half-time nursery school for three-year-olds (soon to include two-year-olds in some areas). Parents don't have to send their children so early; they still have the right to wait for that fifth birthday, but such is the competition to get into particular schools that not going into a school's own nursery or into its reception class may risk a child's place later on. And there is another understandable reason why parents are reluctant to hold these tiny children back: school is free, and child care is not. The situation in the United States is similar in that kindergarten, which used to prepare five-year-old children, part-time, for first grade at age six, is now often full-time and has its own preparation—pre-K—taken a year younger, while nursery school for two-year-olds is widely sought even though it has to be paid for.

The younger children start school, the fewer "older" students there are in child care settings and preschools, which alters the social composition of groups and deprives younger children of role models. "We need more and more potties and pacifiers, fewer and fewer toilets and pens," as one preschool teacher remarked rather sadly. Furthermore, children who move on at four, or even three, have very little continuity of care in the lead-up to compulsory schooling. If there is to be an early childhood sector strong enough to hold its own alongside schools, competing on equal terms for staff and status, an increase in the compulsory school-starting age to six years, the minimum in most of Europe, would certainly help. Furthermore, parents who currently may tolerate poor standards of nursery education in some child care settings because their child will be there only until she nears her fourth birthday would probably get more deeply involved if they knew that "big school" was not going to be available for a further year.

> She's pretty bored with the same old cutting and sticking and blocks
> and circle time, but I'm piling in other activities in the afternoons to
> keep her going until September.   —FCCC mother

MATERNITY/PARENTAL LEAVE

Although childbirth certainly requires a period of paid maternity leave for women, countries that extend this leave through most of the first year or more (as the United Kingdom has done since 2007) should rethink it. What is required from the point of the view of the infant is at least a year, and perhaps more, of *parental leave*. It makes physiological sense (and encourages breast-feeding) if the first three or four months is reserved for the mother, but after that, parents should surely be able, even encouraged, to share parental leave as best suits them. One or two weeks of paternity leave, given at the time of the birth, is better than nothing but not much. Some corporations may complain at having to give leave to fathers rather than only to mothers, but such a change would force a salutary rethink of gender equality. Above all, knowing that either parent may request leave will reverse the apparently increasing tendency of many firms selectively to employ or promote men.

Unpaid leave is not worth considering. Even in the United States, where it is often the only kind of leave available, most parents are not eligible, and many eligible parents don't take it. Along with the obvious reasons—that only the relatively well-to-do can afford it and only the highly qualified can count on their employers to respect it—there are indications that the lack of payment is also seen as an insulting reflection of the low regard in which the corporate world holds parenting.

The rates at which parental leave is paid need careful consideration. While higher payments certainly bring maternity or parental leave within the reach of more families, it seems that as long as such leave is paid at all, the size of payments has less impact on take-up than might be expected. If more money can be made available, giving parents more weeks of leave may be a better use of it than paying fewer weeks at a higher rate. In the Czech Republic as of January 2008, for example, all mothers of newborns got a birth grant of approximately one month's average wage and could then choose one of three government plans extending maternity benefits over two, three, or four years. Those opting for the two-year coverage (which is open only to women earning above-average wages) get 11,300 koruna per month (78 percent of average wages), those opting for three years get 7,600 koruna per month (52 percent of average wages), and those opting for four years get 3,800 koruna per month (26 percent of average wages). Most mothers are choosing the three-year option, and fathers can replace mothers for some of it. Self-employed mothers also qualify, though they tend to have lower income, so they rarely qualify for the two-year benefit.

Paid parental leave, even for the first year, sounds expensive, and proposals to institute or extend it often meet with public objections. Within the wider scheme of child care, though, such leave is good value for the money. The provision of child care for infants is far more expensive than for toddlers and older children. In countries where child care is mostly publicly funded, it is recognized that parents who care for their own children at home during the first year save the taxpayer a great deal of money. In the Nordic countries, it is often said that the enviable child care services available to all families are possible only because they mostly exclude care for babies under one year, who are cared for by parents on leave. So great are the savings that in some countries, such as Sweden, it is still economically advantageous if the stay-at-home parent is paid as much as 80 percent of salary.

Where almost all child care is privately funded, everyone seems to lose financially when a parent stays home from work with a baby;

that is probably why lengths of leave and payments tend to be negligible. Direct payments are not the only way of financing parents' leave, however. There are many ideas that might be worth exploring, especially in countries where public funding and universal (as opposed to targeted) grants are still unacceptable to many politicians and policy makers. "Mortgage holidays" have been suggested, allowing the parent a preplanned payment-free year or two with the accumulated cost spread over the lifetime of the mortgage. Another suggestion is "time banking," in which corporations would allow employees to accumulate any overtime, unsocial hours of work, or unused vacation time in a special account to be topped up by the employer while he benefits from having the money and drawn on by the employee after childbirth. And a range of concessions—on public transportation and admissions to facilities such as museums and swimming pools, for example—could be the right of any adult accompanying a baby and would cost very little, since parents and infants tend to move around and use community facilities at their least busy times, when most people are at work. It is more economical to run a bus or a gallery or a swimming pool with two people in it than with no one, no matter how little they pay.

However it is arranged, it seems that the way forward for child care must include more genuine choice for more parents than is currently the case anywhere in the English-speaking world.

Alternatives to Center Care for Babies

Making even adequate provision for babies in nurseries or child care centers is much more expensive than providing for toddlers and preschool children. Facilities and staff trained to use them have to be provided for mixing formula, for example, storing expressed breast milk, and sterilizing bottles as well as for changing and disposing of diapers. Most countries regulate "milk kitchens" and their hygienic separation from bathrooms.

Since many research findings suggest that the developmental/ emotional needs of children in the first year of life are more likely to be met in individual or domestic-scale settings than in group child care, the way forward should include exploring a starting age of twelve to fifteen months for child care centers. Most babies under that age would probably be at home with parents once parental leave allowed this, as in many European countries, but parents should not be forced into making arrangements at home if they prefer to do otherwise. Ensuring other options for infant care should certainly be part of any policy. Along with nannies and au pairs—the one too costly, the other too unstable for infant care everywhere— such options currently include family day care and care by grandparents. Childminders in the United Kingdom already care for a disproportionate number of infants, often combining this with after-school and perhaps vacation care for school-age children, as in a once-upon-a-time large family. Licensed and inspected, most rate relatively highly for quality. Grandmothers, the preferred caregivers of countless parents, achieve higher-quality care for their grandchildren when they are babies than later on.

There are problems with these types of individual care, as we have seen, but once there was a policy commitment to making them available for infant care, these would be manageable. Family day care settings can be linked in networks with the support of a highly trained care provider, as many are in the United Kingdom, for example. Furthermore, childminders, as well as relatives who are caregivers (and indeed home-bound parents), should be welcomed in children's centers and offered cost-free play facilities for the babies and social interaction for themselves, as well as the up-to-date child care education some grandparents lack.

20. Some Signposts to the Way Forward for Parents and Children

Parents' child care options are dependent on national or state policies or on the priorities chosen by their local authorities, but there are still ways in which they, as individuals, can influence these decision makers and help to advance child care. One important step forward is for parents to have the confidence to listen to their own feelings about the lifestyle they want in the early months and years of bringing up a child or children, and to feel entitled, as far as possible, to do what feels right and comfortable to them.

DIFFERENT CHILD CARE FOR DIFFERENT PARENTS

Mother care

A large body of research links mothers' mental health and sense of well-being with their employment, and their employment with good parenting and good outcomes for children. Further research suggests, however, that the important issue is not so much whether women are employed outside their homes but how satisfied they are with their roles, whether they are employed or full-time mothers. And there is evidence, too, that mothers' satisfaction goes with participation and support from fathers.

It may therefore be that prospective parents who are thinking about their lifestyle after a baby is born—about how much maternity leave the mother should take and whether it will be better for their new baby to have a parent at home rather than at work and using child care—should think seriously about not just practical considerations and the child's well-being but the mother's own feelings in the matter and the extent to which the father shares or supports them. For a mother to do as she pleases in this regard, if she can, is not "selfish," because the more comfortable she is with the balance in her life, the more comfortable she is likely to make her baby. Maternal care may be the very best kind of care for a child if (and only if) and for as long as (but only as long as) being at home is the mother's choice, feels right to her, and is supported by her partner.

Father care

Many families already arrange care for babies among themselves. In the United States, the United Kingdom, and Australia, the first year is the period in which fathers are most likely to take on the major share of their children's care. Evidence suggests not only that those who do it generally do it well, but also that such fathers are more likely than others to stay closely involved as children grow up, to the children's considerable benefit. Paid parental (as opposed to "maternity") leave would certainly make that option easier for more people, but so would a change in attitudes. In most countries, many mothers are ambivalent, even negative, about father care (though those who use it often come to swear by it), and many grandmothers disapprove. Relationship education for both sexes in schools should explore gendered attitudes toward parenting; couples in prenatal classes should be encouraged to discuss the issue, and it should be part of the agenda for child care refresher (or generation-gap-closing) classes offered to grandparents.

Family day care and home care by a nanny

These are often viewed as especially good child care options for babies. However, many parents feel more trusting of a group care setting than of any nonfamily individual. In the United States, regulation of family day care is inadequate, and in all countries lack of regulation of nannies is commonplace and astonishing. These home-based or domestic-scale types of infant care would be better understood and accepted if they were recommended—and perhaps organized—by children's centers. In the meantime, parents could help to raise their quality by being aware of and rejecting the temptation to choose a care provider because she is someone with whom they themselves can be friends rather than because she is someone whom their child will become attached to, and by insisting upon and carefully checking personal references.

DIFFERENT CARE FOR DIFFERENT BABIES

Whatever their child care plans for a baby's first year of life, and however eager they may be to return to the workplace, it is important that parents have some time at home with him after the first chaotic weeks are over and when he is settling down. Time spent in (relatively) peaceful parenting helps mothers and fathers establish attachment bonds with the baby and become familiar with him as an individual. That in its turn will enable them to look for the available child care that will be best for him. Parents do not need to be familiar with the vast literature on infant temperament in order to adjust their expectations and child care arrangements to their particular child. Knowing that a boy is rather more likely to have problems settling into child care encourages parents to allow enough time to do it slowly. Realizing that being fully and still passionately breastfed is a big obstacle to a baby's comfortable separation leads parents to give a baby a few more weeks at home to begin the gradual introduction of daytime bottles before she enters child care. And just observing how a baby currently reacts to a noisy environment, sudden loud sounds, bright lights, and rough-and-tumble play may help parents decide if center care will be overstimulating for her now or if being mostly alone with a nanny or grandmother will be boring. None of these baby characteristics is a reason not to use child care, nor will any of them (except gender!) last for more than a few months, but each is something parents need to be aware of so that they can bear it in mind when looking for the right child care setting or provider.

DIFFERENT CARE FOR DIFFERENT CHILDREN

Acknowledging that child care is for children, not only for adult convenience, is an important signpost toward raising its quality. Parents with more than one child often assume that the care that has worked out well for one will do likewise for another, but it may not. Parents need to put as much thought into arrangements for a

second or third child as they did for the first. They even need to be
prepared to offend the grandmother or family day care provider
who looked after the older sibling and expects to care for the
younger one, if it seems to them that she does not relate comfortably to the second child or that he would be better off in center care
or even at home for a while. Parents who know that a daily nanny
would cost them no more than two places in child care centers
sometimes say that they would love to have a nanny for the baby,
but it wouldn't seem fair to keep him at home when his sister went
into day care at three months. The daughter cannot remember
being three months old, and fairness between the two children is
not the issue. The issue is which of the available alternatives will be
best for this child.

CHILDREN'S "HAPPINESS"

Research has very little to say about the immediate happiness of
babies, toddlers, and preschool children in child care, but the more
parents say, the better. By talking about it, publicly voicing concerns
that almost every parent feels but most are shy to express, parents
can help to bring this issue to the forefront, where it will eventually
be taken as seriously as it deserves. Children cannot learn, socially,
emotionally, or cognitively, when they are anxious and miserable;
none of us can. Not all unhappiness can be avoided in day care, of
course, any more than it can be avoided elsewhere. Separating from
parents is painful for babies and toddlers, sometimes damagingly so,
unless the separation is prepared for and a secondary attachment
figure provided. Some older children will always have difficulty settling into a new group or class. A few days of tears tend to be dismissed as unimportant, but they are not unimportant to the child
(or to her parents), and if they are taken seriously, there is a great
deal that can be done to ease these transitions. Most children in a
group will, at some time or other, feel friendless, isolated, or worse.
But the fact that such unhappiness is commonplace should make
adults more rather than less determined to find ways to prevent it or
at least help children through it.

Parents could encourage better child care if they bravely insisted that a positive experience for their children, whether four months or four years old, is the very least they expect.

Parents' Options and Stress Busting

Keeping work and child care in balance is like being on a tightrope: manageable (maybe even exciting) when everything goes according to plan; disastrous when anything goes wrong. The most common wobbles are the occasions that absolutely require that a parent stay home with a child when she or he is due at work. Since there's no bargain parents can strike with a child's sudden fever or a childminder's migraine, they desperately need a get-out-of-work-free card so one of them can stay home without having to lie to personnel or tell the truth and lose yet another day of precious vacation time. In countries that offer no solution to this conundrum, parents need to work one out for themselves, preferably before it happens: grandmother? neighbor who is a stay-at-home mother?

The European Union's parental leave directive appears to be exactly the card parents need. It allows all parents with children under the age of five to take up to thirteen weeks' extra unpaid holiday for "family reasons." At last, parents can stop panicking every time a child has to stay home—can't they? Not quite. On the face of it, this law, new to the United Kingdom and not, of course, applicable on the other side of the Atlantic, is a triumph for working parents, heralding a new era of family-friendly practices in the workplace. But while the EU directive is a step in the right direction, it is not all it is cracked up to be. Not only is it unpaid, but it must be taken in blocks of one week. It is available only to employees who have been with their companies for more than a year. And, worst of all, it is conditional on the employee giving at least three weeks' notice—which fevers and migraines do not. To top it off, if the employer can prove that granting the parental leave would be detrimental to his business, he can postpone the leave for up to six months. The U.K.'s Department of Trade and Industry's senior policy adviser for employee relations said, "There is a misunderstanding, as it is not meant for emergencies. The kind of situation it might be used for is if care is provided informally by the extended family, who are going on holiday." The parents can then book additional time off from work to stay at home and look after the children themselves, but they would still be forced to take the leave in blocks of one week, each time losing that whole week's wages.

The moral of this account is "Don't plan your life around services or facilities you've only seen reported in the media." The easiest way to check them out is usually on the Internet, using official government Web sites. And that's also where parents might find a service they hadn't heard about on TV.

If your child is sent home with a temperature from a U.K. nursery tomorrow, there is a genuine alternative to fibbing or losing paid vacation days. A benefit allowing time off for employees with dependents was very quietly introduced alongside the parental leave directive and allows the employee to take one or two days off for domestic emergencies, whether the employer is happy about it or not. Sadly, it remains unpaid, but, as notice is not required, it could go a long way toward bridging the gap until paid, flexible parental leave that can be taken at any time (not only in infancy) is finally introduced. Most corporations are global, or at least transatlantic, so if European parents can have this, why not North American or Australian parents? If parents ask that question loudly and persistently enough, politicians might stop huffing and puffing and start addressing it.

What relieves stress for one person increases anxiety for another, and each individual has to find out which is which. Working at home, for example, means that some parents can get their work done while remaining comfortably available to their children, but it means that others can get no work done at all because of constant interruptions by children who are disturbed by a parent being physically present but not fully there for them. Likewise, limiting working hours—to a technically part-time schedule such as a four-day week or to the hours that are actually paid for, such as forty per week—miraculously relieves the pressure on some people but increases it on others. The different responses probably depend partly on the reactions of colleagues and managers to what may be seen as sensible time management or clock-watching. Even cell phones—which make it possible for a parent at work to be almost

Stress busting: control personal technology

Use technological fixes to control the tensions implicit in technological advances, especially when working at home.

- Have voice mail on every phone, including cell phones, and learn to use it. That doesn't only mean learning to ignore the ringing phone when you're wiping your four-year-old's bottom or having dinner in a restaurant; it also means wording your voice mail messages so your mother doesn't decide you've been in a plane crash and your boss doesn't decide (realize!) you're out shopping.

- Use the automatic filter on your e-mail to "trash" messages from any firms, campaigns, or unwelcome contacts whose lists you are stuck on.

- Try to deal with e-mail before it drowns you; answer "in" messages when you first read them and then delete them or move them to another folder.

- Don't let those electronic aids dominate your life. Do you really need to check your e-mail on weekday evenings? If so, can you leave it until your children are asleep? Must you check in during weekends or vacations? An automatic "out of the office" message is a less stressful alternative.

- How many people/firms really need to have your e-mail address/cell phone number? If you've let the list grow out of proportion already, it might even be worth the horrendous upheaval of changing your contact details and then drastically restricting who you give them to.

constantly, and almost infallibly, available in any emergency—are a problem for some people, such as this FCCC mother:

> If I turn it off, I'm worried all the time that the au pair is trying to reach me, but if I leave it on she calls me when I'm in meetings.

Despite the glut of self-help books on the shelves, most people do not really believe that scheduled stress-busting solutions would work for them or that they could follow them. By definition, they already have too much to think about and do. Most parents who take the time to think about what most often threatens their equilibrium get more help from stress relievers that are tailor-made for their particular situations. If the pickup deadline at nursery is so close to the train time that every working day ends in a near crisis, something has to be done—a different understanding with the nursery; an agreement with work that makes an earlier train possible; sharing the pickup on alternate days with the other parent; a baby carpool with a friend; different child care. No one solution solves a particular problem for all parents, but all parents need to take these constant stresses seriously and take the time to find the solution that works for them.

Stress Prevention for Children in Child Care

For most mothers and fathers balancing work and home is a matter of muddling through, wanting only to be as sure as they can be that the best they can do is good enough. If it's not good enough for work, managers or colleagues are usually quick to speak up. But what about the children? There may be ways in which parents can raise the quality not of child care but of their child's life around child care.

Parents who feel they have less time than they would like to spend with their child naturally want it to be "quality time"—for the child as well as for themselves. It's worth working out what that is right now and then thinking about it again every couple of months as children change.

Just because parents have missed out on hugs all day doesn't mean that children want to do nothing but snuggle on the couch. They may want a nap or a walk. And just because parents hate not knowing what their toddlers had for lunch or who they played with doesn't mean those toddlers want to tell. Questions are liable to turn small children off. Progress reports and daily information need to come from caregivers. Communication between parents and care providers is crucial to the quality of care, and anything that improves it is a step forward. Good day care settings make sure parents are given information and are welcome to ask for it; care settings and providers that make parents feel they shouldn't take the caregiver's time at the end of the day should be pressured to rethink and restaff pickup time and change their attitude toward parents.

Some parents feel that quality time means educational time and that they ought to spend it going over flashcards and numbers with their three-year-olds. But if children have missed anything during the day away from home, they've missed mother or father, not teacher. High-quality time means time together that both parents and children enjoy; peaceful time; reconnecting and relaxing time; fun time; recharge-the-batteries time. Parents don't have to devote that precious hour or two to doing things that are just for a child's entertainment or education; it can be for theirs, too. In fact, it doesn't matter what a parent does provided she can do it with the child and talk and laugh (and maybe sing and dance) while she does it. She could make dinner, have a bath, or read a book with her child; she could watch a video if it's one of his, even talk on the phone as long as it's his other parent or grandma on the other end, and the call's for both of them.

Whatever parents do to make that scarce time high-quality, it's important that they make it clear to the children that this time together is valuable to them, too. A parent who checks e-mail or phones or texts someone else during this brief after-work period makes it very clear to children that being with them is not the parent's priority.

Children need to know that parents would like to spend more time with them; that even though they choose to work, they don't like the limits it puts on their family time. One powerful way for parents to give children that message is sometimes to ask a child to play a game or give a hug before she asks them, or to ask a child to please go with the parent on an errand rather than waiting until the other parent gets home and frees the first to go alone.

STAYING CLOSE TO PRE- AND PRIMARY SCHOOL CHILDREN IN CHILD CARE

As other children at day care or school become more important to your child, and her social life and program of after-school activities builds up, it may become even more difficult to spend time together during the week. Different families organize things in different ways, of course, but swapping children for rides to afternoon activities and after-school playdates is a good way to make sure parents stay involved with the new people and things that matter in children's lives and, importantly, with each other. And rosters can mean that coming home early one afternoon a week to drive several children buys a parent four longer days when other parents drive hers.

There is survey information suggesting that two aspects of family life are especially worth trying to hold on to. Some regular family time, in particular eating the evening meal together around a table rather than in front of the TV, really does seem to make a difference to how tuned in and in touch with each other children and adults remain. Having your three-year-old eat supper at child care or with the nanny or babysitter may save you time at too high a cost. Then, parents making an effort for special occasions compensates a lot of children for having them miss out on everyday things. It's worth making sure your child knows that even though another mom takes her to her after-school swimming class, one of her parents will always get to a meet. When the holiday season produces one school-based function after another, and you have to decide if you'll have to leave work early yet again, ask yourself if other parents will be there. If the answer's yes, then your answer is yes.

Once children are old enough to understand the significance of your calendar or BlackBerry, it's a good idea to let them see you put important dates with them in it along with the work stuff. Not only are you telling the child you'll be there, you're also telling her that you're not embarrassed to have your boss or your colleagues know why you left work early that day.

By the time she's ten or twelve, your child may mostly be able to take care of herself in the daytime, but that doesn't mean that she should do so on a regular basis. Latchkey children, as we have seen, face considerable risks, and "independence" from parents easily turns into distance. Once a child loses the habit and expectation of being closely supervised by adults, it's almost impossible to restore it during adolescence, when it may matter even more.

When parents know that children will only come in for two minutes to dump their bags before going back out with their friends until supper and homework time, it can be tempting to stay later at work or to socialize with colleagues afterward. But if parents aren't home, who's going to hear about the Really Bad Day or the Really Good Game, and what do children have to come home for? It's a vicious circle.

For oldest and only children, it's important to continue providing babysitters when you go out in the evening, even when a child seems old enough to stay on her own and spending the money may seem unnecessary. Many children feel very nervous about being on their own after dark, but at this stage they are so busy trying to be grown up that they probably won't admit to it, even if parents ask. Once a child really is too old to have a babysitter (and she and her parents between them will have to decide when that is), arranging for her to have a friend over to keep her company or to go to a friend's house to sleep over can be a good compromise. Either way, parents should try to see to it that one of them comes home first, even if starting the evening out straight from work would cut travel time. Having a parent at home for twenty minutes is infinitely better than nothing, and if a teenager doesn't see his parents from 8 a.m. one day to 8 a.m. the next, he isn't really living with them.

CONCLUSION

We need child care and other children's services out there for children of all ages whether their parents actually need them right now or not—services for children's safety and pleasure, their development and education, their emotional security, their happiness. Parents need those children's services to be available so that they can make whatever arrangements and plans to address the working/caring conundrum are necessary or possible, without feeling overwhelmed by stress and guilt. We shall not get such services unless (or until) everyone comes to acknowledge that while every child is uniquely the responsibility (and the privilege and pleasure) of his or her own family, all children are also everybody's responsibility: not-yet-parents, has-been-parents, the childless, and the child-free. Children will eventually impact their society; their experiences and their feelings actually matter to all of us, not just to those who are currently bringing up children or are children themselves. Right now, scarcity of child-friendly attitudes throughout the English-speaking world weighs even more heavily against high-quality child care than scarcity of financial or other resources. We can do better.

Acknowledgments

Working on the Families, Children and Child Care (FCCC) study gave me the opportunity to focus my attention for several years on the conundrums of child care on both sides of the Atlantic. I am grateful to the Tedworth Charitable Trust and the Glass-House Trust, which funded the study and was unfailingly supportive of it; to my co-directors, Alan Stein and Kathy Sylva; and to the senior researchers, especially Jacqueline Barnes. I also gratefully acknowledge the work of the project team, and of the families, some of whose words help to bring the issues alive.

The literature on child care is too extensive for any one book to do justice to it, and I am conscious of having had to omit more than could be included. In the notes I have tried to cite representative examples of the work of particular researchers and research groups, but I should like to take this opportunity to acknowledge the many other colleagues from whose work I have learned.

A book of this kind relies not only on research but also on opinions and personal experiences. The notes refer readers to only a small selection of these, but I gratefully acknowledge my debt to all the rest.

Despite all this help, though, responsibility for the facts selected, opinions expressed, and conclusions drawn remains mine alone.

Penelope Leach, 2008

Notes

1. The Context for Child Care

3   The 2006 Canadian census shows: Statistics Canada, http://www.statcan.ca/census 2006.

4   we need our populations to produce the next generation of workers: National Center for Health Statistics, final natality data, U.S. Bureau of the Census, 2007. Germany's birth rate is currently lowest, with 8.5 births per 1,000 people: that's fewer than 700,000 babies born in the whole of Germany in 2006, the lowest number since 1945. These figures come from a review article by Luke Harding, "How Parenthood Lost Its Charm," *Guardian*, May 3, 2006.

4   The assumption that countries with very low birth rates: P. McDonald, "Fertility Rates, Women in the Workforce, and Economic Health," *Family Matters* (Australian Institute of Family Studies), no. 63 (Spring/Summer 2002).

4   that situation has now reversed: Organisation for Economic Co-operation and Development (OECD), *Employment Outlook 2005* (Paris).

5   While about 20 percent of women do not want children: C. Hakim, "Work Lifestyle Choices in the 21st Century," *Family Matters* (Australian Institute of Family Studies), no. 63 (Spring/Summer 2002): 2.

5   In a national poll of U.K. adults in 2006: http://www.icmresearxh.co.uk.

5   "This is a particular problem for women": Harriet Harman, speech to Trades Unions Congress Women's Conference, www.harrietharman.org/168html.

6   even the most mother-friendly employment package: McDonald, "Fertility Rates, Women in the Workforce, and Economic Health."

6   "It's really about people who": Ibid., p. 4.

6   selected and colorful versions of which fill hours of prime TV viewing time: Parenting programs on television that are currently widely viewed on both sides of the Atlantic include *Supernanny, Nanny 911, Brat Camp*, and *Family Brat Camp*.

12   Stepfamilies and others: According to the U.S. Census Bureau, there were 10 million single mothers living with a child under age nineteen in 2005 as compared with 3 million in 1970. The U.K. Policy Studies Institute predicts that by the year 2010, serial marriage will become the norm in Britain, with more families breaking down and restructuring than staying together.

13   Traditional gender inequities: British Household Panel Survey, http://www.esds .ac.uk.

13   Recent commentators see couples operating competitively: Man Yee Kan and
      A. Heath, "The Political Values and Choices of Husbands and Wives," *Journal of
      Marriage and Family* 68 (2006): 70–86.

13   Twenty percent more women than men are now graduating: Professor Richard Free-
      man, during discussion after delivering the University of Nottingham World Econ-
      omy Annual Lecture, 2003.

13   Gary Becker, the Nobel Prize–winning American economist: Gary S. Becker and
      Guity Nashat Becker, *The Economics of Life: From Baseball to Affirmative Action to
      Immigration: How Real-World Issues Affect Our Everyday Life* (New York: McGraw-
      Hill, 1997). See also K. Aalto and J. Varijonen, *Cheaper by the Dozen: Economies of Scale
      in Domestic Work*, National Consumer Research Centre Working Paper 95 (Helsinki:
      National Consumer Research Centre, 2006).

16   some nations of continental Europe: E. Melhuish and K. Petrogiannis, eds., *Early
      Childhood Care and Education: International Perspectives* (London and New York: Rout-
      ledge, 2006), pp. 1–5.

17   in the United States the authority of established Protestant institutions: This sugges-
      tion is made by Amanda Porterfield in *The Transformation of American Religion: The
      Story of a Late-Twentieth-Century Awakening* (Oxford and New York: Oxford Univer-
      sity Press, 2001). It was also discussed on the PBS television news program *Religion
      and Ethics Newsweekly*, "Exploring Religious America, Part 4: Spirituality," aired on
      May 17, 2002. It is supported by a 2001 Barna Poll on U.S. Religious Belief, reported
      by Paul Hinlicky, a Lutheran theologian: "[This poll points to] an absolute collapse
      of mainline Protestantism in this country. . . . [There is a] very considerable diversity
      within the Christian community regarding core beliefs. [The study seems to expose
      the] erosion of the church's foundations."

18   "The last time many countries faced a social-capital crisis": Robert D. Putnam,
      Malkin Professor of Public Policy at Harvard University, invited speaker at a Down-
      ing Street seminar on British society, March 27, 2001, www.guardian.co.uk/society/
      2001/mar.

2. The Issues

23   In Scandinavian countries: The level of child care provision varies significantly
      across Scandinavia. Denmark provides publicly funded care for almost half (48 per-
      cent) of all children less than three years of age; Sweden and Iceland provide care to
      37 percent; Norway to 22 percent; Finland to 18 percent.

      Comparisons among the countries are complicated by the existence of other forms
      of assistance. Norwegian parents have access to a cash benefit that can be used to
      support parental care of under-threes on the condition that the child does not also
      use state-supported child care, while Finnish parents can choose between a place in a
      publicly sponsored child care service or a cash benefit.

      The introduction of cash benefits has reduced demand for child care places for the
      under-threes, but there is still unmet demand in both Norway and Finland. See Arn-
      laugh Leira, *Working Parents and the Welfare State: Family Change and Policy Reform in
      Scandinavia* (Cambridge: Cambridge University Press, 2002).

24   In England, the cost of a typical full-time nursery place: Figures are from the annual

survey of child care costs in England, compiled by the Daycare Trust and published in February 2008. The survey covered 150 out of 200 children's and child care information services in the United Kingdom. Costs were based on fifty hours per week in a nursery or center or with a childminder and fifteen hours per week at an after-school club.

25   America's "dramatic increase in the number of children in non-parental childcare": V. Allhusen, A. Clarke-Stewart, and J. Miner, "Childcare in the United States: Characteristics and Consequences," in *Early Childhood Care and Education: International Perspectives*, ed. E. Melhuis and K. Petrogiannis (London and New York: Routledge, 2006), p. 12.

25   In Canada, similarly: An overview report entitled "Early Childhood Education and Care in Canada 2006" describes fourteen separate Canadian child care jurisdictions—ten provinces, three territories, and the federal government.

25   North American parents everywhere: National Childcare Information and Technical Assistance Center, August 2003, http://www.nccic.org.

26   "The dilemma is the majority of parents can't pay": www.kidsource.com/kidsource/content/news/child_care.html.

26   constant stress with which many poor American mothers struggle: Ajay Chaudry, *Putting Children First: How Low-Wage Working Mothers Manage Child Care* (New York: Russell Sage Foundation, 2004).

28   "While Project Child Care provides state-mandated training": www.kidsource.com/kidsource/content/news/child_care.html.

28   Having more children to care for does not automatically preclude: P. Leach, J. Barnes, L.-E. Malmberg, K. Sylva, A. Stein, and the FCCC team (2006), "The Quality of Different Types of Child Care at 10 and 18 Months: A Comparison Between Types and Factors Related to Quality," *Early Child Development and Care* 178, no. 2 (February 2008): 177–209.

28   "Attachment," used in the context of infant development: M. Ainsworth, M. Belhar, E. Waters, and S. Wall, *Patterns of Attachment: A Psychological Study of the Strange Situation* (Hillsdale, N.J.: Lawrence Erlbaum Associates, 1978).
        In the original study, ten- to twenty-four-month-old infants were subjected to a strange playroom, the entrance of an unfamiliar female, and two brief separations from the parent. Their behavior on being reunited with the parent was observed and classified into three attachment patterns:
        Insecure-avoidant, or A Turns away or moves away from parent upon reunion; mood is flat, and play is not effective or animated.
        Secure, or B Happy to see the parent upon reunion, settles if distressed, and returns to often joyful play.
        Insecure-resistant/ambivalent, or C Both seeks contact and angrily (or passively) rejects it when offered, remaining upset and ineffectual at play.
        These have come to be regarded as organized strategies for maintaining the relationship with a predictable caregiver. A more recent categorization:
        Disorganized, or D The infant has no consistent strategies for maintaining the relationship because the caregiver is not predictable but frightened or frightening.

29   Attachment figures: There is a very extensive literature on attachment theory and its applications over more than two generations that is beyond the scope of this book. A

useful discussion of the place of attachment theory in current thinking and research by Dr. Howard Steele, co-director of the Center for Attachment Research at the New School for Social Research in New York, was published by the British Psychological Society: H. Steele, "State of the Art: Attachment Theory," *The Psychologist* 15, no. 10 (October 2002): 518–23. See, in particular, "But What About Fathers?," pp. 519–20, and "Day Care and Attachment," p. 521.

30   "The attention that we receive as babies": This quotation is from an interview given by Sue Gerhardt to the *Guardian* newspaper soon after the publication of her book *Why Love Matters: How Affection Shapes a Baby's Brain* (New York: Brunner-Routledge, 2004).

30   Mothers teach inner-world emotional lessons: Steele, "State of the Art: Attachment Theory."

31   the risk that leaving her with somebody else during adult working hours: National Institute of Child Health and Human Development (NICHD) Early Child Care Research Network, "The Effects of Infant Child Care on Infant-Mother Attachment Security: Results of the NICHD Study of Early Child Care," *Child Development* 68 (1997): 860–79; NICHD Early Child Care Research Network, *Child Care and Child Development: Results from the NICHD Study of Early Child Care and Youth Development* (New York and London: Guilford Press, 2005), pp. 208–23.

31   The truly tragic outcomes of "maternal deprivation": World Health Organization, "Deprivation of Maternal Care: A Reassessment of Its Effect" (Public Health Papers No. 14) (Geneva: WHO, 1962). After Romania's Communist regime collapsed in 1989, it was found that the physical and emotional deprivation that children in Romania's orphanages had endured had had long-term effects on their cognition and behavior and caused structural changes in the brain, too. A recent magnetic resonance imaging study shows that the uncinate fasciculus, the major fiber tract that connects the anterior temporal and inferior frontal cortical regions, is thin and poorly organized in orphans who survive; see *Pediatrics* 117, no. 6 (June 2006): 2093–2100.

31   "The attachment literature does not demand exclusive parental care": Sebastian Kraemer, consultant child and adolescent psychiatrist, Tavistock Clinic, London, advice to Ten-Year Strategy for Childcare, HM Treasury, 2004.

32   Finally, even the words of the father of attachment theory, John Bowlby: Two works by John Bowlby are the bibles of attachment theory: the brief volume, written at the request of the British government to be accessible to nonspecialist readers, *Maternal Care and Mental Health* (Geneva: World Health Organization, 1951); and the first volume of his later trilogy, *Attachment and Loss: Vol. 1. Attachment* (New York: Basic Books, 1969).

32   In an even less well known paper: J. Bowlby, "The Study and Reduction of Group Tensions in the Family," *Human Relations* 2 (1949): 123–28.

33   "The point is that more than one caregiver is necessary": Sebastian Kraemer, personal communication, 2007.

34   children who had spent more time in child care: NICHD Early Child Care Research Network, "Early Child Care and Children's Development in the Primary Grades: Follow-up Results from the NICHD Study of Early Child Care," *American Educational Research Journal* 42, no. 3 (2005): 537–70.

35   Other studies that have looked at social development: Lower-quality child care has been found to be associated with a wide range of undesirable social outcomes for

children, including more solitary play, aimless wandering, and noninvolvement in classroom activities; more frowning and crying and less sustained verbal interactions; more behavior problems; and poorer social adjustment.

However, child care of high quality has been found to be associated with a range of positive social outcomes for children, including better peer interactions and social development, and more advanced social skills (Cost, Quality and Child Outcomes Study Team, "Cost, Quality and Child Outcomes in Child Care Centers Public Report," 1995); more complex play behaviors with peers; and higher levels of social problem-solving skills. In higher-quality centers, children also comply more with adult requests; are more cooperative, responsive, and innovative; are more securely attached to their teachers; and are more sociable. This large body of research, spanning thirty years, is exemplified in E. C. Melhuish, "A Literature Review of the Impact of Early Years Provision upon Young Children, with Emphasis Given to Children from Disadvantaged Backgrounds," Report to the Comptroller and Auditor General, London. National Audit Office, 2004, http://www.nao.org.uk. See also E. C. Melhuish, "Day-care," in *Cambridge Encyclopedia of Child Development*, ed. B. Hopkins, et al. (Cambridge: Cambridge University Press, 2005).

36   conduct studies in the light of national or state contexts and perspectives: M. Lamb, K. Sternberg, C. Hwang, and A. Broberg, eds., *Childcare in Context* (Hillsdale, N.J.: Lawrence Erlbaum, 1992); J. Love, L. Harrison, A. Sagi-Schwarz, M. H. Van Ijzendoorn, et al., "Child Care Quality Matters: How Conclusions May Vary with Context," *Child Development* 74, no. 4 (July–August 2003): 1021–33; K. Sylva, A. Stein, P. Leach, J. Barnes, L.-E. Malmberg, and the FCCC team, "Family and Child Factors Related to the Use of Non-Maternal Infant Care: An English Study," *Early Childhood Research Quarterly* 22, no. 1 (2007): 118–36.

36   If poor-quality care is bad enough: A. Sagi, N. Koren-Karie, M. Gini, Y. Ziv, and T. Jocls, "Shedding Further Light on the Effects of Various Types and Quality of Early Child Care on Infant-Mother Attachment Relationship: The Haifa Study of Early Child Care," *Child Development* 73, no. 4 (July–August 2002): 1166–86.

38   But when women are actually consulted: The idea that women's policies should be based on women's choices has been dignified with the term "preference theory" along with a detailed analysis of the choices made by women all over the Western world concerning not only motherhood but also careers and marriage. Research shows that while the social and economic changes of the last thirty years have created new opportunities for women, these have neither made all women alike nor given most of them the desire to emulate men in their working lives. C. Hakim, *Work-Lifestyle Choices in the 21st Century* (Oxford: Oxford University Press, 2000), describes modern women as falling into three groups: (1) home-centered women who give priority to children and family life and prefer not to work for money—about 20 percent of women in America and Britain; (2) work-centered women who give priority to careers—again about 20 percent; (3) adaptive women who combine work and family life—about 60 percent. Hakim believes it is the work-centered 20 percent who conform to feminist and economic expectations and in whose interests most policies are made. However, policies designed to suit this group ignore the needs of the home-centered 20 percent, and often the adaptive 60 percent, too, because many of them would prefer to work shorter hours or take on less responsibility in order to give greater priority to the needs of their children.

38   Home care allowances: C. Hakim, "Fertility Rates, Women in the Workforce, and
     Economic Health," *Family Matters* (Australian Institute of Family Studies), no. 63
     (Spring–Summer 2002): 42–43.

39   "Education is an investment": Committee for Economic Development, Research
     and Policy Committee, *The Unfinished Agenda: A New Vision for Child Development
     and Education* (Washington, D.C.: Committee for Economic Development, 1991),
     pp. 27–28.

40   "The question is not whether we can afford": Elliot L. Richardson, quoted ibid.

40   "Investing in early childhood education": Isabel Sawhill, cited in *Washington Post*,
     February 17, 1999.

3. How Much Child Care? What Kinds and Where?

43   "most of the over 70% of children": *The State of ECEC in Canada in 2005: An
     Overview*, www.childcarecanada.org; Early Childhood Education and Care, *Child
     Care 1996–2001* (2005), Statistics Canada, www.statcan.ca.

43   The U.S. Child Care Bureau: U.S. Childcare Bureau, *Child Care and Development
     Fund (CCDF): Report to Congress* (Washington, D.C.: U.S. Department of Health and
     Human Services, 2003), http://www.acf.hhs.gov.

43   In Australia, a government survey of child-rearing practices: *Growing Up in Australia:
     A Government Survey of Child Rearing Practices*, Australian Institute of Family Studies,
     September 29, 2006; http://www.aifs.gov.au.

43   Official figures for England published by the inspection body OFSTED: In October
     2005, the total number of registered child care places in England rose to more than
     1.5 million for the first time, with quarterly data showing an increase of 200 full day
     care providers (10,400 full day care places) since the previous figures were published
     in June 2005.

44   two major follow-up studies of child care, one American and the other English: Early
     Childhood Longitudinal Study, Birth Cohort (hereafter ECLS-B), a representative
     national study of ten thousand American babies born in 2001.

     C. Bryson, A. Kazimirski, and H. Southwood, *Childcare and Early Years Provision
     [hereafter CEYP]: A Study of Parents' Use, Views and Experiences* (London: National
     Centre for Social Research, 2006). A study of just under eight thousand English fam-
     ilies interviewed in 2004–05, it was commissioned by the DfES and carried out by
     the National Centre for Social Research (NatCen). As well as providing information
     in its own right, this report continues the time series data from two earlier survey
     series: the Parents' Demand for Childcare series and the Survey of Parents of Three-
     and Four-Year-Old Children and Their Use of Early Years Services series. Two sets
     of figures extracted from this survey are shown on the facing page:

NUMBER OF PARENTS USING DIFFERENT TYPES OF CARE BY CHILDREN'S AGES

FORMAL Early years provision and child care	Age 0–2 (%)	Age 3–4 (%)	Age 5–7 (%)	Age 8–11 (%)	Age 12–14 (%)
Nursery school	2	10	+	o	o
Nursery class	1	22	+	o	o
Reception class	0	28	5	o	o
Day nursery	18	12	+	o	o
Playgroup or preschool	9	18	+	o	o
Child minder	5	5	4	3	1.
Nanny or au pair	1	2	1	1	1
Babysitter	3	2	3	3	1
Out-of-school club on-site		2	13	13	
Out-of-school club off-site	+	1	4	4	
INFORMAL child care					
Parent's ex-husband/wife/partner	3	4	5	6	4
The child's grandparent(s)	29	26	22	22	13
The child's older brother/sister	1	1	2	5	7
Another relative		6	5	4	3
A friend or neighbor	5	6	9	10	
All families (Weighted base)	1,451	1,507	1,348	1,916	1,578

NUMBER OF PARENTS USING FORMAL SCHOOL-AGE CHILD CARE, BY TYPE

Institutional Providers	**75 %**	**Informal Providers**	**26 %**
Breakfast club/after-school club on-site	36	Grandparents	52
Reception class attached to a primary or infants school	21	Ex-husband/partner/child's other parent	14
Breakfast club/after-school club off-site	13	A friend or neighbor	14
Special day school or nursery or unit	1	Child's older brother/sister	12
Nursery class attached to primary or infants school	1	Another relative	8
Individual Providers	**19 %**		
Childminder	9		
Babysitter	7		
Nanny/au pair	3		
Other	9		
Sport/leisure activity	9		

n 100% base (families with a school-age child using mainly formal care) 1,363
n 100% base (families with a school-age child using mainly informal care)1,336

44   The NICHD Study of Early Child Care and Youth Development: This study has generated several hundred papers. Unless otherwise stated, those cited in this book can be found in NICHD Early Child Care Research Network, *Child Care and Child Development: Results from the NICHD Study of Early Child Care and Youth Development* (New York: Guilford Press, 2005).

44   The Families, Children and Child Care study: Details of the design, sample, and methods of the Families, Children and Child Care study (FCCC), together with published and forthcoming papers, can be found at www.familieschildrenchildcare .org. Published papers are cited individually.

45   In North America, the United Kingdom, and Australia: Australia embarked on a new "child-friendly" tax policy, including a new child care tax rebate effective from July

2006. In preparation for this, in May 2006 the Australian Bureau of Statistics revealed the results of a major survey of child-rearing practices. In Canada, Fleishman Hillard Canada (formerly GPC Research), released the Canadian Survey of Child Care Policy in July 2006. The preelection survey of 2,012 families in seven provinces was carried out in November 2005. See also C. D. Hayes, J. L. Palmer, and M. J. Zaslow, *Who Cares for America's Children? Child Care Policy for the 1990s* (Washington, D.C.: National Academy Press, 1990).

46 parents use child care when they are not working: S. Dunlevy and E. King, "Yuppies Blamed for Clogging Childcare," May 23, 2006; www.news.com.au/story/0,10117, 1922827/.

49 an increase in part-time women employees holding down professional or managerial jobs: S. Driver and L. Martell, "New Labour, Work and the Family," *Social Policy & Administration* 36, no. 1 (February 2002): 46–61.

50 The contribution of biological fathers, especially black fathers: Jennifer Hamer, *What It Means to Be Daddy* (New York: Columbia University Press, 2001).

51 child care is something of a jigsaw puzzle: A. Chaudry, *Putting Children First* (New York: Russell Sage Foundation, 2004).

52 the percentage cared for in their own homes: Alison Clarke-Stewart, "Characteristics and Quality of Child Care for Toddlers and Preschoolers," *Applied Developmental Science* 4 (2000).

53 a major European study carried out in the United Kingdom: K. Sylva, E. Melhuish, P. Sammons, I. Siraj-Blatchford, B. Taggart, and K. Elliot, *The Effective Provision of Pre-School Education (EPPE) Project: Findings from the Pre-School Period* (London: Institute of Education, University of London, 2003).

54 15 percent of those between the ages of five and fourteen: Data from the 2002 American Census and the National Household Survey 2001, reported by the National Center for Education Statistics, 2004.

55 Perhaps the best-known school vacation care in the world: Figures from the American Camp Association, http://www.acacamps.org.

55 childminders look after many children before and after school and during school vacations: The former Department for Education and Skills (DfES) (now the Department for Children, Schools and Families) commissioned BMRB (British Market Research Bureau) to undertake four surveys to collect information about child care providers and the child care workforce. One, published in 2005, was about childminders. Findings are based on interviews with 1,132 childminder samples from the OFSTED database and weighted and grossed to provide national estimates.

56 "Farrah is currently in her first year of compulsory schooling": Excerpted with permission from B. Cohen, P. Moss, P. Petries, and J. Wallace, *A New Deal for Children?: Re-forming Education and Care in England, Scotland and Sweden* (Bristol, Eng.: Policy Press, 2004), p. 136.

4. Parents and Child Care

58 there is considerable evidence, especially from Scandinavian countries: The evidence is well surveyed and summarized in A. Leira, *Working Parents and the Welfare State: Family Change and Policy Reform in Scandinavia* (Cambridge: Cambridge University Press, 2002).

59   if early education with a group of other children: Quotes from mothers in this chapter are from participants in the Families, Children and Child Care (FCCC) study unless otherwise stated, and specifically from P. Leach, J. Barnes, M. Nichols, J. Goldin, A. Stein, K. Sylva, and L.-E. Malmberg, "Child Care Before 6 Months of Age: A Qualitative Study of Mothers' Decisions and Feelings about Employment and Non-maternal Care," *Infant and Child Development* 15, no. 5 (2006): 471–502.

59   However, choosing child care is not like choosing a refrigerator: E. P. Pungello and B. Kurtz-Costes, "Why and How Working Women Choose Child Care: A Review with a Focus on Infancy," *Developmental Review* 19 (1999): 31–96. Pungello and Kurtz-Costes's influential review put forward a theoretical model of child care choice behaviors relating choices to environmental contexts (such as availability of care), maternal beliefs about child care, child factors (such as temperament), and demographic characteristics of the mother.

Subsequent research has been additionally concerned with the macroenvironment of institutions and government policies. Studies from the United States and from Europe have explored the relationship between external circumstances, including different economic opportunities and labor market conditions, and personal attitudes in women's child care choices.

61   first children were twice as likely as others: K. Sylva, A. Stein, P. Leach, J. Barnes, L.-E. Malmberg, and the FCCC team, "Family and Child Factors Related to the Use of Non-maternal Infant Care: An English Study," *Early Childhood Research Quarterly* 22, no. 1 (2007): 118–36.

62   suitable child care seems so difficult: G. A. Bogat and L. K. Gensheimer, "Discrepancies Between the Attitudes and Actions of Parents Choosing Day Care," *Child Care Quarterly* 15 (1986): 159–69.

62   An Australian study of child care: S. Wise and A. Sanson, *Children in Cultural Context: Issues for New Research*, research paper no. 22 (Melbourne: Australian Institute of Family Studies, 2000); M. Rosenthal, "Out-of-Home Child Care Research: A Cultural Perspective," *Journal of Behavioural Development* 23, no. 2. (1999): 477–518.

63   In the American study of ten thousand babies born in 2001: Early Childhood Longitudinal Study, Birth Cohort (ECLS-B), 2002.

64   Both the provision and the financing of child care are different: P. Peltola, ed., *Working Time in Europe: Towards a European Working Time Policy* (Finnish EU Presidency Conference Report) (Helsinki: Hakapaino Oy, 2000); C. Hakim, *Work-Lifestyle Choices in the 21st Century: Preference Theory* (Oxford: Oxford University Press, 2001); E. Pungello and B. Kurtz-Costes, "Working Women's Selection of Care for Their Infants: A Prospective Study," *Family Relations* 49 (2000): 245–55. A study from the United Kingdom analyzed the "choices" recent government policies have made available to mothers, the relationships in their child care decision making between external constraints and existing attitudes and preferences, and the policy implications. C. Bryson, A. Kazimirski, and H. Southwood, *Childcare and Early Years Provision* [hereafter *CEYP*]: *A Study of Parents Use, Views and Experiences* (London: National Centre for Social Research, 2006).

65   the Child Care Action Campaign: "Tracking Down Quality Child Care," www .kidsource.com/kidsource/content/news/child_care.html. The Child Care Action Campaign was a national not-for-profit child advocacy organization based in New York City that sought better standards for child care. In 2001, it reported that nationwide, parents paid an average of $3,500 a year for care; that one-third of work-

ers nationwide needed child care; and that absenteeism from work due to child care breakdowns cost businesses $3 billion each year. According to the Florida Children's Forum, another advocacy group, 61,000 income-qualified Florida parents are receiving public child care subsidies, with another 25,000 parents on waiting lists. In Manatee County, 1,175 parents receive subsidies while another 279 working parents are eligible for subsidies, but there isn't enough money to help them. "Those parents are paying for child care and struggling," said a representative. "Or they have their kids in compromising situations, either juggling them between friends and family or leaving them alone."

66 There is a great deal of evidence, especially from North America: The situation of low-earning single mothers in the United States is vividly described by A. Chaudry, *Putting Children First: How Low-Waged Working Mothers Manage Child Care* (New York: Russell Sage Foundation, 2004). A wider-reaching perspective for the whole of North America is provided by C. Michaelopoulos and P. K. Robins, "Employment and Child-Care Choices of Single-parent Families in Canada and the United States," *Journal of Population Economics* 15, no. 3 (2002): 465–93.

66 many parents, especially women, can describe the child care arrangements: J. Barnes, P. Leach, K. Sylva, A. Stein, and L.-E. Malmberg, "Infant Care in England: Mothers' Aspirations, Experiences, Satisfaction and Caregiver Relationships," *Early Child Development and Care* 176, no. 5 (July 2006): 553–73.

66 two clusters of beliefs: An attitude scale named Beliefs About the Consequences of Maternal Employment for Children (BACMEC; E. Greenberger, W. Goldberg, and J. Granger, "Beliefs About the Consequences of Maternal Employment for Children," *Psychology of Women Quarterly* 12, no. 1 [1988]: 35–59) has been widely used in child care research all over the world. The scale yields two scores: one for "belief in the costs of maternal employment for children" and the other "belief in the benefits of maternal employment for children." Mothers who score higher on costs than benefits almost invariably use less child care, while mothers who score higher on benefits use more.

67 relationships between the types of child care: S. Himmelweit and M. Sigala, "Choice and the Relationship Between Attitudes and Behaviour for Mothers with Preschool Children: Some Implications for Policy" (Working Paper Series No. 23, Hawke Research Institute, 2003).

68 Recent data suggest: Barnes et al., "Infant Care in England."

68 hindsight often confuses the issue: In two large-scale American studies in the 1990s, about one-quarter of mothers using a range of care types were not using their preferred type. S. L. Hofferth and D. A. Wissoker, "Price, Quality and Income in Child Care Choice," *Journal of Human Resources* 28 (1992): 70–111; S. Kontos, C. Howes, M. Shinn, and E. Galinsky, *Quality in Family Child Care and Relative Care* (New York: Teachers College Press, 1995). In a study of parents who were using family day care settings, almost two-thirds (62 percent) wanted a different type of care. Specifically, two in five (39 percent) would have preferred nursery or school care, and one in five (19 percent) would have preferred to care for the child themselves. R. W. Fuqua and R. Schieck, "Child Care Resource and Referral Programs and Parents' Search for Quality Child Care," *Early Childhood Research Quarterly* 4 (1989): 357–65.

72 In American studies, a majority of mothers have said: For instance, in a large sample of American mothers, the item "caregiver-child interaction" had the highest mean rating of importance (M = 2.99 on a scale of 1 to 3) for mothers of infants and tod-

dlers. D. Cryer and M. Burchinal, "Parents as Child Care Consumers," *Early Childhood Research Quarterly* 12 (1997): 35–58. In another large-scale study, this time of American mothers using family or relative day care, caregiver attributes were the most important reasons for parents' choice of care arrangement: S. Kontos, C. Howes, M. Shinn, and E. Galinsky, *Quality in Family Child Care and Relative Care* (New York: Teachers College Press, 1995).

73   their own, very personal and subjective, assessments of care providers: G. M. Rassin, P. A. Beach, D. P. McCormick, B. N. Niebuhr, and S. Weller, "Health and Safety in Day Care: Parental Knowledge," *Clinical Pediatrics* 30 (1991): 344–49.

74   Reasons for Choosing a Type of Formal Child Care: This table and table on facing page from *CEYP.*

74   Mothers of under-threes, and especially of under-ones: For example, a pre-election survey of Canadian child care policy (released July 2006) asked two thousand respondents in six provinces for their views. Over 80 percent said that parental care in the home was the best arrangement for young children (84 percent of low-income Canadians compared with 78 percent of high-income Canadians). If parental care was not an option, 53 percent preferred relative care, 20 percent family day care, 17 percent nonprofit group care, and 7 percent for-profit group care.

77   making supportive contact with one another: www.urbanbaby.com.

77   gathering information about child care from experts and retailers: www.mumsnet.com.

77   a secure means for parents who need childminders or nannies: www.childcarelink.gov.uk.

Introduction: Family Care, the Baseline

82   in some countries, the choice is contrary to government social policy: The Swedish tax system is one that pressures households to have two earners. The single-earner breadwinner starts paying 32 percent income tax on incomes as low as the equivalent of $2,200 a year, and many feel that this pressure is designed so that a dual-earner home is essential. Sweden heavily subsidizes use of day care and has withdrawn much financial support for any other style of child rearing. Some parents have become so concerned that benefits do not flow to all children, only to those in day care, that two groups have taken an official complaint to the UN High Commissioner for Human Rights in Geneva, former Canadian Supreme Court justice Madame Louise Arbour. HARO, Riksorganisationen for Valfrihet, Jamstalldhet och Foraldraskap, is a UN NGO (non-governmental organization): For Freedom of Choice, Gender Equality & Parenthood. Foreningen Barnens Ratt Till Foraldrarnas Tid is the Association for the Right of Children to Their Parents.

82   A review of ethnographic reports from 156 cultures: This was part of the first World Summit on Fatherhood held in Oxford, England, in 2003. The summit, backed by the United Nations and organized by Fathers Direct, was attended by delegates from five continents; www.fathersdirect.com/home.

82   the introduction of one to two weeks' paternity leave: In 2003, fathers in the United Kingdom became entitled to leave for which they receive Statutory Paternity Pay, provided they have worked for the same employer for six months; currently this is £117.18, or 90 percent of average weekly earnings, whichever is less. This is the same

rate at which mothers are paid after the first six weeks of maternity leave. However, despite the fact that almost two-thirds of fathers had taken time off for the births of babies in the year 2000, usually utilizing vacation time, only 19 percent took up this new paid entitlement in the first year it was available. The likely explanation is that the flat-rate payment is inadequate. European comparisons show that universal take-up of paternity leave, as opposed to maternity leave, depends on replacement income levels of between 80 percent and 100 percent. This illustrates the danger of assuming that mothers and fathers will react in the same way to measures directed at them without gender differentiation as parents. Women, facing childbirth and often breast-feeding, will take all the paid maternity leave that is offered to them; the payment may be inadequate, but it is certainly better than nothing. Fathers have more choice about whether and when to stay off work at the time of a birth, and they will exercise it.

83   recent research into attachment has shown: H. Steele, "Attachment," *The Psychologist* 15, no. 10 (2002): 518–23.

83   The Pre-School Learning Alliance: http://www.pre-school.org.uk/research.

5. Shared Care by Mothers and Fathers

85   a 1.5 dual-earning couple: P. Gregg and E. Washbrook, "The Effects of Early Maternal Employment on Child Development in the UK" (working paper series no. 03/070, Centre for Market and Public Organization, Department of Economics, University of Bristol, 2003).

86   "Overall, time spent by fathers": *Fathers: Balancing Work and Family* (Equal Opportunities Commission, March 2003), p. 3.

86   "fathers of infants spend less than an hour a day": *Growing Up in Australia: The Longitudinal Study of Australian Children* (Melbourne: Commonwealth of Australia, 2005), p. 24; L. Craig, "The Hidden Cost of Parenthood: The Impact of Children on Adult Time" (PhD diss., School of Social Science and Policy, University of New South Wales, 2004), p. 133. These figures are based on time-use diaries of parents of infants in the Longitudinal Study of Australian Children, Department of Family and Community Services and Australian Institute of Family Studies.

87   Some groups of fathers are far more hands-on: See international time-budget diary comparisons from the Multinational Time-Use Study held at the University of Essex and extensively analyzed, mainly by Jay Gershuny: "Gender, Class and Family," International Conferences, City University, 2008; http://www.genet.ac.uk/events.

87   father involvement in the first year of life: The Avon Longitudinal Study of Parents and Children (ALSPAC); Gregg and Washbrook, "Effects of Early Maternal Employment."

87   Fathers who do not live with their children: E. Maris Hetherington and John Kelly, *For Better or Worse: Divorce Reconsidered* (New York: Norton, 2002).

88   In what workplace specialists are calling "The Daddy Wars": Stephanie Armour, "Workplace Tensions Rise as Dads Seek Family Time," *USA Today*, December 11, 2007.

90   not only a glass ceiling but also a motherhood crash barrier: A useful account of this issue in both the United States and the United Kingdom was written by Viv Groskop, "Mothers Need Not Apply," *Guardian*, February 22, 2008. In 2007, a sur-

vey by Britain's Equality and Human Rights Commission reported that more than two-thirds of recruitment agencies had been instructed not to hire women who were pregnant or likely to get pregnant.

In March 2008, the Trades Unions Congress revealed the full extent of the gender pay gap: "Women's wages start to stagnate as early as their thirties and many are paying an unacceptable penalty simply for having children."

The *Guardian* focused on part-time work as "the great divide" in pay both between women and men and between full-time and part-time women. Lucy Ward, "The Baby Blues: Study Finds a Third of Mothers Slip Down Career Ladder," *Guardian*, February 27, 2008, p. 3.

6. Care by Full-Time Mothers

93 In Australia, for example, where there is no state-funded maternity leave: Relative to comparable countries, Australian women have a low level of workforce involvement, as the table below shows. In the year 2000, only 43 percent of Australian women with two or more children were in the labor force as compared with 82 percent in Sweden, 65 percent in the United States, and 62 percent in the United Kingdom. Only Ireland (41 percent), Spain (43 percent), and Italy (42 percent) have rates as low as Australia.

AUSTRALIAN COUPLES' ENGAGEMENT IN THE LABOR FORCE BY NUMBER OF DEPENDENT CHILDREN

Labor Force Status	No children	One child	Two or more
Husband *employed*, wife *employed*	55.9	14.5	29.6
Husband *employed*, wife unemployed	36.5	20.3	43.2
Husband employed, wife not in labor force	36.9	19.0	44.1
Husband *unemployed*, wife *employed*	59.0	12.3	28.6
Husband *unemployed*, wife unemployed	40.8	24.3	34.9
Husband *unemployed*, wife not In labor force	34.9	23.0	42.1
Husband not in labor force, wife not in labor force	93.6	2.2	4.2
Husband not in labor force, wife employed	77.6	9.7	12.7

Source: ABS Labour Force Status and other Characteristics of Families 2000 Cat. No. 6224_0, p. 15.

93 Countries that have coupled the carrot of subsidized child care: The Canadian tax system discriminates in favor of households that have two wage earners and use formal child care. Complaints of similarly one-sided funding that amounts to discrimination have been made by other nations at the UN—for example, Endeavour Forum in Australia in 1997 and Low Income Families Together from Canada in 1998. Also in 1998, Beverley Smith made a complaint as an individual homemaker at the Division for the Advancement of Women at the UN, supported by three Canadian organizations and by the European Federation for Women Working in the Home, UNICA in Rome, and the World Movement of Mothers. An Irish organization, WITH, Women in the Home, is currently working with many other groups to get the European Union to recognize unpaid caregiver homemaking as a profession.

94 Talking with mothers about care in the first year of life: Personal interview conducted by author, 2000.

95   Choices of child care: Data from Australia in 2003 illustrates the fact that in all West-
      ern countries, more mothers are at home with younger children than with older chil-
      dren, and that many mothers work part-time when their children are young.

          Comparative figures for all mothers were 35.5 percent employed part-time and
      25 percent employed full-time, with just under 40 percent not employed.

MOTHERS EMPLOYMENT BY AGE OF YOUNGEST CHILD, 2003

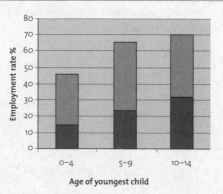

• Mothers part-time employment • Mothers full-time employment
Source: ABS *Labour Force Australia 2003* Data Cubes, cited in Iain Campbell and Sara
Charlesworth, *Background Report: Key Work and Family Trends in Australia*
(Melbourne: Centre for Applied Research, RMIT Melbourne, 2004), p. A2-7.

95   legislation passed in November 2006 brought the United Kingdom more into line:
      British regulations that entitle women to a year's maternity leave, regardless of the
      length of time they have worked at a particular company, came into force on Novem-
      ber 1, 2006, as part of the Work and Families Act 2006. The regulations apply to
      women who give birth on or after April 1, 2007. Statutory maternity and adoption pay
      periods have been increased from twenty-six weeks to thirty-nine weeks. The law also
      introduces "keeping in touch days," allowing women to work up to ten days during
      their maternity leave without losing statutory maternity pay. S. Buirgess, P. Gregg,
      C. Propper, E. Washbrook, and the ALSPAC study team, "Maternity Rights and
      Mothers' Return to Work" (working paper series no. 02/055, Centre for Market and
      Public Organization, Department of Economics, University of Bristol, 2002).

95   how wide the differences in paid maternity leaves are: Tanaka Sakiko, "Parental
      Leave and Child Health Across OECD Countries, *Economic Journal* 115 (February
      2005): F7–F28.

          In North America and in Australia, although different states and different corpo-
      rations offer some women a range of benefits, there is no national paid maternity
      leave. Furthermore, the Family and Medical Leave Act (FMLA, 1993), which gives
      Americans the right to ask for unpaid leave, applies only to those who have worked
      for at least twelve months and at least 1,250 hours in a firm with fifty or more
      employees. Firms with fewer than fifty employees do not have to hold open the posi-
      tion of a woman taking maternity leave.

95   most of the women who were part of the FCCC study stayed out of work: P. Leach,

J. Barnes, M. Nichols, J. Goldin, A. Stein, K. Sylva, and L.-E. Malmberg, "Child Care Before 6 Months of Age: A Qualitative Study of Mothers' Decisions and Feelings About Employment and Non-maternal Care," *Infant and Child Development* 15, no. 5 (2006): 471–502.

101 Children certainly make a difference in women's employment rates: In the United Kingdom in 2002, 88 percent of women with educational qualifications and no dependent children were employed, and 48 percent of women with neither qualifications nor dependent children. In comparison, the numbers of employed women with a child under five were 72 percent and 23 percent. Employment rates were lower for women with young children, but figures for women with a child under five include those with an infant, even those on paid maternity leave. The highest levels of employment (higher even than in the United States) were in Sweden, with 80 percent of women with a child under six in the workforce and a much smaller difference in the employment rates of qualified and unqualified women. The relative impact of children may be lessening, however. In April 2006, Statistics Canada released results of a study of paid workforce participation, noting that women in their mid-thirties to mid-forties are choosing to leave paid work for a time to begin a family or work in the household. Across Canada, paid labor force participation fell in 2005 for the first time ever outside of a recession. The trend has surprised observers, who thought that labor force participation might go up since unemployment is at a thirty-year low, and wages are accelerating. However, it is becoming evident that many women prefer to be home for a time with the children, while younger women may also want to stay in further education. The trend is applauded by many women but described by some observers as "disturbing."

101 the have-it-all culture of the 1990s is softening: In October 2005, *Chatelaine* magazine (French edition) ran an article called "Mamans à la Maison—les Nouvelles Rebelles." This lengthy analysis of women at home raising their children pointed out that though some think taking care of a baby at home is a traditional role and that the rebellious thing to do is to use day care, societal and tax pressures to use day care are so strong that in Quebec, at least, the rebellious thing to do is to be home with the child. The cutting-edge daring of women, then, is to confront the prejudices against this role, according to Manon Lavoie and friend Isabelle Deslandes, who have formed a group called Le Mouvement Inspiration (www.mouvementinspiration .com) to make their voices heard and their choices respected by government. Anthropologist Bernard Arcand has observed the trend to devalue the role of mother, which he says is a prejudice dating from the industrial era, when we started to count only paid work as work. He has said that it takes a lot of courage to go against the current. One small child observed the irony of the care role at home: "Mummy doesn't work. She has too much to do."

Leslie Steiner has put together a volume of essays by twenty-five writers called *Mommy Wars: Stay-at-Home and Career Moms Face Off on Their Choices, Their Lives, Their Families* (New York: Random House, 2006). Reviewers, such as Lisa Fitterman of the *Montreal Gazette*, note that choosing either way can be seen as a feminist decision. In the book itself, Helene Mitci, for example, argues that it is possible to have a full-time career and be a good mother, while Lois Shea feels that to leave her reporter job to be home with her daughter is also a feminist statement because "I am doing exactly what I want to be doing." For Shea, being able to choose is the real victory.

101 one in twenty children in the United States is said to be homeschooled: www
.raisingkids.co.uk.

102 However, satisfaction with work and the mental health advantages associated with it:
Consideration of social class is important, especially as research has also shown more
consistent advantages for children in working-class families than in the middle class
when their mothers are employed. S. Desai, P. L. Chase-Lansdale, and R. T.
Michael, "Mother or Market? Effects of Maternal Employment on Four-Year-Olds'
Intellectual Abilities," *Demographics* 26 (1980): 546–61; L. W. Hoffman, "Effects of
Maternal Employment in the Two-Parent Family," *American Psychologist* 44 (1989):
283–92. It is possible that the greater advantage of maternal employment for working class children is produced by its more positive effect on the mother's sense of
well-being.

103 Research comparing the child-rearing behavior: D. DeMeis, and H. W. Perkins,
" 'Supermoms' of the Nineties," *Journal of Family Issues* 17, no. 6 (1996): 777–92.

104 negative effects from the first year last well into the school years: L. Youngblade,
"Peer and Teacher Ratings of Third- and Fourth-Grade Children's Social Behavior
as a Function of Early Maternal Employment," *Journal of Child Psychology and Psychiatry* 44, no. 4 (2003): 477–88.

105 A few studies have found that sons of middle-class mothers: P. Gregg and E. Washbrook, "The Effects of Early Maternal Employment on Child Development in the
UK" (working paper series no. 03/070, Centre for Market and Public Organisation,
Department of Economics, University of Bristol, 2003). A greater emphasis on their
children's achievement by employed mothers was also found in the longitudinal
research of: A. E. Gottfried, A. W. Gottfried, and K. Bathurst, "Maternal and Dual-
Earner Employment Status and Parenting," in *Handbook of Parenting*, vol. 2, *Biology
and Ecology of Parenting*, ed. M. H. Bornstein (Mahwah, N.J.: Lawrence Erlbaum,
1988), pp. 139–60. In this study, based on a middle-class sample of two-parent families, contemporaneous and earlier maternal employment predicted higher educational aspirations for both boys and girls at ages five and seven, as well as more
after-school lessons and less TV viewing. Employed mothers were also more
involved in discussing school activities with their children. Although these parental
behaviors themselves predicted a variety of measures of the children's academic competence, there was no direct relationship between the mother's employment status
and the indices of child competence.

105 These relationships between mothers working outside the home: M. Rutter,
J. Dunn, R. Plomin, E. Simonoff, A. Pickles, B. Maughan, J. Ormel, J. Meyer, and
L. Eaves, "Integrating Nature and Nurture: Implications of Person-Environment
Correlations and Interactions for Developmental Psychology," *Development and Psy-
chopathology* 9 (1997): 335–64; M. Rutter, "Family and School Influences on Behav-
ioural Development," in *Research and Innovation on the Road to Modern Child
Psychiatry*, vol. 2, *Classic Papers by Professor Sir Michael Rutter*, ed. E. Taylor and
J. Green (London: Gaskell/Royal College of Psychiatrists, 2001); K. Lyons-Ruth
and C. Zeanah, "The Family Context of Infant Mental Health: Affective Development in the Primary Caregiving Relationship," *Handbook of Infant Mental Health*
(New York: Guilford Press, 1993), pp. 14–37.

105 mothers' mental health or sense of well-being: V. C. McLoyd, "The Impact of Economic Hardship on Black Families and Children: Psychological Distress, Parenting
and Socioemotional Development," *Child Development* 61 (1990): 311–46. In this

study, all three levels—employment status, maternal depressed mood, and parenting styles—were examined in a study of lower-class, single African American mothers of adolescents. Full-time homemakers were more depressed than employed mothers, and depression was significantly related to both a negative perception of the maternal role and to the use of power-assertive discipline. However, no attempt was made to see if depression carried into the relationship between the mother's employment status and her parenting style.

106 mothers' satisfaction with their roles: E. Hock, D. DeMeiss, and S. McBride, "Maternal Separation Anxiety: Its Role in the Balance of Employment and Motherhood," in *Maternal Employment and Children's Development: Longitudinal Research*, ed. A. E. Gottfried and A. W. Gottfried (New York: Plenum Press, 1988), pp. 191–239.

7. Fathers as Principal Care Providers

107 This occurs in a very small group of families: In 2006, Dr. Aron Rochlen of the University of Texas estimated a rapidly growing trend toward more father care in the United States, both full-time (159,000) and part-time (perhaps 2 million). U.K. fathers are estimated by the Equal Opportunities Commission to provide about 2 percent of nonmaternal child care across all age groups.

Many of the U.K. statistics in this chapter are from the WLB2000 Employee Survey data set. This comprises data from a nationally representative survey of 7,500 persons employed in workplaces with five or more staff, including 1,486 fathers and 2,260 mothers with dependent children. The employer data set comprises data from a nationally representative survey of 2,500 workplaces with five or more employees. The MORI Social Research Institute conducted sixty-one qualitative in-depth interviews with fathers, their partners, and HR managers in six case-study organizations, and three focus groups with fathers, between April and June 2002.

Useful papers from this study published in the EOC Research Discussion series include: M. O'Brien and I. Shemilt, *Working Fathers: Earning and Caring* (London: Equal Opportunities Commission, 2003); W. Hatter, L. Vinter, and R. Williams, *Dads on Dads: Needs and Expectations at Home and at Work* (Manchester: Equal Opportunities Commission, 2002). In October 2007, the EOC became part of the Equality and Human Rights Commission. For further information about EOC research and statistical work, see http://www.equalityhumanrights.com/cn/policyresearch.

107 In the NICHD study of early child care: NICHD Early Child Care Research Network, *Child Care and Child Development: Results from the NICHD Study of Early Child Care and Youth Development* (New York and London: Guilford Press, 2005), pp. 39–59.

107 In the FCCC study, only 8 percent of babies: K. Sylva, A. Stein, P. Leach, J. Barnes, L.-E. Malmberg, and the FCCC team, "Family and Child Factors Related to the Use of Non-maternal Infant Care: An English Study," *Early Childhood Research Quarterly* 22, no. 1 (2007): 118–36.

108 young fatherhood is more common in the United States: In 1990, about 33 million Americans (14 percent of the population), but that figure was made up of 11.4 percent whites, 31.3 percent blacks, and 29 percent Hispanics; by 1993, the difference had slightly increased to 11.6 percent whites, 33.3 percent blacks, and 29.3 percent Hispanics.

108 They took on more caregiving responsibilities for sons than for daughters: NICHD
     Early Child Care Research Network, "Factors Associated with Fathers' Caregiving
     Activities and Sensitivity with Young Children," in *Child Care and Child Development*,
     pp. 395–406.

108 when 1,201 mothers of three-month-old babies: J. Barnes, P. Leach, K. Sylva,
     A. Stein, and L.-E. Malmberg, "Infant Care in England: Mothers' Aspirations, Expe-
     riences, Satisfaction and Caregiver Relationships," *Early Child Development and Care*
     176, no. 5 (2006): 553–73.

108 When a group of these mothers who had returned to work: P. Leach, J. Barnes,
     M. Nicols, J. Goldin, A. Stein, K. Sylva, and L.-E. Malmberg, "Child Care Before
     6 Months of Age: A Qualitative Study of Mothers' Decisions and Feelings About
     Employment and Non-maternal Care," *Infant and Child Development* 15, no. 5
     (2006): 471–502.

110 The relatively poor outcomes in social and emotional development: P. Gregg and
     E. Washbrook, "The Effects of Early Maternal Employment on Child Development
     in the UK" (working paper series no. 03/070, Centre for Market and Public Organi-
     sation, Department of Economics, University of Bristol, 2003).

111 the gender gap in pay is exacerbated: Equal Opportunities Commission, *Fathers: Bal-
     ancing Work and Family*, 2003.

111 Dual-earner households in which women earn more: A. S. Fulgini and J. Brooks-
     Gunn, "Measuring Mother and Father Shared Caregiving: An Analysis Using the
     Panel Study of Income Dynamics," *Child Development Supplement* (paper presented at
     the Workshop on Measuring Father Involvement, Bethesda, Md., February 8–9,
     2001).

112 Detailed study, using video recordings: S. Lewis, A. West, A. Stein, L.-E. Malmberg,
     K. Bethell, K. Sylva, J. Barnes, and P. Leach, "A Comparison of Father-Infant Inter-
     action Between Primary and Non-Primary Care Giving Fathers," *Child Care, Health
     and Development*, submitted February 2008.

112 Nevertheless, those progressive and traditional attitudes: NICHD Early Child Care
     Research Network, "Factors Associated with Fathers' Caregiving Activities."

112 Powerful narratives collected in the study *Dads on Dads:* Hatter, Vinter, and
     Williams, *Dads on Dads.*

113 The outcomes that go with fathers' involvement: M. E. Lamb and C. Lewis, "The
     Development and Significance of Father-Child Relationships in Two-Parent Fami-
     lies," in *The Role of the Father in Child Development*, ed. M. E. Lamb, 4th ed. (Hobo-
     ken, N.J.: Wiley, 2004).

113 when both parents involve themselves: J. Dunn, L. Davies, T. O'Connor, and
     W. Sturgess, "Parents' and Partners' Life Course and Family Experiences: Links
     with Parent-Child Relationships in Different Family Settings," *Journal of Child Psy-
     chology and Psychiatric and Allied Disciplines* 41, no. 8 (2000): 955–68.

114 When fathers in particular show greater interest: R. Goldman, *Fathers' Involvement in
     Their Children's Education* (London: National Family and Parenting Institute, 2005).

8. Grandparent Care

115 grandparents in many communities on both sides of the Atlantic: G. Dench and
     J. Ogg, *Grandparenting in Britain*, BSA survey (London: Institute of Community

Studies, 2002); P. Uhlenberg and B. Hammill, "Frequency of Grandparent Contact with Grandchild Sets: Six Factors that Make a Difference," *The Gerontologist* 38 (1998): 276–85.

115 In a recent U.K. magazine survey: The 21st Century Gran Survey, conducted by *Yours* magazine in July 2004. Given the lack of detailed, focused information about contemporary grandmothers, it is tempting to supplement research with less scientific sources, such as this survey.

> The 21st century granny—a character composed from 2,000 replies—is as far from the traditional scone-making biddy with a steel grey hairbun as any image-maker could contrive. Feeling, on average, 21 years younger than her actual age [which is 54], the modern grandmother is adept at picking up modern technology—mobile phones and computers are a must. Half of all respondents had recently been to a theme park, 15% said they always try out new roller-coasters and 7% like to go skinny-dipping. A fifth said they have an alcoholic drink every day, 94% like dressing up regularly for a night out, and half are on the lookout for love.

Quotation from the *Guardian*, July 1, 2004; see http://www.literacytrust.org.uk/talktoyourbaby/grandparents/html.

116 Once they had any regular care from anyone but the mother: The NICHD Early Child Care Research Network, *Child Care and Child Development: Results from the NICHD Study of Early Child Care and Youth Development* (New York and London: Guilford Press, 2005), pp. 39–49; K. Sylva, A. Stein, P. Leach, J. Barnes, L.-E. Malmberg, and the FCCC team, "Family and Child Factors Related to the Use of Nonmaternal Infant Care: An English Study," *Early Childhood Research Quarterly* 22, no. 1 (2007): 118–36.

116 In the United States, about one-third of children under six: H. Boushey, "Who Cares? The Child Care Choices of Working Mothers" (data brief no. 1, Center for Economic and Policy Research, 2003); P. Meadows and Volterra Consulting, *The Economic Contributions of Older People* (London: Age Concern England, 2004). Scottish Executive Survey suggests that parents' enthusiasm for grandparent care is due to its "affordability" (i.e., most parents do not have to pay anything). In 2002, for example, 89 percent of all Australian informal child care was at no cost: *Child Care* (Australian Bureau of Statistics, 2002), p. 6.

116 A very large survey of child care in the United Kingdom: C. Bryson, A. Kazimirski, and H. Southwood, *Childcare and Early Years Provision: A Study of Parents' Use, Views and Experience* (London: National Centre for Social Research, 2006).

116 And in Australia in 2002: D. de Vaus, *Diversity and Change in Australian Families: Statistical Profiles* (Melbourne: Australian Institute of Family Studies, 2004), p. 243.

117 The British Daycare Trust stated, in 2006: www.LiteracyTrust.org.uk/talktoyourbaby/grandparents.html.

117 The particular importance of grandparents' care for teenage grandchildren is highlighted: M. Anderson, J. Tunaly, and J. Walker, *Relatively Speaking: Communication in Families* (Newcastle: University of Newcastle Family Studies Centre, 2000).

118 Grandparents, such as those in a U.S. AARP study: Curt Davies et al., *The Grandparent Study*, 2002 Report, AARP Knowledge Management, www.aarp.org.

119 "When grandfathers reported looking after grandchildren": Christine Millward, *Family Relationship and Intergenerational Exchange in Later Life* (working paper no. 15, Australian Institute of Family Studies, Melbourne, 1998), pp. 23–24. See also Barbara Pocock, *The Work/Life Collision* (Sydney: Federation Press, 2003), p. 64.

119 In the United States, where relative (including grandmother) care: NICHD Early Child Care Research Network, *Early Child Care and Youth Development;* Bensley, "Who Cares?"; Meadows and Volterra, *Economic Contributions.*

120 more mothers selected care by their own mothers: J. Barnes, P. Leach, K. Sylva, A. Stein, and L.-E. Malmberg, "Infant Care in England: Mothers' Aspirations, Experiences, Satisfaction and Caregiver Relationships," *Early Child Development and Care* 176, no. 5 (2006): 553–73; P. Leach, J. Barnes, M. Nicols, J. Goldin, A. Stein, K. Sylva, and L.-E. Malmberg, "Child Care Before Six Months of Age: A Qualitative Study of Mothers' Decisions and Feelings About Employment and Non-maternal Care," *Infant and Child Development* 15, no. 5 (2006): 471–502.

120 Responsibility for grandchild care may clash: J. Goodfellow and J. Laverty, "Grandparents Supporting Working Families: Satisfaction and Choice in the Provision of Child Care," *Family Matters* 66 (2003): 14–19.

121 A majority would prefer to step back: P. Cotterill, "Women's Attitudes Towards Grandmother Care," *Sociology* 26 (1992): 614.

121 suggest a more combative relationship between the generations: L. M. Drew, M. H. Richard, and P. K. Smith, *Grandparenting and Its Relationship to Parenting* (The Foundation for Grandparenting, 2002), www.grandparenting.org/Research.htm.

121 A recent report on 8,752 English families: E. Fergusson, B. Maughab, and J. Golding, "Which Children Receive Grandparental Care and What Effect Does It Have?" *Journal of Child Psychology and Psychiatry* 49, no. 2 (February 2008): 161–69.

122 Grandmothers in multigenerational households often provide: D. Oyserman, N. Radin, and R. Benn, "Dynamics in a Three-Generation Family," *Developmental Psychology* 29 (1993): 564–72.

122 around 4 million children in the United States: S. Gilbert, "Rising Stress of Raising a Grandchild," *New York Times,* July 28, 1998.

122 In Australia in 2003, 22,500 families: M. Fitzpatrick and P. Reeve, "Grandparents Raising Grandchildren: A New Class of Disadvantaged Australians," *Family Matters* 66 (2003): 54–57. See also B. Cornelius, of Cangrands Kinship Support Group, reporting data from Statistics Canada (2006), www.cangrands.com; M. E. Sinovacz, ed., *Handbook on Grandparenting* (Westport, Conn.: Greenwood Press, 1999); E. Fuller-Thomson, "Grandparents Raising Grandchildren in Households Where Parents Are Not Present" (University of Toronto, 2005).

123 training and interest in child care as a career: A. R. Pence and H. Goelman, "The Relationships of Regulation, Training and Motivation to Quality of Care in Family Day Care," *Child and Youth Care Forum* 20 (1991): 83–101.

123 found lower-quality ratings for relative homes: S. Kontos, C. Howes, M. Shinn, and E. Galinsky, *Quality in Family Child Care and Relative Care* (New York: Teachers College Press, 1995).

123 higher-quality care for babies in grandparent care: NICHD Early Childcare Research Network, "Characteristics of Infant Child Care: Factors Contributing to Positive Caregiving," *Early Childhood Research Quarterly* 11 (1996): 269–306. See also P. Leach, J. Barnes, L.-E. Malmberg, K. Sylva, and A. Stein, "The Quality of Differ-

ent Types of Child Care at 10 and 18 Months: A Comparison Between Types and Factors Related to Quality," *Early Child Development and Care* 178, no. 2 (2008): 177–209.

123 informal familial child care arrangements: R. Bernal and J. Moore, *Maternal Time, Child Care and Cognitive Development: The case of Single Mothers*" (2005), www.ucl.ac .uk/childcare29/08/2005.

123 grandparents are at higher risk for physical and emotional health problems: Fitzpatrick and Reeve, "Grandparents Raising Grandchildren."

9. Care by Nannies, Au Pairs, and Other In-Home Child Care Providers

125 In the U.K. Department of Education and Skills: C. Bryson et al. *Childcare and Early Years Provision: A Study of Parents' Use, Views and Experiences* (Research Report No. 723, National Centre for Social Research, Department for Education and Skills, 2006).

125 A report by the U.S. Center for Economic and Policy Research: H. Boushey, *Who Cares? The Child Care Choices of Working Mothers* (data brief no 1, Center for Economic and Policy Research, 2003).

126 The NICHD study showed that 15 percent of infants: NICHD Early Child Care Research Network, *Child Care and Child Development: Results from the NICHD Study of Early Child Care and Youth Development* (New York and London: Guilford Press, 2005), pp. 50–77.

126 In the FCCC study, 3.6 percent of the mothers: J. Barnes, P. Leach, K. Sylva, A. Stein, and L.-E. Malmberg, "Infant Care in England: Mothers' Aspirations, Experiences, Satisfaction and Caregiver Relationships," *Early Child Development and Care* 176, no 5 (2006): 553–73.

127 demand, according to the London *Times*, is increasing: R. Bennett, "Reality Shows Convince World the British Nanny Knows Best," *Times*, January 4, 2008.

131 The irony, of course, is that many of these exploited women: Joanna Moorehead, "Who Is Looking After the Baby?" *Guardian*, May 19, 2004, p. 15.

132 Although the outcomes of nanny care for children: P. Leach, J. Barnes, L.-E. Malmberg, K. Sylva, A. Stein, and the FCCC team (2006), "The Quality of Different Types of Child Care at 10 and 18 Months: A Comparison Between Types and Factors Related to Quality," *Early Childhood Development and Care* 178, no. 2 (February 2008): 177–209.

134 The correspondence in the box: P. Leach, *Your Baby and Child* (New York: Knopf, 2003), p. 316.

10. Family Day Care

139 The lower fees for family day care, however: J. Statham and A. Mooney, "Across the Spectrum: An Introduction to Family Day Care Internationally," in *Family Day Care: International Perspectives on Policy, Practice and Quality*, ed. A. Mooney and J. Statham (London: Jessica Kingsley, 2003).

139 "[There can be] conflict between the affective, caring aspects": Ibid., p. 16.

139 family day care as a formal service: Statham and Mooney, " 'Across the Spectrum.' "

140 During the 1990s, the National Childminding Association: The National Childminding Association in the United Kingdom and the National Association for Family Child Care in the United States played a role in professionalizing family child
care. See especially National Childminding Association with the Children's Workforce Development Council, "Taking Training," February 2007, www.cwdcouncil
.org.uk.

140 in many countries family day care: M. Cochran, "European Childcare in Global Perspective," *European Early Childhood Education Research* 3, no. 1 (1995): 61–72.

141 "No one says anything about family day care": Ibid., p. 66.

143 "After these two short spells in kin care": A. Chaudry, *Putting Children First: How
Low-Wage Working Mothers Manage Child Care* (New York: Russell Sage Foundation,
2004), p. 35.

145 And in the last ten years, the enormous importance of childminding: Department for
Education and Skills, *Choice for Parents, the Best Start for Children: A Ten-Year Strategy*
(London: Her Majesty's Stationery Office, 2004).

> The British Government is committed to providing an out-of-school
> childcare place for all children aged 3 to 12 between the hours of
> 8 a.m. and 6 p.m. each weekday by 2010 (with half of parents access-
> ing this by 2008 or before). Targets have also been set for a children's
> centre in every community—that's 3500 by 2010. The strategy recog-
> nises that registered childminding will play an essential part in the
> success of these schemes, providing home-based care on their
> behalf—essential for offering choice to parents.

146 the National Childminding Association: www.ncma.org.uk; S. Owen, "The Development of Childminding Networks in Britain: Sharing the Caring," in Mooney and
Statham, *Family Day Care*, pp. 78–92.

146 the early years education of three- and four-year-olds: OFSTED, "Better Education
and Care," *The Annual Report of Her Majesty's Chief Inspector of Schools* (London: Her
Majesty's Stationery Office, 2006).

148 In the United States, approximately a million family day care providers: K. Smith,
Who's Minding the Kids? Child Care Arrangements: Winter 2002, Current Population
Reports, Household Economic Studies (Washington, D.C.: U.S. Department of
Commerce, 2002), pp. 70–86.

148 However, U.S. family day care is still viewed somewhat skeptically: National Association for Family Child Care (United States), 2002, www.nafcc.org.

149 Recent estimates indicate that 90 percent of American family day care: A. Clarke-
Stewart and V. Allhusen, *What We Know About Childcare* (Cambridge, Mass.: Harvard
University Press, 2005).

149 When licensing is required and enforced: The Children's Foundation, *Licensing
Study* (Washington, D.C., 2002).

149 The hope is that by setting higher standards: K. Modigliani, "Who Says What Is
Quality?" in Mooney and Statham, *Family Day Care*, pp. 215–33.
    Modigliani says that by 2002 more than three thousand providers were accredited
or studying to become so, and a number of states (notably California) were beginning to offer essential financial assistance and training. Furthermore, she reported

that "a number of states pay higher purchase-of-care rates to family childcare providers that are accredited, and this can provide a particular incentive for providers serving low-income families who are eligible for such subsidies. Some parents who are aware of the importance of accreditation in communities where centre-based accreditation has become popular are seeking accredited family childcare providers." However, she concludes: "If there are approximately one million family childcare providers in the United States, less than 1 percent of them are expected to go through the accreditation process in the next few years. Raising standards through a voluntary accreditation system will take time, and requires support—financial and otherwise—if it is to reach providers in all communities" (p. 231).

149 Some of the highest-quality family day care in the country: MilitaryHOMEFRONT is the official Web site of the Department of Defense for "Quality of Life" information for troops and their families. It includes information for those who prefer family day care for their children and for those whose military commitments require them to seek very flexible and unpredictable hours of care for their children.

150 Ajay Chaudry found that at least three-quarters of poor mothers: Chaudry, *Putting Children First.*

11. Child Care Centers or Nurseries

153 the popular image of such group day care centers: U.K. national sample: C. Bryson, A. Kazimirski, and H. Southwood, *Childcare and Early Years Provision (CEYP): A Study of Parents' Use, Views and Experiences* (London: National Centre for Social Research, 2006), a study of just under eight thousand English families interviewed in 2004–05, commissioned by the Department for Children, Schools and Families. As well as providing information in its own right, this report continues the time series data from two earlier survey series: the Parents' Demand for Childcare series and the Survey of Parents of Three and Four Year Old Children and Their Use of Early Years Services series.

154 Around 80 percent of American and more than 90 percent of British three- and four-year-olds: U.S. national sample: I. Iruka and P. Carver, *Initial Results from the 2005 NHES Early Childhood Program Participation Survey* (Washington, D.C.: National Center for Education Statistics, U.S. Department of Education, 2006). Center-based arrangements, including all early years education settings and pre-K but not K: under one year—28 percent; one to two—43 percent; three to five—78 percent. Nursery and other group arrangements: 0–2-year-olds 18 percent (+ playgroup/preschool 9 percent) = 27 percent 3–4-year-olds 12 percent (rest in nursery schools/classes/preschools) = 89 percent.

154 Furthermore, in countries in which child care is mainly in the private sector: Laing & Buisson, *Children's Nurseries U.K. Market Report 2004,* www.laingbuisson.co.uk. See also S. Vevers, "Running on Empty: Special Report on the State of the Market," *Nursery World,* April 28, 2005.

157 policy "carrots" to encourage improvements in quality: K. Modigliani, "Who Says What Is Quality?" in *Family Day Care: International Perspectives on Policy, Practice and Quality,* ed. A. Mooney and J. Statham (London and Philadelphia: Jessica Kingsley, 2003), pp. 215–33; OFSTED, "Better Education and Care," *The Annual Report of*

Her Majesty's Chief Inspector of Schools (London: Her Majesty's Stationery Office, 2006).

157 In the United States, the National Association for the Education of Young Children: NAEYC, www.naeyc.org/accreditation.

157 American group care is mostly of low quality: Cost, Quality, and Child Outcomes Study Team, *Cost, Quality, and Child Outcomes in Child Care Centers* (Denver: Department of Economics, University of Colorado, 1995). This study rated four hundred randomly selected child care centers on a scale of 1 to 7 for the following characteristics: 1) Inadequate—children's need for health and safety are not met, there is no observed warmth or support from adults, and no learning is encouraged; 2) Minimal—children's basic health and safety needs are met, a little warmth and support is provided by adults, and few learning experiences are provided; 3) Good—health and safety needs are fully met, warmth and support is provided for all children, and learning is encouraged in many through interesting, fun activities; 4) Excellent—all of the characteristics of good care are present, and children are encouraged to become independent, teachers plan for children's individual learning needs, and adults have close, personal relationships with each child. The study found that one in ten preschool centers and fully four in ten infant care centers were of such poor quality (scoring 1–2 on their scale) that they may jeopardize the children's development. In contrast, on average only 14 percent of all the centers studied achieved developmentally adequate quality (scoring 5–7). http://carolinacommunicationproject.org.

157 Ten years later, data from the National Child Care Information Center: A National Child Care Information Center, "Child Care Center Licensing Regulations" (April 2005): Child: Staff Ratios and Maximum Group Size Requirements," http://nccic.org.

157 The quality of British centers is only now being reported: P. Leach, J. Barnes, L.-E. Malmberg, K. Sylva, and A. Stein, "The Quality of Different Types of Child Care at 10 and 18 Months: A Comparison Between Types and Factors Related to Quality," *Early Child Development and Care* 178, no. 2 (2008): 177–209.

157 and Italy, especially the city of Reggio Emilia: M. Pace, "An Inspiring New Language," *Nursery World*, May 19, 2005, p. 34.

159 "With preschool, [starting age] is an important consideration": N. Schulman and E. Birnbaum, *Practical Wisdom for Parents: Demystifying the Preschool Years* (New York: Knopf, 2007), p. 17.

159 the most important predictor of a secure attachment between mother and baby: NICHD Early Child Care Research Network, *The Effects of Infant Child Care on Infant-Mother Attachment Security* (New York: Guilford Press, 2005), 193–223.

160 the relationship between group care and very young children's levels of the hormone cortisol: A. Dettling, S. Parker, S. Lane, A. Sebanc, and R. Gunnar, "Quality of Care and Temperament Determine Changes in Cortisol Concentrations over the Day for Young Children in Child Care," *Psychoneuralendocrinology* 25 (2000): 819–36; J. Bruce, E. P. Davis, and M. R. Gunnar, "Individual Differences in Children's Cortisol Response to the Beginning of a New School Year," *Psychoneuralendocrinology* 27 (2002): 635–50. See also M. de Haan, M. R. Gunnar, K. Tout, J. Hart, and K. Stansbury, "Familiar and Novel Contexts Yield Different Associations Between Cortisol and Behavior Among 2-year-old Children," *Developmental Psychobiology* 31, no. 1 (1998): 93–101; E. P. Davis, B. Donzella, W. K. Krueger, and M. R. Gunnar, "The Start of the New School Year: Individual Differences in Sali-

vary Cortisol Response in Relation to Child Temperament," *Developmental Psychobiology* 35 (1999): 188–96.

160 The concern that has hit most media headlines: James Meikle and Lucy Ward, "Children Spending Long Hours in Nursery More Prone to Poor Behaviour Says Study," *Guardian Education/Early Years*, April 5, 2007.

160 The effects are small: NICHD Early Child Care Research Network, "Early Child Care and Self-control, Compliance, and Problem Behavior at Twenty-four and Thirty-six Months," *Child Development* 69 (1998): 1145–70; T. Smith, K. Coxon, M. Sigala, K. Sylva, S. Mathers, L. La Valle, R. Smith, S. Purdon, L. Dearden, J. Shaw, L. Sibieta, *National Evaluation of the Neighbourhood Nurseries Initiative: Integrated Report* (2007), http://www.dfes.gov.uk/research.

161 "If parents or researchers or policy makers": Alison Clarke-Stewart, "Characteristics and Quality of Child Care for Toddlers and Preschoolers," in NICHD Early Child Care Research Network, *Child Care and Child Development: Results from the NICHD Study of Early Child Care and Youth Development* (New York and London: Guilford Press, 2005), pp. 91–104.

161 "which observable characteristics of the care arrangement predict higher quality care": NICHD Early Child Care Research Network "Characteristics of Infant Care: Factors Contributing to Positive Caregiving," *Early Childhood Research Quarterly* 11 (1996): 269–306.

161 a high ratio of adults to infants was overwhelmingly the most important: Clarke-Stewart, "Characteristics and Quality of Child Care for Toddlers and Preschoolers."

162 "Observed child-carer ratios in the nurseries": Leach et al., "The Quality of Different Types of Child Care at 10 and 18 Months," p. 22.

163 "The keyperson approach": P. Elfer, "Building Intimacy in Relationships with Young Children in Nurseries," *Early Years* 16, no. 2 (1996): 30. See also P. Elfer, E. Goldschmied, and D. Selleck, *Key Persons in the Nursery: Building Relationships for Quality Provision* (London: David Fulton, 2003), p. 30; D. Selleck and S. Griffin, "Quality for the Under Threes," in *Contemporary Issues in the Early Years*, ed. G. Pugh, 2nd ed. (London: Paul Chapman/Sage, 1996), pp. 152–69.

163 "It's hard for a child being in a nursery": Quoted in Selleck and Griffin, "Quality for the Under Threes," p. 160.

165 The Effective Provision of Pre-School Education (EPPE) project: K. Sylva, E. Melhuish, P. Sammons, I. Siraj-Blatchford, B. Taggart, and K. Elliot, *The Effective Provision of Pre-School Education (EPPE) Project: Findings from the Pre-School Period*, Summary of findings, Institute of Education, University of London, 2003.

167 Former President Clinton, in a 1997 speech: http://www.ed.gov/PressRelease/04-1997/970417d.html.

167 A 2000 report by the U.K. Daycare Trust: U.K. Daycare Trust, *No More Nine to Five: Childcare in a Changing World*, September 2000. The following quotations from nursery managers come from this report.

12. Integrated Care and Education: Children's Centers and Extended Schools

170 Treating the care and education of infants, toddlers, preschool, and school-age children as separate services: OECD (Organisation for Economic Cooperation Devel-

opment), *Starting Strong* (Paris: OECD, 2001). All OECD quotations are from this publication.

170 "[There is] a welcome trend towards increased cooperation": Ibid., p. 28.

171 there are already many Sure Start children's centers up and running: J. Belsky, J. Barnes, and E. Melhuish, *The National Evaluation of Sure Start: Does Area-Based Early Intervention Work?* (Bristol: The Policy Press, 2007).

171 The best-known program is Head Start and Early Head Start: Mathematica Policy Research, Inc., *Early Head Start: Making a Difference in the Lives of Infants and Toddlers and Their Families: The Impacts of Early Head Start* (Princeton, N.J., 2002).

171 Early Head Start: http://www.acf.hhs.gov/programs/opre/ehs/ehs_resrch/reports/building_summary/building_exesum.pdf.

172 Sure Start children's centers are being rapidly rolled out: National Audit Office report to Parliament, December 19, 2006. According to this report, by the end of 2006, children's centers were already serving more than 650,000 children.

172 other state initiatives have wider briefs: See Web site for National Child Care Information and Technical Assistance Center, www.nccic.org.

172 In 2001, when the No Child Left Behind Act was signed: www.whitehouse.gov/infocus/earlychildhood. Although "Good Start, Grow Smart" is primarily focused on Early Learning Guidelines aimed at school readiness, the Child Care Bureau encourages states to include its objectives in their plans for administering the Child Care and Development Fund and is carrying out research and evaluation on integrated early years provisions including: research and evaluation of the effectiveness of strategies to improve children's early learning; the impact of professional development efforts in changing caregiver skills and practice, including coordination of training efforts across early care and education systems; the impact of partnerships and collaborations among Head Start, child care, and pre-K in promoting child, provider, and family incomes.

175 In Sweden, the education and training of all those working with children: B. Cohen, P. Moss, P. Petrie, J. Wallace, *A New Deal for Children?: Re-forming Education and Care in England, Scotland and Sweden* (Bristol, Eng.: Policy Press, 2004).

176 Pedagogy is the most popular degree course in Denmark: J. North, *Support from the Start: Lessons from International Early Years Policy* (London: The Maternity Alliance, 2005), p. 60.

177 Child places fifteen years ago: P. Leach, *Children First: What Society Must Do—and Is Not Doing—for Children Today* (New York: Vintage, 1994), pp. 251–52.

179 providing a very small proportion of the available child care places: The number is so small that centers are not even separately labeled in the exhaustive study published in 2006 by the National Centre for Social Research. C. Bryson, A. Kazimirski, and H. Southwood, *Childcare and Early Years Provision: A Study of Parents' Use, Views and Experience* (London: National Centre for Social Research, 2006).

180 Integrated children's centers are not yet commonplace: While "Good Start, Grow Smart" is focused primarily on early learning guidelines aimed at school readiness, the Child Care Bureau encourages states to include its objectives in their plans for administering the Child Care and Development Fund and is carrying out research and evaluation on integrated early years provisions including: research and evaluation of the effectiveness of strategies to improve children's early learning; the impact of professional development efforts in changing caregiver skills and practice, includ-

ing coordination of training efforts across early care and education systems; the impact of partnerships and collaborations among Head Start, child care, and pre-K in promoting child, provider, and family incomes.

180 In its 2001 review of early childhood education and care services: OECD, *Starting Strong*.

181 Schools Partnership Training Institute (SPTI): See www.ncrel.org/sdrs.

182 the British government has an ambitious ongoing program: See Evaluation of the Full-Service Extended Schools Initiative, final 2007, www.desf.gov.uk/research.data.

183 An extended school in a deprived English community: http://www.teachernet.gov .uk/wholeschool/8509/extendedschools/practicalknowhow.

184 such as the New Jersey school-based youth services program: Constancia Warren, *The New Jersey School-Based Youth Services Program Evaluation* (1997; 2000), http:// scs.aed.org/publications. C. Warren, M. Feist, and N. Neverez, *A Place to Grow: Evaluation of the New York City Beacons* (New York: AED Center for School and Community Services, 2002).

184 Most of the argument and exhortation seems to be aimed: M. Eberstadt, "Home Alone America," *Policy Review*, no. 107 (June–July 2001).

184 extended or community schools will gradually be recognized: KidZinc, the School Age Care Society of Alberta, April 2007 campaign to get government to value afterschool care equally with preschool care.

184 a cost of around $275 per month: These figures are cited in Canadian dollars.

13. Quality of Care from Research Viewpoints

189 The accepted scientific way of judging the quality of child care: Following are some examples of studies relating child care quality to outcomes for children.

C. Howes and M. Olenick, "Family and Child Care Influences on Toddlers' Compliance," *Child Development* 57 (1986): 202–16. In a study of center care and compliance in a sample of American infants at eighteen, twenty-four, and thirty-six months at home, in day care, and in a structured observation, quality of care was the best predictor of children's overall noncompliance, with children from high-quality centers showing more compliance and cooperativeness than children from low-quality centers.

C. Howes, "Can the Age of Entry into Child Care and the Quality of Child Care Predict Adjustment in Kindergarten?" *Developmental Psychology* 26 (1990): 292–303; E. K. Beller, M. Stanke, P. Butsz, W. Stahl, and H. Wessels, "Two Measures of the Quality of Group Care for Infants and Toddlers," *European Journal of Psychology of Education* 11 (1996): 151–67. An American and a German study each reported positive correlations between quality of care and a range of other aspects of social competence.

C. Howes, E. Smith, and E. Galinsky, *The Florida Child Care Quality Improvement Study* (New York: Families and Work Institute, 1995). Research carried out immediately before and after changes in Florida child care regulations showed that improvement in quality was associated with improvements in peer interactions.

Cost, Quality, and Child Care Outcomes Study Team, *Cost, Quality, and Child Outcomes in Child Care Centers, Public Report* (Denver: University of Colorado, Center for

Research in Economics and Social Policy, 1995). Results from a multisite study in four American states found that after controlling for family background, higher quality of care was associated with better social competence.

B. L. Volling and L. V. Feagans, "Infant Day Care and Children's Social Competence," *Infant Behaviour and Development* 18 (1995): 177–88. Socially withdrawn infants developed better peer relations in high-quality day care centers, and these peer relations deteriorated if they were placed in centers with low-quality care.

Recent studies have shown links between child care quality and measures of the stress hormone cortisol. In full-time day care, children's cortisol levels tend to rise throughout the day, in contrast to the typical diurnal pattern, an endocrine response indicative of increased stress. Cortisol levels are more likely to increase as the quality of day care decreases. Some studies report associated increases in behavior problems. J. Bruce, E. P. Davis, and M. R. Gunnar, "Individual Differences in Children's Cortisol Response to the Beginning of a New School Year," *Psychoneuroendocrinology* 27 (2002): 635–50.

Child care quality has been shown to impact not only on social-emotional development but also on cognitive and language development. When the NICHD sample reached fifty-four months, children with child care in the highest tercile of quality achieved significantly higher scores on "pre-academics" and language compared with children in child care in the lowest tercile. D. Vandell, "Early Child Care and Children's Development Prior to School Entry," *American Educational Research Journal* 39 (2002): 133–64.

189 "There is an extraordinary international consensus": Sandra Scarr, "American Child Care Today," *American Psychologist* 53 (1998): 100.

190 And even that correlation did not fully explain the difference: S. Scarr, M. Eisenberg, and K. Deater-Deckard, "Measurement of Quality in Child Care Centers," *Early Childhood Research Quarterly*, 9, no. 2 (1994): 131–51.

191 A large study in the United States: C. Howes, D. Phillips, and M. Whitebook, "Thresholds of Quality: Implications for the Social Development of Children in Center-Based Child Care," *Child Development* 63 (1992): 449–60.

191 Official ratios cannot be relied upon: J. McGuire and N. Richman, "Management of Behavior Problems in Day Nurseries," *Early Childhood Development and Care* 45 (April 1989): 1–128.

191 In a study of the "climate": B. Ekholm, A. Hedin, and B. E. Andersson, "Climates in Swedish Day Care Centres: A Methodological Study," *Journal of Research in Childhood Education*, 9, no. 2 (1995).

191 Structural features seem to provide: E. C. Melhuish, E. Lloyd, S. Martin, and A. Mooney, "Type of Childcare at 18 Months—II. Relations with Cognitive and Language Development," *Journal of Child Psychology and Psychiatry* 31 (1990): 861–70.

191 the largest U.S. study to focus on child care staff: M. Whitebook, C. Howes, and D. A. Phillips, *Who Cares? Childcare Teachers and the Quality of Care in America*, final report, National Childcare staffing study (Oakland, Calif.: Child Care Employee Project, 1989).

192 The measures themselves are complex and detailed: Some observational measures widely used to assess quality in international studies of child care are: T. Harms and R. Clifford, *Early Childhood Environment Rating Scale (ECERS)* (1980); T. Harms and R. Clifford, *Family Day Care Rating Scale (FDCRS)* (1989); T. Harms, D. Cryer,

and R. Clifford, *Infant/Toddler Environment Rating Scale (ITERS)* (1990); NICHD Study of Early Child Care, *Observational Record of the Caregiving Environment (ORCE)* (1998).

192 different methods may be needed instead or as well: D. Cryer and L. Phillipsen, "A Close Up Look at Child Care Program Strengths and Weaknesses," *Young Children* 52 (1997): 51–61.

193 Measures focusing on individual caregivers: J. Barnes, "Using Observations to Evaluate Paid Child Care Settings," in *The Preschool Period: Care—Education—Development: Findings from International Research*, ed. K. Petrogiannis and E. C. Melhuish (Athens: Kastaiotis, 2001), pp. 395–440.

193 Children's relationships with the people who take care of them: Elfer, "Building Intimacy"; Selleck and Griffin, "Quality for the Under Threes."

193 Warm personal relationships between care providers and children: J. Lindon, "Relationships Matter: Making It Personal," *Practical Professional Child Care*, November 2005; J. Grenier, "Developing Positive Relations with Children," *Nursery World*, June 2, 2005; Department for Education and Skills (DfES), *Key Elements of Effective Practise* (London: Her Majesty's Stationery Office, 2004). Department for Education and Skills (DfES), *Staffing Continuity, Consistency and Ratios* (London: Her Majesty's Stationery Office, 2005); P. Elfer, E. Goldschmied, and D. Selleck, *Key Persons in the Nursery: Building Relationships for Quality Provision* (London: David Fulton, 2003).

193 These findings also link closely with the concept of the key person: In the autumn of 2008, a statutory Early Years Foundation Stage (EYFS) came into force in England. The provision of a "key worker" for every child in group care, which had long been part of government guidance, became statutory; www.standards.dfes.gov.uk.

194 Children who experience greater caregiver stability: NICHD Early Child Care Research Network, "Child Care in the First Year of Life," *Merrill-Palmer Quarterly* 43 (1997): 340–60. See also NICHD Early Child Care Research Network, "The Effects of Infant Child Care on Infant-Mother Attachment Security," *Child Development* 68 (1997): 860–79.

194 Adult-child ratios, group sizes, children's age at entry: K. A. Clarke-Stewart, D. L. Vandell, M. Burchinal, M. O'Brien, and K. McCartney, "Do Regulable Features of Child Care Homes Affect Children's Development?" *Early Childhood Research Quarterly* 17 (2002): 52–86; A. Clarke-Stewart and V. Allhusen, *What We Know About Childcare* (Cambridge, Mass.: Harvard University Press, 2005); NICHD Early Child Care Research Network, "Structure-Process-Outcome: Direct and Indirect Effects of Caregiving Quality on Young Children's Development," *Psychological Science* 13 (2002): 199–206.

194 A comparison between the quality of different types of child care in the FCCC study: P. Leach, J. Barnes, L.-E. Malmberg, K. Sylva, and A. Stein, "The Quality of Different Types of Child Care at 10 and 18 Months: A Comparison Between Types and Factors Related to Quality," *Early Child Development and Care* 178, no. 2 (2008): 177–209.

194 In the NICHD study, children's outcomes were predicted: NICHD Early Child Care Research Network, *Child Care and Child Development: Results from the NICHD Study of Early Child Care and Youth Development* (New York: Guilford Press, 2005), 376–91.

194 in an American study of Early Head Start: J. Love, L. Harrison, A. Sagi-Schwartz, M. van Ijzendoorn, C. Ross, J. Ungerer, H. Raikes, C. Brady-Smith, K. Boller,

J. Brooks-Gunn, J. Constantine, E. Kisker, D. Paulsell, and R. Chazan-Cohen, "Child Care Quality Matters: How Conclusions May Vary with Context," *Child Development* 74, no. 4 (July–August 2003): 1021–33.

195 It is likely that in such circumstances: McGuire and Richman, "Management of Behavior Problems."

195 ways in which relevant national and professional standards are interpreted and implemented: C. Kam, M. Greenberg, and C. Walls, "Examining the Role of Implementation Quality in School-Based Prevention Using the PATHS Curriculum," *Prevention Science* 4, no. 1 (2003).

196 In the United Kingdom, for example, there is a new interest: A. G. Munton, A. Mooney, and L. Rowland, "Deconstructing Quality: A Conceptual Framework for the New Paradigm in Day Care Provision for the Under Eights," *Early Child Development and Care* 114 (1995): 11–23.

196 The best-known theoretical framework for child care: The "Reggio approach" is well described in L. Thornton and P. Brunton, *Understanding the Reggio Approach* (London: David Fulton, 2005).

196 "Reggio practitioners are united in their view": Martin Pace, Dolphin Nurseries, "A Regular Visitor Describes the Reggio Philosophy," *Nursery World*, February 2004.

198 Standards, settings, and staffing vary: M. Rosenthal, "Out-of-Home Child Care Research: A Cultural Perspective," *Journal of Behavioural Development* 23, no. 2 (1999): 477–518.

199 the Nordic conceptualization, known as "dual socialization": D. Sommer and O. Langsted, "Modern Childhood: Crises and Disintegration, or a New Quality of Life?" *Childhood* 2, no. 3 (1994): 129–44.

199 One Danish researcher stated in 1994: Ibid., p. 136.

200 "The Nordic countries, notwithstanding some variations": Ibid.

200 Yet in a study conducted in Haifa: A. Sagi, N. Koren-Karie, Y. Ziv, T. Joels, and M. Gini, "Shedding Further Light on the NICHD Study of Early Child Care: The Israeli Case," paper presented at the International Conference on Infant Studies, Atlanta, Georgia, 1998.

14. Quality of Care from Parents' Viewpoints

201 As we have seen, parents' judgments may also be affected: M. Rosenthal, "Out-of-Home Child Care Research: A Cultural Perspective," *Journal of Behavioral Development* 23, no. 2 (1999): 477–518; G. Dahlberg, P. Moss, and A. Pence, *Beyond Quality in Early Childhood Education and Care: Postmodern Perspectives* (London: Falmer Press, 1999).

Research Connections: Research-to-policy connections No. 1. National Center for children in poverty. ICPSR The information is well-summarized in J. L. Kreader, et al., *Infant and Toddler Child Care Arrangements* (2005), www.childcareresearch.org.

K. Sylva, A. Stein, P. Leach, J. Barnes, L.-E. Malmberg, and the FCCC team, "Family and Child Factors Related to the Use of Non-maternal Infant Care: An English Study," *Early Childhood Research Quarterly* 22, no. 1 (2007): 118–31.

202 The extent to which parents from diverse cultural backgrounds: J. Gonzalez-Mena, *The Child in the Family and Community* (New York: Merrill, 1993); B. Fuller, S. Hol-

loway, and X. Liang, "Family Selection of Child-Care Centers: The Influence of Household Support, Ethnicity and Parental Practices," *Child Development* 67, no. 6 (1996): 3320–37.

202 Most early child care research assumed: E. Poznanski, A. Maxey, and G. Marsden, "Clinical Implications of Maternal Employment: A Review of Research," *Journal of the American Academy of Child Psychiatry* 9 (1970): 741–61.

202 what were then referred to as "mother substitutes": J. B. Perry, "The Mother Substitutes of Employed Mothers: An Exploration Inquiry," *Marriage and Family Living* 23 (1961): 362–67.

202 the basis for the Parent Satisfaction with Child Care Scale: L. F. Myers, V. Elliott, J. Harrell, and M. J. Hostetter, "The Family and Community Day Care Interview" (technical report no. 6, The Pennsylvania Day Care Study Project, Pennsylvania State University); J. E. Harrell and C. A. Ridley, "Substitute Child Care, Maternal Employment and the Quality of Mother-Child Interaction," *Journal of Marriage and the Family* 37 (1975): 556–64; L. C. Buffardi and C. J. Erdwins, "Child Care Satisfaction: Linkages to Work Attitudes, Inter-Role Conflict and Maternal Separation Anxiety," *Journal of Occupational Health Psychology* 2 (1997): 84–96; J. Barnes, P. Leach, K. Sylva, A. Stein, L.-E. Malmberg, and the FCCC team, "Infant Care in England: Mothers' Aspirations, Experiences, Satisfaction and Caregiver Relationships," *Early Child Development and Care* 176, no. 5 (July 2006): 553–73.

202 parents are predisposed to be enthusiastic: D. Cryer and M. Burchinal, "Parents as Child Care Consumers," *Early Childhood Research Quarterly* 12 (1997): 35–58.

204 In one very large sample of American parents: G. A. Bogat and L. K. Gensheimer, "Discrepancies Between the Attitudes and Actions of Parents Choosing Day Care," *Child Care Quarterly* 15 (1989): 159–69.

204 the opinions of low-income African American parents: M. R. Burchinal, F. A. Campbell, D. M. Bryant, B. H. Wasik, and C. T. Ramey, "Early Intervention and Mediating Processes in Cognitive Performance of Children of Low-Income African American Families," *Child Development* 68 (1997): 935–54.

204 Parents often tell researchers that they would prefer a different type: S. L. Hofferth and D. A. Wissoker, "Price, Quality and Income in Child Care Choice," *Journal of Human Resources* 28 (1992): 70–111; S. Kontos, C. Howes, M. Shinn, and E. Galinsky, *Quality in Family Child Care and Relative Care* (New York: Teachers College Press, 1995); R. W. Fuqua and R. Schieck, "Child Care Resource and Referral Programs and Parents' Search for Quality Child Care," *Early Childhood Research Quarterly* 4 (1989): 357–65.

205 That mother is then likely to revise her earlier beliefs: E. P. Pungello and B. Kurtz-Costes, "Why and How Working Women Choose Child Care: A Review with a Focus on Infancy," *Developmental Review* 19 (1999): 31–96.

205 The FCCC study, being prospective rather than retrospective: P. Leach, J. Barnes, M. Nicols, J. Goldin, A. Stein, K. Sylva, and L.-E. Malmberg, "Child Care Before 6 Months of Age: A Qualitative Study of Mothers' Decisions and Feelings About Employment and Non-maternal Care," *Infant and Child Development* 15, no. 5 (2006): 471–502. See also Barnes et al., *Infant Care in England.*

206 The personal characteristics of caregivers: Cryer and Burchinal, "Parents as Child Care Consumers."

207 American parents using care at home by a relative or nanny: M. van Ijzendoorn,

L. Tavecchio, G. Stams, M. Verhoeven, and E. Reiling, "Attunement Between Parents and Professional Caregivers: A Comparison of Child Rearing Attitudes in Different Child Care Settings," *Journal of Marriage and the Family* 60 (1998): 771–81.

209 Like mothers in earlier studies on both sides of the Atlantic: D. J. Erdwins, W. J. Casper, and L. C. Buffardi, "Child Care Satisfaction: The Effects of Parental Gender and Type of Child Care Used," *Child and Youth Care Forum* 27 (1998): 111–23.

210 A major pre-election poll of all provinces in Canada: Statistics Canada, Fleishman-Hillard Pre-election Survey, November 2005, results July 2006.

210 "Ease of communication with the caregiver": R. W. Fuqua and D. Labensohn, "Parents as Consumers of Child Care," *Family Relations* 35 (1986): 295–303; M. Owen, A. Ware, and B. Barfoot, "Caregiver-Mother Partnership Behavior and the Quality of Caregiver-Child and Mother-Child Interactions," *Early Childhood Research Quarterly* 15, no. 3 (2000): 413–28; S. Wise and A. Sanson, *Child Care in Cultural Context: Issues for New Research*, Research Paper no. 22. Melbourne: Australian Institute of Family Studies, 2000.

211 A paper aptly called "Who Says What Is Quality?": K. Modigliani, "Who Says What Is Quality?: Setting Childcare Standards with Respect for Cultural Differences," *Family Day Care: International Perspectives on Policy, Practice and Quality*, ed. A. Mooney and J. Statham (London and Philadelphia: Jessica Kingsley, 2003), pp. 215–33.

211 This was a survey of two thousand mothers of children under five: Discovery Home and Health Channel survey, 2006.

15. Quality of Care from Children's Viewpoints

213 It is still important to look at child care quality from children's points of view: A. Clark, A. T. Kjorholt, and P. Moss, *Beyond Listening: Children's Perspectives on Early Childhood Services* (Bristol: Policy Press, 2005). See also Childcare Act 2006, http://www.opsi.gov.uk/acts/acts2006/ukpga_20060021_en_1; J. Lepper, "The Planning Experts," *Children Now*, February 21, 2007, pp. 18–19.

214 instead, they focused on children's attitudes to their parents' work: B. Pocock and J. Clarke, "Time, Money and Job Spillover: How Parents' Jobs Affect Young People," *Journal of Industrial Relations* 47, no. 1 (2005): 62–76. See also Department for Work and Pensions, *Working Parents Do Their Kids Proud*, August 14, 2007, http://www.gds.col.gov.uk/Content/Detail.asp?ReleaseID=30726&NewsAreaID=2; NSW Commission for Children and Young People, Submission to the Human Rights and Equal Opportunity Commission [Australia] Discussion Paper, "Striking the Balance: Women, Men, Work and Family," November 2005.

214 "Formal child care not only helps parents": Pocock and Clarke, "Time, Money and Job Spillover," p. 75.

215 Some children, perhaps especially boys, might be better off: A. Phillips, *The Trouble with Boys* (London: Pandora/HarperCollins, 1993).

215 policy has moved toward ever more tightly defined and all-embracing "frameworks": Early Years Foundation Stage, Department for Education and Skills, London, 2007.

The Early Years Foundation Stage (EYFS): A comprehensive framework that sets statutory standards for the care, development, and learning of all children from birth to five in all nonfamilial care settings in the United Kingdom. The framework builds on and replaces the nonstatutory Birth to Three Matters guidance, the Foundation Stage curriculum for three- and four-year-olds, and the National Standards for Daycare.

Alongside the statutory guidance is one hundred pages of practical guidance on putting its principles into practice, including many examples: e.g., caregivers with babies eight to twenty months should talk to them about the patterns and marks they make with fingers or biscuits on highchair trays or with crayons on paper.

It also sets out what children should be able to do by the end of the EYFS (usually age five) and thirteen formal scales of development on which children will be regularly assessed during its final year and their progress against the early learning goals and assessment scales recorded.

The framework states that childcare providers should aim to deliver individualized learning, development, and care that enhances each child's development: Each child should be supported to "make progress at their own pace." . . . "The learning and development grids are not about ticking children off against them. They're about thinking what children need."

216 "and for their parents, who may perceive the effects": L. Beardsley, *Good Day/Bad Day: The Child's Experience of Child Care* (New York: Teachers College Press, 1991), p. xi.

217 acute or chronic stress—manifested in levels of the hormone cortisol: The topic is clearly explained in a paper written by Robin Balbernie, "Cortisol and the Early Years," published in 2006 by What About the Children?, http://www.whataboutthe children.org.uk.

The following papers are some of those on which Balbernie's summary relies: M. R. Gunnar and R. G. Barr, "Stress, Early Brain Development, and Behaviour," *Infants & Young Children* 11, no. 1 (1998): 1–14; M. R. Gunnar and B. Donzella, "Social Regulation of the Cortisol Levels in Early Human Development," *Psychoneuroendocrinology* 27 (2002): 199–220. M. R. Gunnar and C. L. Cheatham, "Brain and Behaviour Interlace: Stress and the Developing Brain," *Infant Mental Health Journal* 24, no. 3 (2003): 195–211; T. S. Parry, M. Sims, and A. Guiltoyle, "Salivary Cortisol Levels in Children as a Biomarker of Quality Child Care," poster presentation, WAIMH Congress, Paris, 2006.

219 "There is quite a good database": Sebastian Kraemer, consultant child and adolescent psychiatrist, Tavistock Clinic, London, advice to Ten-Year Strategy for Childcare, HM Treasury, 2004.

219 The security of that secondary attachment: P. Elfer, E. Goldschmied, and D. Selleck, *Key Persons in the Nursery: Building Relationships for Quality Provision* (London: David Fulton, 2003); D. Selleck and S. Griffin, "Quality for the Under Threes," in *Contemporary Issues in the Early Years*, ed. G. Pugh, 2nd ed. (London: Paul Chapman/Sage, 1996), pp. 152–69.

219 many aspects of their development may suffer: E. C. Melhuish, E. Lloyd, S. Martin, and A. Mooney, "Type of Daycare at Eighteen Months: I. Differences in Interactional Experience," *Journal of Child Psychology and Psychiatry* 31 (1990): 849–60; E. C.

Melhuish, E. Lloyd, S. Martin, and A. Mooney, "Type of Daycare at Eighteen Months: II. Relations with Cognitive and Language Development," *Journal of Child Psychology and Psychiatry* 31 (1990): 861–70.

220 In a longitudinal study of children from birth to six years: C. Howes, D. Phillips, and M. Whitebook, "Thresholds of Quality: Implications for the Social Development of Children in Center-Based Child Care," *Child Development* 63 (1992): 449–60.

220 Staff turnover in child care centers in the United States: M. Whitebrook, L. Sakai, E. Gerber, and C. Howes, *Then and Now: Changes in Child Care Staffing, 1994–2000* (Washington, D.C.: Center for the Child Care Workforce, 2001); http://www.ccw .org/then&now.html.

221 Stable groups of children: Research carried out immediately before and after changes in Florida child care regulations showed that improvement in child care quality was associated with improvements in peer interactions. C. Howes, E. Smith, and E. Galinsky, *The Florida Child Care Quality Improvement Study* (New York: Families and Work Institute, 1995); J. M. Love, "Quality in Child Care Centers," *Early Childhood Research and Policy Briefs* 1, no. 1 (1997) (Chapel Hill, N.C.: National Center for Early Development & Learning, 1997); J. M. Love, P. A. Schochet, and A. L. Meckstroth, *Are They in Any Real Danger? What Research Does and Doesn't Tell Us About Child Care Quality and Children's Well-being* (Princeton, N.J.: Mathematical Policy Research, 1996).

222 Indeed, some of the research on stress in child care: R. A. Fabes, N. Eisenberg, S. Jones, M. Smith, I. Guthrie, R. Poulin, S. Shepard, and J. Friedman, "Regulation, Emotionality, and Preschoolers' Socially Competent Peer Interaction," *Child Development* 70, no. 2 (1999): 432–42; A. C. Dettling, S. W. Parker, S. K. Lane, A. M. Sebanc, and M. R. Gunnar, "Quality of Care and Temperament Determine Whether Cortisol Levels Rise over the Day for Children in Full-Day Child Care," *Psychoneuroendocrinology* 25 (2000): 819–36; N. Schulman and E. Birnbaum, *Practical Wisdom for Parents: Demystifying the Preschool Years* (New York: Knopf, 2007).

222 professionally staffed and run preschools produced better outcomes: K. Sylva, E. Melhuish, P. Sammons, I. Siraj-Blatchford, and B. Taggart, *The Effective Provision of Pre-School Education (EPPE) Project: Final Report*, a longitudinal study funded by the DfES 1997–2004 (London: DfES, 2004).

The Effective Provision of Pre-School Education (EPPE) project is the first major European longitudinal study of a national sample of young children's development (intellectual and social/behavioral) between the ages of three and seven years.

To investigate the effects of preschool education, the EPPE team collected information on over three thousand children, their parents, their home environments, and the preschool settings they attended. In the study, 141 preschool settings were randomly sampled to include the full range in England (local authority day nursery, integrated centers, playgroups, private day nurseries, nursery schools, and nursery classes). A sample of "home" children (who had no or minimal preschool experience) was recruited to the study when they entered school for comparison with the preschool group. In addition to investigating the effects of preschool provision on young children's development, the project explored effective practice through twelve intensive case studies.

225 In fact, in light of the comments on some well-known early years programs: Fight Crime: Invest in Kids, *America's Child Care Crisis: A Crime Prevention Tragedy*, 2nd ed. (Washington, D.C.: Fight Crime: Invest in Kids, 2000). See also A. Reynolds,

J. Temple, D. Robertson, and E. Mann, *Age 21: Cost-Benefit Analysis of the Title 1 Chicago Child-Parent Centers* (Madison, Wisc.: Institute for Research on Poverty, 2002); J. M. Love, E. Kisker, R. Ross, P. Schocket, J. Brooks-Gunn, K. Boller, D. Oasell, A. Fuligni, and L. Berlin, *Building Their Futures: How Early Head Start Programs Are Enhancing the Lives of Infants and Toddlers in Low-Income Families* (Washington, D.C.: Department of Health and Human Services, 2001); Administration on Children, Youth and Families, *Making a Difference in the Lives of Infants, Toddlers and Their Families: The Impacts of Early Head Start* (Washington, D.C.: Department of Health and Human Services, 2002).

225 The best-known and internationally most admired of all U.S. preschool programs: http://www.kidsfirstcanada.org/daycare.htm.

227 Poor-quality care can negatively affect: E. Peisner-Feinberg and M. Burchinal, "Relations Between Pre-School Children's Child Care Experiences and Concurrent Development: The Cost, Quality, and Outcomes Study," *Merrill-Palmer Quarterly* 43 (1997): 451–77.

227 "58 African American kids aged 3–4": Ibid.

227 research projects whose findings suggest that poor-quality child care: Ibid.

229 When the United Kingdom's universal (though taxed-as-income) child benefit was discussed: Commission on Social Justice/Institute for Public Policy Research, *Social Justice: Strategies for Renewal* (London: Vintage, 1994); P. Hewitt and P. Leach, "Social Justice, Children and Families," issue paper, Commission on Social Justice, 1993.

16. Choosing Child Care

231 Some of the FCCC mothers who started back to work: J. Barnes, P. Leach, K. Sylva, A. Stein, L.-E. Malmberg, and the FCCC team, "Infant Care in England: Mothers' Aspirations, Experiences, Satisfaction and Caregiver Relationships," *Early Child Development and Care* 176, no. 5 (July 2006): 553–73; P. Leach, J. Barnes, M. Nicols, J. Goldin, A. Stein, K. Sylva, and L.-E. Malmberg, "Child Care Before 6 Months of Age: A Qualitative Study of Mothers' Decisions and Feelings About Employment and Non-maternal Care," *Infant and Child Development* 15, no. 5 (2006): 471–502.

236 This is illustrated by the NICHD study's findings: NICHD Early Child Care Research Network, "Characteristics of Infant Child Care: Factors Contributing to Positive Caregiving," in *Child Care and Child Development: Results from the NICHD Study of Early Child Care and Youth Development* (New York: Guilford Press, 2005), pp. 50–66.

236 Findings from the American NICHD study are echoed: P. Leach, J. Barnes, L.-E. Malmberg, K. Sylva, and A. Stein, "The Quality of Different Types of Child Care at 10 and 18 Months: A Comparison Between Types and Factors Related to Quality," *Early Child Development and Care* 178, no. 2 (February 2008): 177–210.

242 The differences between aspects of quality that are important: Alison Clarke-Stewart, "Characteristics and Quality of Child Care for Toddlers and Preschoolers," in NICHD Early Child Care Research Network, *Child Care and Child Development: Results from the NICHD Study of Early Child Care and Youth Development* (New York and London: Guilford Press, 2005), pp. 91–104.

242 For example, U.K. children who attended nursery education in the 1980s: E. Melhuish, "The Quest for Quality in Early Day Care and Preschool Experience Continues," *International Journal of Behavioral Development* 25, no. 1 (2001): 1–26.

242 Part-time is quite enough: K. Sylva, E. Melhuish, P. Sammons, I. Siraj-Blatchford, and B. Taggart, *The Effective Provision of Pre-School Education (EPPE) Project: Final Report*, a longitudinal study funded by the DfES 1997–2004 (London DfES, 2004).

242 However, the quality of preschool education is crucial: NNI Research Team, *National Evaluation of the Neighbourhood Nurseries Initiative (NNI)*, March 2007, www .dfes.gov.uk/research/data/uploadfiles/ssu2007FR024.pdf.

244 A planned curriculum appropriate to the developmental stage: Department for Education and Skills, *Early Years Foundation Stage* (London: DfES, 2007).

Introduction: Is Better Child Care a Priority?

256 there are multiple methods for measuring various aspects of child care environments: NICHD Early Child Care Research Network, *Child Care and Child Development: Results from the NICHD Study of Early Child Care and Youth Development* (New York: Guilford Press, 2005).

256 "The vast majority of [American] child care is of unacceptably low quality": S. L. Ramey, "Commentary," in NICHD Early Child Care Research Network, *Child Care and Child Development*, p. 432.

258 "I judge that the basic descriptive findings": Ibid.

17. Politics and Policies, Models and Money

261 "To what extent the scientific community will focus on discovering effective ways": S. L. Ramey, "Commentary," in NICHD Early Child Care Research Network, *Child Care and Child Development: Results from the NICHD Study of Early Child Care and Youth Development* (New York: Guilford Press, 2005), p. 434.

262 "In the professional and political circles I know best": Ibid., p. 435.

262 When the government-funded Effective Provision of Pre-School Education (EPPE) project showed clear developmental benefits: K. Sylva, E. Melhuish, E. Sammons, I. Sirak-Blatchford, B. Taggart, *The Effective Provision of Pre-School Education (EPPE) Project: Final Report* (London: DfES, 2004).

263 Even the theoretical frameworks of those northern European countries: M. E. Lamb, C. P. Hwang, F. L. Bookstein, A. Broberg, G. Hult, and M. Frodi, "Determinants of Social Competence in Swedish Preschoolers," *Developmental Psychology* 24 (1988): 58–70.

18. Families and Child Care

277 "Enrolling children from age one in full-day preschools": Gunilla Dahlberg and Hillevi Lenz-Taguchi, *Preschool and School—Two Different Traditions and a Vision of a Meeting Place* (2003). This quote comes from the important report written by Swedish researchers for a Swedish government commission with another revealing title: *The Base for Lifelong Learning: A School Ready for Children*.

277 In the home, children can express a range of emotions: D. Sommer and O. Langsted, "Modern Childhood: Crises and Disintegration or a New Quality of Life," *Childhood*

2, no. 3 (1994): 129–44. This paper remains a classic exposition of the concept of dual socialization.

279 It's the *wrong question:* M. Sims, "Are We Asking the Right Question When We Ask 'Is Child Care Bad for Children?'" *Australian Journal of Early Childhood* 28, no. 4 (December 2003).

280 "This study [NICHD] unequivocally demonstrates": S. L. Ramey, "Commentary," in NICHD Early Child Care Research Network, *Child Care and Child Development: Results from the NICHD Study of Early Child Care and Youth Development* (New York: Guilford Press, 2005), p. 433.

19. Some Signposts to the Way Forward for Politicians, Policy Makers, and Professionals

285 "Mortgage holidays" have been suggested: "Mortgage holidays" were suggested to me in 2004 by Dilys Davis, founder of AIMH-UK, the U.K. affiliate of the World Association for Infant Mental Health (WAIMH).

Index

RAISING AMERICA
Experts, Parents, and a Century of Advice About Children
by Ann Hulbert

Since the beginning of the twentieth century, millions of anxious parents have turned to child-rearing manuals for reassurance. Instead, however, they have often found yet more cause for worry. In this rich social history, Ann Hulbert analyzes one hundred years of shifting trends in advice and discovers an ongoing battle between two main approaches: a "child-centered" focus on warmly encouraging development versus a sterner "parent-centered" emphasis on instilling discipline. She examines how pediatrics, psychology, and neuroscience have fueled the debates but failed to offer definitive answers. And she delves into the highly relevant and often turbulent personal lives of the popular advice givers, from L. Emmett Holt and Arnold Gesell to Bruno Bettelheim and Benjamin Spock to the prominent (and ever conflicting) experts of today.

Sociology/978-0-375-70122-1

CHILDREN FIRST
What Society Must Do—and Is Not Doing—for Children Today
by Penelope Leach

Penelope Leach's groundbreaking, extensively researched book places parenting in a social context. For in case after case, Leach argues that, for all our vocal espousal of family values, our laws, employment policies, and culture are actually inimical to children and disastrous for committed parents. *Children First* is above all a call to action. It boldly spells out: what specific policies our society must adopt in order to discriminate in favor of children and the grownups who care for them; how measures like paid parental leave and universal preschool education will actually end up saving us money; why "family friendly" workplaces and communities turn out to be good for employers and ordinary taxpayers. The resulting volume is likely to revolutionize the status of children and parents both—reminding us that the former are our heirs and that the latter do their job best when it is a practical, pleasureable choice.

Parenting/Current Affairs/978-0-679-75466-4

PRACTICAL WISDOM FOR PARENTS
Raising Self-Confident Children in the Preschool Years
by Nancy Schulman and Ellen Birnbaum

This reassuring guide to navigating nursery school life—both at home and in the classroom—is the most comprehensive book on the subject. Nancy Schulman and Ellen Birnbaum draw on their decades of experience at the 92nd Street Y Nursery School to respond to parents' hunger for practical information on a wide range of topics including: what to look for in a preschool; strategies for separation, discipline, toilet training, and bedtime; the best toys, books, and activities at every stage; how to stimulate our children without over-scheduling them; ways to talk about difficult topics like divorce, illness, or death; how to support your child's social and intellectual development. Schulman and Birnbaum have devoted their lives to listening to and understanding young children, and the advice they offer is as warm and humorous as it is comforting and wise.

Family/Parenting/978-0-307-27538-7

VINTAGE BOOKS
Available at your local bookstore, or visit
www.randomhouse.com